To my dear friend &

Gerald Wright,

An inspirational leader who always

wants to do the right things in any

transformation.

With highest regards

Behnam N. Tabrizi

Stanford, CA

Oct 23, 07

Rapid
Transformation

Rapid Transformation

A 90-DAY PLAN
FOR FAST AND
EFFECTIVE CHANGE

Behnam N. Tabrizi

HARVARD BUSINESS SCHOOL PRESS
Boston, Massachusetts

To Nazanin and Sheila

Copyright 2007 Harvard Business School Publishing Corporation
All rights reserved
Printed in the United States of America

11 10 09 08 07   5 4 3 2 1

Library of Congress Cataloging-in-Publication Data
Tabrizi, Behnam N.
   Rapid transformation: a 90-day plan for fast and effective change / Behnam
Tabrizi.
        p.   cm.
   Includes index.
   ISBN-13: 978-1-4221-1889-4 (hardcover: alk. paper)
   1. Organizational change. 2. Reengineering (Management) I. Title.
   HD58.8.T33 2007
   658.4'06--dc22

                                                              2007014157

The paper used in this publication meets the requirements of the American National Standard for Permanence of Paper for Publications and Documents in Libraries and Archives Z39.48-1992.

Contents

Acknowledgments

In the mid 1990s, while traveling the globe on research and business, I became committed to live a life that I loved. Thus I searched for the path that would lead to fulfillment for me. I vigorously pursued this quest as well as answers to the ultimate existentialist questions: "Who am I?" and "What am I doing here?" For me, these answers are summed up in the personal paragraph that I read every morning and that is the true compass in my life: "I stand for the purpose of unconditional love, infinite and abundant energy, with powerful and inspirational presence to transform people and organizations while upholding my highest integrity." This statement is profoundly intertwined with my DNA!

This book is the current culmination of my journey, and one that I am very excited about. It is based on a decade of rigorous research and hands-on experience of working with CEOs and senior executives on their organizational transformation. The study included turning large volumes of data into a useful framework for an iterative process of developing ideas based on data and further revising and for testing once conflicting evidence arose. Having an able research team ensured that rigorous standards were applied every step of the way.

I was truly fortunate to work with outstanding research assistants. First and foremost, Athena Mak played a leading role in contributing to this book. Athena's passion, intellect, attention to details, and wonderful demeanor were outstanding. Jacqueline del Castillo contributed to the earlier incarnations of the diagnosis and the implementation phases. Jackie's enthusiasm for and keen interest in the topic was remarkable. Having experienced so many all-day working meetings around our dining-room table, often with my family present, my wife and I now consider Athena and Jackie our special daughters! I also thank Aman Govil, Cyrous Jame, and Yiduo Yu, and Naseem Delan for their contributions to the Appendix and the analysis. Anand Jha, Jacqueline del Castillo, Athena Mak, Drew Bennett, Brett Hofer, Gaurav

Singh, and Ryan Akkina contributed to developing cases. Professor Paul Leonardi of Northwestern Business School provided valuable advice regarding the methodology.

I would also like to express my appreciation to Professor Saikat Chaudhuri of Wharton Business School and Faraj Alaei, CEO of Centillium, for their valuable and detailed feedback on the early version of the manuscript. Industry leaders such as David House, Lloyd Carney, Gale England, George Haddad, Vernon Irvin, Faraj Alaei, Kimm Hershberger, and Ava Butler have truly shaped my first-hand experience with transformation. I also owe a great deal of gratitude to the thought leaders who have had a major impact on my thinking: Kathy Eisenhardt, Jim March, Bob Sutton, Steve Barley, Henry Mintzberg, Jeff Pfeffer, Karl Weick, John Kotter, Jim Collins, and Tom Peters.

Finally, I am indebted to Jacqueline Murphy, senior editor of HBSP for her encouragement and commitment throughout this book project, and Deborah English and Stacey Sawyer for their admirable efforts on editing and completing this book.

Introduction

*If you do not change direction, you may
end up where you are heading.*

—Lao Tzu

Many of us are afraid of change. We establish our daily routines and, over time, become comfortable with our patterns of behavior. To change is to take a risk—to give up a current state in an attempt to reach a potentially more desirable one. We tend to resist change. We may fear failure or be uncomfortable with the uncertainty surrounding change.

Corporations are no different. Over time, employees become comfortable with their daily work schedules. Processes become embedded in the inner workings of the organization. Gradually, the energy and competitive temperature of the business settles down to room temperature. As Alan Lafley, CEO of Procter & Gamble, once said, "People get used to being a player without being a winner."[1]

However, despite a natural resistance to change, employees want to be part of a successful company; they want to win! Take a trip to your local bookstore and you will find that achieving success in business is quite a hot topic. Lining the best-seller shelves are titles such as *Good to Great*, *Winning*, and *Ahead of the Curve*. Business leaders devour these books in hopes of discovering the secrets to keeping their businesses on the cutting edge.

In practice, however, there are no secrets. Competing in today's marketplace is like competing in any other game. To stay competitive, a player must be dynamic in the marketplace, constantly revising its own strategy in response to the strategies of its opponents, as well as aligning itself with the changing demands of its customers. The organizations that can most quickly respond to the marketplace, particularly those that adapt faster than their competitors, are the ones that make it to the top.

HOW DO ORGANIZATIONS CHANGE?

Change can come either in small, baby steps or in large, giant steps.

Baby steps feel safer and can be conceptualized as evolution, or gradual, incremental change. However, in organizations, incremental change is effective insofar as all else is constant and maintaining the status quo is the goal. According to Procter & Gamble's Lafley, evolutionary change is "like a classic military strategy, where you just keep putting on the pressure, you just keep extending the lines, you just keep rolling up the weakest competitors" to gain "another half a share point and another half a margin point."[2] Although incremental change should be a routine part of any good manager's or leader's job, it promotes a parochial outlook and attitude in the rank and file if it becomes too routine. After a while, people show up at work to play rather than to win. Through incremental change, the thirst for outside-the-box thinking is lost.

When tiptoeing around is no longer effective in the existing environment, the organization may consider taking large, giant steps to improve the organization's performance by leaps and bounds. These drastic moves are often better understood as revolution, or transformations. Leaders often turn to transformations when they are in dire need of a cure for their ailing organizations, though transformations can be quite effective in less desperate situations.

So what exactly is a transformation in the organizational sense? At its core, a transformation is a fundamental shift in the company's functioning, and its goal is to significantly improve the current performance of an organization by better aligning it to changing market conditions and demands. It typically encourages change at every level of the organization, from the executive-level management down to the individual employee of a company.

Historically, leaders who have tried to revolutionize, or transform, their companies have tried to do so through reengineering, which in practice turned out to be attacking one key section at a time. Typically, some of these sections are finances via cost cutting, culture, services or products, strategy, and processes (usually one, or at most several, at a time).

Such piecemeal, serial efforts, however, have not proved to be very effective in improving the company's overall performance. A study conducted in the mid-1990s found that approximately 70 percent of reengineering efforts were considered failures within five years after they were undertaken.[3] Why are these popular reengineering efforts ineffective? Below, we highlight the interplay between some characteristics of reengineering efforts that cause their ineffectiveness (see figure I-1).

- *They're piecemeal.* The piecemeal nature of reengineering efforts is often their core problem and a root cause leading to the manifestation of other symptoms, such as being lengthy and tactical.

- *They're lengthy.* Reengineering is lengthy not only because it's piecemeal but also because companies undertake these piecemeal changes serially.

- *They're tactical.* Tactical changes, as opposed to long-term changes, are more focused on the immediate and short-term future. Reengineering efforts are tactical mainly because they are lengthy and piecemeal. The lengthy nature means that quite often, the cycle of internal change becomes lengthier than the cycle of external change. Hence, by the time the reengineering effort has been completed, external market conditions have changed beyond what was anticipated when the effort was first undertaken. Ironically, the effort initiated by a need to adjust to the changing market conditions is the same effort that prevents the organization from catching up to those changes. Additionally, the piecemeal nature of reengineering translates to an oversight of the interplay between different processes and functions. By failing to take advantage of the synergies among various functions, processes, and business units, reengineering fails to provide a holistic perspective or a strategic plan of attack.

Despite these deficiencies, reengineering efforts have been rather popular and have been packaged and repackaged in different shapes and forms over time. While we highlighted the demerits of reengineering efforts, there must have been some advantages that created the hype. If we give reengineering the benefit of the doubt and assume that it was at one time effective, then has anything changed about the business landscape that can explain why reengineering has failed to live up to its expectation? Thirty-year General Electric veteran Dennis Donovan hints at some of the reasons for the ineffectiveness of reengineering in today's society: "From 1981 through the

FIGURE I-1

Reasons for reengineering ineffectiveness

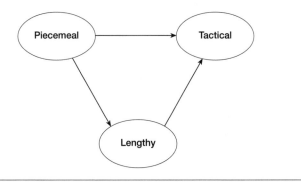

1990s, Jack Welch [former CEO of General Electric] focused on one area of business at a time: structural revolution in the early '80s, followed by cultural revolution, such as the workout. Next, it was the process revolution, such as Six Sigma, followed by the digitalization revolution in the '90s. Today, we don't have that luxury. If you have an eight-cylinder engine, you have to run on all cylinders; you have to have an integral model that would focus on all aspects of business in parallel and quickly."[4]

To elaborate, the 1990s represented a major, fundamental shift in the corporate environment that transformed both the way companies were run and the way business was conducted. In that decade, the entire landscape shifted from an industrial, international economy to an informational, truly global economy, a shift that was facilitated and accelerated by the advent of the World Wide Web and rapid globalization. Amid these changes, an organization in the 1990s needed to address numerous new management challenges and reexamine its culture and processes because of the ready access to information. Companies had to rethink what they were doing and how to address the new and different challenges they were encountering.

This major shift resulted in what we call a postmodern or post-Web corporate world. In this new, hypercompetitive environment, market transitions are a lot faster, and the cycle of innovation has gotten increasingly shorter. Because people and companies learned to innovate from anywhere in the world, new products and services started appearing more and more frequently, resulting in even more competition. Furthermore, this landscape change also saw the rapid adoption of e-mail and work group tools, and the rise of the power of real-time information.

It is amid these changes that reengineering found itself outdated. With the shorter cycles of innovation and hence increasingly frequent breakthroughs, the piecemeal, serial model was no longer effective in the new, fast-paced society. Hence, the interplay between the information revolution, the rapid pace of globalization, and fierce competition requires a new model of change.

Given the criticisms of reengineering and its ineffectiveness in the postmodern or post-Web society, our research was hence interested in identifying the key effective principles and practices of transformation used in today's world. In thinking about the post-Web industries, however, we quickly realized that the turn of the millennium also saw another major event in the corporate environment: the so-called Y2K, telecom, and dot-com bubble. This bubble saw unprecedented heights in company valuation by financial markets in the years preceding 2000, followed by an equally remarkable decline in the years following 2000. The prebubble phase was characterized by abundance, the postbubble by scarcity. During the research, however, it was less clear whether this bubble reflected as major a change in the landscape as did the advent of the Internet and rapid globalization in the 1990s. The research team was hence further interested in dissecting the findings into the prebubble and postbubble phases to identify whether the same tools, principles, and processes of change could be applied in both eras.

RESEARCH METHODOLOGY

This book is based on over ten years of research led by the author with the assistance of a panel of experts and a team of a dozen researchers.[5] The panel of experts consisted of:

- The CFO of a billion-dollar company, with senior management background in one of the Big Four accounting firms as an auditor

- A former partner of a well-known consulting firm, with over twenty years of experience in organizational change

- An expert in company valuation who works for a large hedge fund on the East Coast

- A finance expert at Stanford University

The research started with the quantitative analysis, using the *transformation performance index model* detailed in the appendix, which aimed at distinguishing between successful and unsuccessful transformation efforts. Of an initial sample of over five hundred companies that underwent changes in the past twenty years, fifty-six transformation efforts were deemed relevant for further analysis, and this final sample of fifty-six companies was categorized and ranked using the model.

With the companies categorized, the team proceeded to the qualitative analysis to identify the principles and tools that affected the outcome of the various efforts. The research team used its tremendous direct industry experience, in-person interviews with top executives, case studies, and archival studies to identify not only the high-level critical success factors but also the specific principles and tools used by the successful companies.

KEY FINDINGS: CRITICAL SUCCESS FACTORS

Our research found several critical success factors that differentiated successful transformations from unsuccessful efforts.[6] Particularly, successful transformation efforts were all-encompassing, integrative, and fast and had full, passionate commitment and buy-in, especially at the top layers of the organization. Unsuccessful efforts, on the other hand, were missing either one or several of these factors. Note also that reengineering efforts typically lack several of these factors.

We discuss these factors further in the next chapter.

OVERVIEW OF THE 90 DAYS
TRANSFORMATION MODEL

In addition to discovering the critical success factors of transformation efforts, in-depth research of the companies led to the development of the *90 days transformation model* (see figure I-2). The 90 days reflects the planning stage of the effort, meaning the problems are diagnosed and the blueprint for implementation is set. Actual, full-fledged implementation of the effort, however, will extend well beyond the 90 days. In spite of this, however, the 90 days model is effective in providing a framework for accelerating typical transformation efforts.

The 90 days model is particularly effective not only because it solves the problems associated with reengineering but also because it embraces the critical success factors. We reexamine the reason for the effectiveness of the 90 days model in the next chapter, and the rest of the book will be devoted to explaining the step-by-step processes of executing each phase.

FIGURE I-2

90 days transformation model
(90 Days Transformation is a registered trademark of Tabrizi, LLC)

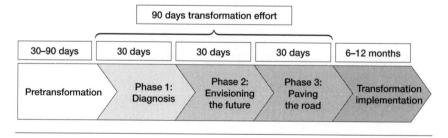

HOW IS THIS BOOK ORGANIZED?

This book is divided into the following chapters: Model Overview, Pretransformation, Cross-Functional Rapid Response Teams, Phase 1, Phase 2, Phase 3, and Transformation Implementation. Each chapter details the processes, practices, tools, and methodology needed to carry out the 90 days transformation effort, and gives numerous examples of the best-in-class practices that constitute the proposed methodology. The appendix details the transformation performance index model, as well as the results of the analysis.

WHAT SHOULD I TAKE AWAY FROM THIS BOOK?

Whether you're in industry or academia, this book illustrates an effective model of accelerating transformations. If you are a current or future leader, we advise you to read through the steps and think through the variations and adjustments you can make to tailor the model to different situations and environments.

If you are a manager, an executive, a CEO, a divisional manager of a for-profit or nonprofit firm, this book will serve as a guidebook for implementing a successful transformation effort by introducing you to a set of best practices. While we often discuss full organizational transformations in this book, the same processes can be applied on a smaller scale, such as in a department or business unit.

If you are a professor in management, we invite you to use this book as learning material to spark a discussion about corporate transformations. Alternatively, if you are a student in management, such as an MBA student, this book's practical concepts will add to your knowledge of different aspects of corporate transformations and will further prepare you to support, and one day lead, these types of efforts in your professional career.

CONCLUSION

When business leaders learn about the 90 days transformation model for the first time, their initial reaction is typically "That's impossible! There's no way a company can transform itself that quickly!" However, one intriguing finding from our research is that even in companies that engaged in accelerated transformation efforts, the transformation leaders often look back and wish that they could have carried out the transformation more quickly. For example, when asked if there's anything in the process he would have done differently,

Bay Networks' CEO Dave House said, "I would have done it more quickly."[7] Hence, difficult as the 90 days model sounds, organizations that have successfully carried out the 90 days effort demonstrate not only that it is feasible and effective but that they can continue to push the boundaries in speed and effectiveness.

We now invite you to join us in the coming chapters to explore and learn more about the 90 days transformation model and how you can use it to quickly become a high-performance organization.

1

Model Overview
The 90 Days Transformation Model

A man who does not plan ahead will find trouble right at his door.

—Confucius

Companies need to constantly reinvent themselves to remain competitive in today's world. However, they don't need to keep reinventing the wheel. The 90 days transformation[1] model provides companies with a framework with which to transform themselves in order to stay ahead of the curve.

In the introduction, we described how change efforts have evolved, and how transformation efforts provide significant leaps in improvement as opposed to the incremental change that occurs daily in an organization.

In this chapter, we revisit the critical success factors, look more in depth at the general 90 days transformation model, examine why it's effective, and meet six companies that used the 90 days model.

CRITICAL SUCCESS FACTORS REVISITED

Through an extensive and intensive analysis of transformation efforts, we identified several critical success factors that differentiated between successful and failed transformation efforts.[2] In particular, successful transformations had the following characteristics: (1) all-encompassing, (2) integrative, (3) fast, and (4) had full, passionate commitment and buy-in, especially at the top layers of the organization (see figure 1-1).

- *All-encompassing.* In their transformation efforts, successful companies first and foremost looked at and analyzed all aspects of the company, looking under all the rocks and leaving no stones unturned. As General Electric's Donovan mentioned, all eight cylinders of an eight-cylinder engine must be used—no longer can companies afford to use only one cylinder at a time.

- *Fast.* By using all eight cylinders at a time, companies reduce downtime and hand-off periods. Successful companies engaged in all their efforts in parallel, looking at everything at once.

- *Integrative.* Successful transformation efforts also integrated and synchronized various functions and processes within the organization to take advantage of the cross boundary synergies in parallel.

- *Had full, passionate commitment and buy-in.* While complete buy-in is important at all levels of the organization, it is especially critical from the top. Lack of buy-in at the top level may, in fact, impede the transformation effort by stalling it and creating, rather than removing, obstacles.

We found that most successful transformation efforts fully embraced all these critical success factors, while failed efforts typically lacked at least one, though often more, of these factors.

FIGURE 1-1

Critical success factors

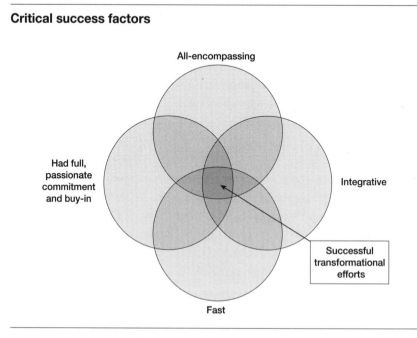

CRITICAL SUCCESS FACTORS APPLIED

Having seen the critical success factors, let's now look at how these critical factors are applied and how they affect the transformation effort. Their power can be seen in particular by comparing companies that used them and companies that didn't. Specifically, the dyads we will introduce here are companies that are comparable in many ways.

Apple Versus Sony

Sony's transformation efforts from 1999 to 2003 were almost exclusively targeted at improving operational efficiency, cutting costs, and implementing a new organizational structure across the organization. These initiatives were purely internal-facing—none of them was visible to the consumer. In contrast, in addition to streamlining its operations, Apple in 1997 implemented a new product line strategy and focused on developing exciting and innovative new products. Furthermore, Apple rolled out a series of impressive advertising campaigns that managed to rekindle the interest of consumers and revive Apple's brand message. As Board Member Gareth Chang of Hughes International wisely stated, "We forgot sometimes who pays the bills—it's the customer who pays the bills."[3] Thanks to these customer-focused initiatives, Apple was able to rectify its situation; Sony did not (see figure 1-2).

At Apple, the leadership was completely overhauled with a new CEO and board of directors, bringing not only a new energy but also a new sense of direction and focus for the organization. Steve Jobs, considered the heart of the organization, was warmly welcomed back to lead Apple. His return alone was enough to inspire Apple's customers and employees. This kind of fresh perspective can be essential for building buy-in and shaping the transformation. At Sony, the leadership situation was very different. The CEO, Nobuyuki Idei, was a long-standing presence in the organization, and although Howard Stringer was recruited in 1997 to be the CEO of Sony Corporation USA, he had no direct power—until 2005 when he was named CEO of Sony Corporation—and was controlled by Idei. This situation, coupled with the Sony leadership's lack of charisma, stifled the energy that was needed to implement a successful transformation. To make matters worse, when Stringer entered his new leadership role his credibility was immediately questioned, because his background did not match the strong engineering and technical tradition that was at the heart of Sony.

FIGURE 1-2

Critical success factors: Apple vs. Sony

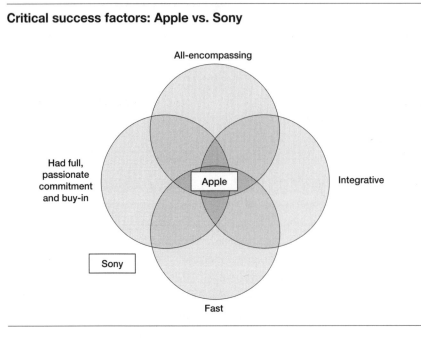

Since these two transformation efforts originated in very different environments, with different types of leadership, they resulted in different focuses and results. The Sony transformation became a relatively uninspiring, piecemeal corporate reform to better the position of the company. A lack of urgency, combined with less than compelling leadership, resulted in superficial cost-cutting techniques that did not yield the desired effect. Conversely, Apple's transformation was born of necessity. The inherent sense of urgency, combined with Jobs's stellar leadership and holistic approach, produced a consistent strategy with good focus on the customer and excellent support from inside the company. The opposing results of the two transformations are well reflected by BusinessWeek's 2003 rankings of best and worst managers: Jobs was categorized among the best managers, whereas Idei was ranked among the worst.[4]

Hewlett-Packard (Fiorina) Versus Hewlett-Packard (Hurd)

Hewlett-Packard (HP) is one of the world's largest information technology corporations, providing products, services, and solutions. Following the retirement of Lewis Platt, Carly Fiorina joined HP to lead the company into the new millennium, but she failed on two major accounts: (1) She failed to get buy-in from the company, and (2) she failed to execute, or hold people accountable, leading to a slow and lagging effort. When Mark Hurd replaced her in 2005, HP was arguably in a worse situation than when Fiorina arrived. In his efforts, Hurd leveraged the critical success factors to his advantage, building on Fiorina's work but achieving a more desirable outcome (see figure 1-3).

When Fiorina joined the company, HP was a decentralized organization without a company-wide strategy. The silo structure resulted in customer dissatisfaction, slow responses to the changing business environment, and brand diffusion. Lack of accountability was also problematic, as sometimes managers were required to clear their decisions with dozens of executives.[5] Additionally, then-CEO Lewis Platt failed to capitalize on the Internet revolution, putting HP in a less-than-desirable situation.

Fiorina entered with the dazzle of marketing under her belt and attacked many different aspects of the company, including reorganization, cost-cutting, vision-setting. However, she did not have support and buy-in; she never took the time to develop rapport with individual employees. Additionally, employees didn't completely support her initiatives because Fiorina failed to execute, or

FIGURE 1-3

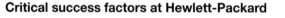

Critical success factors at Hewlett-Packard

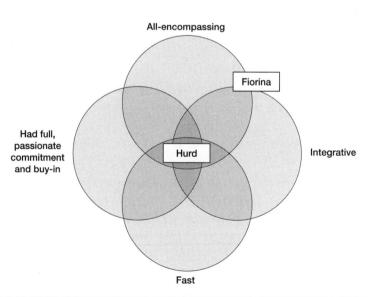

hold employees accountable, as mentioned above. Often, she would speak of the grandiose vision but fail to follow through on it, which lost her credibility and support of the organization. The HP-Compaq merger, a key tipping point in her tenure, illustrated this clearly: employees, stockholders, and the board of directors were divided in the decision, but Fiorina managed to push the decision through by a narrow margin. This meant that a portion of the company didn't support the merger, resulting in conflicts during her tenure.

As her replacement, Mark Hurd has brought the company back to the fundamentals by focusing on data and execution. Building credibility and establishing rapport with the employees, Hurd has gained buy-in throughout the organization. Additionally, he has addressed many different aspects of the company, building on the strategy and vision initially set by Fiorina. Through his efforts, HP's stock price has more than doubled within two years of Hurd's arrival, EBIT margin has increased by 60 percent, and revenues have increased by nearly 20 percent at the expense of fierce competitors, such as Dell.

General Motors Versus Nissan

General Motors (GM) and Nissan are both large automobile manufacturers that faced dire circumstances at the turn of the millennium. After undertaking their respective transformation efforts, however, General Motors has remained troubled, while Nissan has been extremely successful and has been internationally acknowledged and recognized. A big part of the difference in their respective outcomes can be accounted for by the extent to which they used the critical success factors: Nissan fully embraced all of them, while General Motors struggled with embracing even one (see figure 1-4).

In 2001, six months after Rick Wagoner took the helm of GM officially as CEO and informally as GM's transformation leader, GM posted a net profit of $420 million. By 2005, however, net income turned into a loss of over $10 billion. Aside from poor management and decision making, how can we understand this tremendous failure? The lack of any critical success factor may provide some insight, for the GM transformation was piecemeal, not integrated, executed serially, and lengthy.

The lack of integration of different parts of the transformation resulted directly from the nature and culture of GM. According to Jay Conger, a professor of management at the London Business School, "GM has always been a very siloed corporation with all of its different divisions really operating like separate companies. There have been numerous reorganization efforts at GM,

FIGURE 1-4

Critical success factors at Nissan and GM

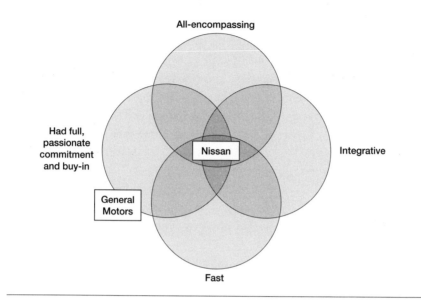

and most have not fared well, because of the turf battles and independent nature of GM's divisions."[6]

Additionally, the transformation effort at GM has been extremely piecemeal, with the company addressing a few key issues at a time, such as human resources, information technology, lead time, and dealer location.[7] Furthermore, cost cutting, a poor long-term strategy, has been a major part of GM's transformation effort—in June 2005, GM announced plans to eliminate twenty-five thousand jobs in the United States, or 17 percent of its U.S. workforce, by closing several plants in the coming years.[8]

Partly because of this tremendous cost-cutting effort, GM has encountered tremendous difficulty in getting buy-in for the change effort from middle management. This has in turn resulted in senior-level executives' view that their transformation is an "evolution not a revolution," and that the transformation process will be a lengthy one.[9] This has ironically become a self-fulfilling prophecy. For example, the IT aspect of the transformation itself took six years![10] Interestingly, this lack of a sense of urgency has often been connected with many unsuccessful transformation efforts.

However, consider the case of Nissan. Carlos Ghosn joined as COO and transformation leader, and in a few short months had involved a big portion of the company to develop an integrative plan that addressed many of Nissan's pain points. This plan, called the Nissan Revival Plan, incorporated not only cost-cutting efforts to reduce debt but also strategies for long-term growth.[11] In developing the plan, Ghosn made sure he had support from the top levels of the organization, which in turn gave him more influence and respect in the organization. At the same time, he also made sure he had buy-in from other levels of the organization. Through an integrated, all-encompassing, and speedy transformation effort, the goals stated in the Nissan Revival Plan, such as introducing twenty new models, reducing debt in half, and becoming profitable were all met within two years, an entire year ahead of schedule.

Nortel Networks Versus Bay Networks

The transformation efforts of both Bay Networks and Nortel Networks, two telecommunications companies, were headed by Dave House. Shortly after House's stunningly successful transformation of Bay Networks, Nortel acquired the company and hired House officially as president and unofficially as Nortel's transformation leader. However, various factors, especially lack of top-down buy-in and integration at Nortel, made House incapable of replicating his success at Nortel (see figure 1-5).

FIGURE 1-5

Critical success factors at Bay Networks and Nortel

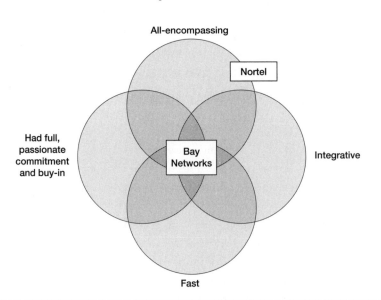

At Bay Networks, House was able to harness the capabilities of his workforce to bring about a successful change effort. Using a model similar to the 90 days model, House attacked every aspect of the organization, especially its dysfunctional culture, and developed an integrated strategic solution that addressed the key problems plaguing the company. As the CEO of Bay Networks at the time, House was able to get buy-in from the top levels of his organization, which were then able to get buy-in at the lower levels. This top-down buy-in was important in analyzing and solving the problems in a timely and efficient manner. Furthermore, the buy-in was also important in keeping Bay Networks focused and aligned with the transformation effort.

At Nortel, however, House encountered numerous obstacles that led to an unsuccessful transformation effort. First of all, Nortel engaged in a piecemeal transformation that was neither integrative nor effective. The divisions within the company were unable to cooperate and create the cross-boundary synergies that are so powerful in a transformation effort. More importantly, House was not given the authority necessary to lead the transformation effort, nor did he have adequate buy-in from the top levels of the organization. Because Nortel was controlled by a board of directors that was focused more on managing the company than attending to the transformation effort, even CEO John Roth didn't have the power or mandate to work with House to drive the transformation through the organization. Therefore, even when employees would claim and promise to do something, House could not enforce execution and delivery of their promises. This lack of support created unnecessary obstacles, and House's efforts were ineffective against the long-standing bureaucracies and inertia of the organization. Therefore, lack of power and authority undermined House's attempt to transform Nortel, despite his understanding and knowledge of the critical success factors for transformation efforts.

OVERVIEW OF THE 90 DAYS
TRANSFORMATION MODEL

The previous section used brief case studies to illustrate how the critical success factors can impact the outcome of a transformation effort. Further in-depth analysis and case studies of companies and their best-in-class transformation practices revealed a striking similarity in the path taken by several successful companies: 3M, ACI (Asian Company Inc., a pseudonym), Bay Networks, Nissan, Apple, and VeriSign. The similarities between these companies' transformation efforts led to the development of the 90 days transformation model, which embraces the critical success factors. The key principles and tools described in this model were extracted from our analysis of not only these six companies but all the successful transformation efforts. And, failed transformation efforts identified several practices to avoid and obstacles to anticipate.

In the introduction, we noted that the corporate landscape changed significantly because of the information revolution, rapid globalization, and fierce competition in the 1990s. We also noted that we were interested in seeing whether the Y2K, Telecom, and dot-com bubble at the turn of the millennium had the same effect. In particular, would we find the tools and practices identified in our analysis to be different in the prebubble (before the dot-com bubble burst in 2000) and postbubble (post-2000) periods? Was the dot-com bubble substantial enough to effectively change the rules of the game?

Through both our quantitative and qualitative research, we found striking consistency between successful companies that transformed before the bubble and those that transformed after the bubble. Hence, even though the environment had changed in the hype of the bubble and the following correction period, the entire landscape wasn't overhauled the same way it was with the emergence of postmodern society. Hence, the tools, processes, and practices that have been identified as best-in-class are relevant to today's world, regardless of whether the company the practice was drawn from was a prebubble or postbubble company.

Also noted in the introduction, the 90 days portion of the 90 days transformation model refers not to the full transformation implementation of the effort but to the diagnosis and planning stages. By the end of the 90 days, the organization should have identified the root causes of the problems and developed a detailed blueprint for the actual implementation, which will take an additional six to twelve months.

The 90 days transformation model consists of three main phases, each lasting 30 days: phase 1, phase 2, and phase 3. Flanking both sides of the 90 days are two additional phases: the pretransformation and the transformation implementation phases. A day-long integration meeting attended by all the key players of the effort highlights the end of each phase. Figure 1-6 gives a visual representation of the timeline of the 90 days transformation model.

The 90 days effort is run in parallel with the normal inner workings of the company, so that the organization is not put on hold for the sake of the transformation effort. Rather, employees involved in the effort carry out both their day jobs and the tasks associated with the transformation. By doing so, nothing in the organization is sacrificed, though employees must be prepared

FIGURE 1-6

90 days transformation model

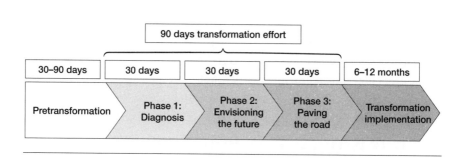

to put in extra time and energy to ensure that their schedules do not slip in either their daily job functions or the transformation effort.

The heart of the pretransformation phase is the transformation leader's preparation before the actual engagement. In this phase, he not only plants the seeds for a successful transformation, he also begins creating momentum by getting buy-in from key players throughout the organization. The most significant deliverable of the pretransformation phase is the creation of cross-functional rapid response teams, after which the organization enters phase 1.

During phase 1, the transformation leader assigns each cross-functional rapid response team to each major business function and drives a company-wide diagnosis of its problems and their respective causes. By working in parallel, cross-functional teams save time, involve employees, and provide a more holistic and thorough perspective on the organization's situation.

Once the company has completed its analysis and diagnosis, the teams progress to phase 2, where they develop a detailed vision of where their respective function should be. This vision should address the problems found in phase 1, and the company should conduct a gap analysis to determine what is missing between the current situation of the company and the envisioned future.

Phase 3 is the development of a detailed implementation plan to move the company from its current state to its future state. This phase also involves the planning for a new organizational structure and a publicity campaign to be implemented in the transformation implementation phase.

As implied by the name, the transformation implementation phase involves actual execution of the implementation plans. The original cross-functional rapid response teams are disassembled here, and former team members are sprinkled throughout the organization, spreading their enthusiasm, newly gained knowledge, and expertise.

Note that the 90 days model can be tailored to meet an organization's particular needs. The practices and tools explained in each phase can be modified as necessary, depending on the particular situation of the organization. Let us now look at the model as a whole and see what makes the model so powerful when all these steps are combined.

WHY IS THE 90 DAYS MODEL SO EFFECTIVE?

The 90 days model is particularly effective because it incorporates the critical success factors into its DNA. Key reasons for its success are that it's participatory, all-encompassing, integrative, and fast.

It's Participatory

Cross-functional rapid response teams, the heart of the 90 days transformation, get buy-in from thought leaders and other key enthusiastic employees of the company and involve them in the transformation effort. Instead of calling in an army of consultants, assembling these teams early on in the effort creates a powerful coalition of individuals who support the transformation effort. Not only does this reduce the level of resistance to the change effort, it also breaks down many barriers within the organization, including functional barriers and the vertical chain of command. Upon completion of the effort, the organization will have grown and developed a set of leaders who have a broader perspective of company goals and logistics. The knowledge and expertise gained during the effort will aid them in taking responsibility in their daily work environment, leading to more sustained changes. Because the change effort and associated skills have been internalized, former members of the cross-functional rapid response teams can become change agents who have the experience and know-how to lead future change efforts. In this way, best practices are pushed down through the organization by leaders who were developed through the transformation effort. As Lou Gerstner, CEO and transformation leader of IBM, recognized, it is important that the employees themselves get involved in the transformation because "in the end, management doesn't change culture. Management invites the workforce itself to change the culture."[12]

It's All-Encompassing and Integrative

In the 90 days model, change is all-encompassing, holistic, and integrative, meaning that every aspect of the business—including culture, strategy, cost cutting, organizational structure, process, IT, and values—is diagnosed. Collaboration across the boundaries of an organization, from geographies to functions, improves the ability of the organization to create value, especially in a large corporation. Without changing holistically, an organization may overlook key synergies that could bring significant value to it.

It's Fast

Even with this holistic change effort, the 90 days model is fast and cost-effective because the thorough and exhaustive diagnoses are conducted in parallel internally by cross-functional rapid response teams. By using employees in the change effort, the 90 days model capitalizes on the expertise and know-how of the company itself, saving the time, money, and energy associated with hiring an army of consultants. Using internal employees also accelerates the transformation effort, especially in implementation, not only because involved employees will be less likely to misunderstand their own solutions, but also because they will feel more ownership and accountability in implementation. An accelerated effort is important, since transformation efforts often fail because they take too long and lose momentum and support. Additionally, long transformation efforts consume a tremendous amount of time and money. Hence, decreasing the length of efforts not only increases their likelihood of success but also prevents the company from spending otherwise unnecessary resources.

BEST-IN-CLASS TRANSFORMATIONS

Throughout this book, we will present numerous insightful stories from the transformation efforts in our research sample. These stories will highlight the major transformation steps, common successful practices, and even common pitfalls and practices to avoid. While they often come from tremendously successful companies, these stories more importantly represent specific instances of successful change. Few companies do *everything* well—it is therefore important to extract best practices from different companies, even if other aspects of their organization or behavior are slightly lacking.

Before we begin, however, we would like to provide you with a brief background of the six companies that used a model that closely resembled the 90 days transformation model: 3M, VeriSign, Nissan, Bay Networks, Apple, and ACI.

3M

In 1998, 3M was experiencing declining profits and revenue, on top of stagnant growth and a bloated infrastructure. Culturally, employees were content with the status quo, for there was no fear of being fired. In fact, employees referred to the company as "Mother Mining" for its maternal attitude.[13] As a result, employees were cutting corners and delivering mediocre performances. In an attempt to cut costs, however, then-CEO L.D. DeSimone cut over 5,000 jobs and decommissioned 10 percent of its global factories. This proved ineffective, as profits only improved slightly by 2000, and 3M began to seek out a new leader.

In 2000, James McNerney was brought in to heal the company's ailments. In the first ninety days, McNerney announced a global strategic plan and five company-wide performance initiatives that would help cut costs, create standards, and increase efficiencies. These five initiatives were Six Sigma, 3M Acceleration, sourcing effectiveness, indirect cost control, and eProductivity. In fact, McNerney had begun to implement four of these five initiatives within sixty days of joining the company. Furthermore, McNerney led the company through a cultural transformation, emphasizing accountability, efficiency, structured innovation, and a focus on market strengths.

Through McNerney's efforts, 3M's net sales and net income increased every year from 2001 through 2004. By the end of 2004, in fact, annual net sales had increased $4 billion, or 25 percent over the 2001 mark, topping $20 billion for the first time. In that same four-year period, stock price increased $23, peaking at $85 per share.

VeriSign

In the second quarter of 2002, as the industry recovered from the deteriorating domain name market and weak technology and telecommunication services environments, VeriSign Communications Services (VCS), a division inside Verisign Inc., did not find itself in a very competitive position.[14]

Facing mature products with decreasing margins and a lack of innovations in the product pipeline in the VCS division, Verisign's visionary CEO,

Stratton Sclavos, hired Vernon Irvin as the new executive vice president to help revive VCS and take advantage of market transition.

Irvin recruited several teams in September 2003 to help design strategies to turn VCS from a $400 million division into an $800 million one. Instead of proposed solutions, Irvin received replies like "We don't think we can do it," "We've tried everything," and "We don't know how to do what you want us to do to grow that business, because we don't think it's there."

Despite these disparaging remarks, Irvin raised the bar, setting a new revenue goal of $1 billion by 2006. He initiated a cross-functional rapid response team effort and assembled a "$1 Billion team" to drive the transformation effort. Within ninety days, the core teams developed a set of detailed implementation plans that later guided the execution of the transformation effort.

Irvin's sense of urgency and deep-seated commitment made the transformation effort highly successful. In just ninety days, he was able to empower people to take ownership over the future of the organization; he created a burning platform for change. Over the next twenty months following the ninety days, VCS met its goal of $1 billion two years ahead of schedule, and has positioned itself as "the leading provider of intelligent infrastructure services for the Internet and telecommunications networks."[15] In recognition of its leadership in creating and marketing its third-party mediation offerings to the telecommunications industry, VeriSign won the Telecommunications Service Provider of the Year Award for 2004.[16]

Nissan

In 1999, Nissan, a major Japanese automotive manufacturer, was experiencing a severe set of problems. With an insurmountable amount of debt, inflated supplier costs, standstill new product development, and no profit for nearly eight years, the company was in a state of crisis. There was a lack of focus on the customer, and employees had little concern for the pursuit of profits. Brand power had eroded, with Nissan giving away nearly $1,000 for every car it sold in the United States. Nissan's global market share had decreased from 6.6 percent in 1991 to 4.9 percent in 1999. To top it off, executives and managers felt a deep sense of resignation and helplessness.[17]

In an attempt to rescue the corporation, the company signed an alliance agreement with French automaker Renault. Immediately thereafter, Renault sent Carlos Ghosn, who was appointed as COO of Nissan, with a team of Renault employees to start "one of most aggressive and comprehensive restructuring efforts ever attempted by a manufacturing company the size of Nissan."[18]

After talking with suppliers and customers, and learning as much as possible about the company within a short time span, Ghosn initiated a cross-functional team effort to examine the problems within the organization and to examine potential solutions. He set up nine cross-functional rapid response teams to cover the areas that needed reform.

In just three months, these teams came up with solutions and significantly contributed to the development of the Nissan Revival Plan, which was unveiled in October 1999. The plan reflected a precise course of action to revive the company and was very precise in its metrics, focusing on a quick return to profitability, debt reduction, and cost cutting. Specifically, the plan called for a return to profitability in fiscal year 2000, a profit margin in excess of 4.5 percent of sales by fiscal year 2002, and a 50 percent reduction in the level of debt that existed at the time the plan was revealed.

The implementation of the plan was so successful that Ghosn announced in May 2002 that the plan that was proposed for a three-year span was completed in just over two years. In terms of financial results, the operating profit increased from $6.8 million to $2.9 billion, and net profit from a loss of $5.7 billion to $2.8 billion. Operating margin increased from 1.4 to 5.5 percent, and capacity utilization increased from 53 to 82 percent. While the Nissan Revival Plan in 2000 was a huge success, currently Ghosn is leading a second transformation of Nissan to increase the number of product lines and improve operations.

Bay Networks

In 1996, there were a few key competitors in the computer networking industry, including Cisco, Wellfleet, and SynOptics. In an effort to become a major networking company and to compete against Cisco, which was growing through the acquisition of a series of smaller companies, Wellfleet and SynOptics merged to become Bay Networks. However, soon after the signing of the contract, the two companies experienced the difficultly of integrating two corporations with very different corporate cultures. Wellfleet, headquartered in Boston, boasted a very formal, East Coast culture, while SynOptics, headquartered in Silicon Valley, exhibited a more Western, entrepreneurial style. The differing managerial styles and the difference in geography exacerbated the problem. Therefore, with the company never fully integrated, Bay Networks plunged into a phase of decreasing profits. Furthermore, there were problems in the product pipeline, with products having bugs, lacking features, and often missing deadline. In January 1997, the company realized that something had to be done, and hired Dave House, former executive vice president of Intel, as CEO, chairman, and president of Bay Networks to come and rescue the company.

House worked to "Intelize" the Bay Networks culture through his "House-Training" program, which was designed to educate his employees on the art of decision making, conflict management, effective meetings, and straight talk. Furthermore, he set out to refurbish the product pipeline in order to encourage innovation of new products. In just two months, Bay Networks had finished the planning phase of the transformation effort and was ready to implement the change effort.

As a result of his effort, Bay Networks successfully transformed itself and was acquired in 1998 by Nortel Networks for $9.1 billion. As mentioned earlier, House was appointed as president of Nortel and hired to help transform Nortel, especially its culture.

Apple

In January 1996, Apple reported a loss of over $60 million.[19] Sales had plummeted and customer satisfaction was very low. Although Mike Spindler had just taken the helm in 1993, Apple decided to bring in a new CEO in 1996. The new CEO, Gil Amelio, however, fared no better. Focusing on cutting costs, Amelio failed to address some of the more critical aspects facing Apple and turned to Steve Jobs as an advisor. When Jobs officially took over as interim CEO in 1997, Apple's market share was around 3 percent, and its share price was at the lowest point in its history.[20] To illustrate the dire situation Apple was facing, Michael Dell replied to the question of how he would handle the situation with, "What would I do? I'd shut it down and give the money back to the shareholders."[21]

Steve Jobs recognized the deep-rooted problems Apple faced. In particular, the lack of a uniform agenda and overarching strategy led to disjointed decisions and poor sales. To address these issues, Jobs turned the company back to its core competencies, narrowing its product line and refocusing the company on its customers rather than on its competitor Microsoft, going so far as to partner with Microsoft. In this vein, Jobs not only ensured that Apple developed products that customers would want but also decided to leverage one of Apple's greatest assets—its brand. The hallmark result of Jobs's efforts was the introduction of the iPod in 2001, which quickly became one of Apple's best-selling products ever. Additionally, Jobs also turned Apple around operationally, revamping its distribution system and inventory management processes.

Jobs transformed Apple from a struggling computer manufacturer to a highly successful company that also provides consumer devices and multimedia services. In 2006, Apple was ranked as having the 39th most valuable brand in the entire world.[22] Furthermore, since 1997, Apple share price has increased from $4 (split adjusted) to well over $100 in 2007.[23]

ACI

ACI (Asian Company Inc.) is a pseudonym for a midsize systems integration and consulting company based in Bangalore, India, with offices in Paris and Silicon Valley. Before the transformation in 2002, ACI lacked a clear vision and strategy and was very deal focused, even at the expense of profit and a unique value proposition by the company. The company had a loosely decentralized organization with considerable redundancies between the various business units and had no clear metrics to measure the performance of the company. Human resources was mainly a secretarial function, and there was no clear control and budgeting process. On the sales and marketing side, processes were ad hoc, a situation that was exacerbated by the exodus of a top sales and marketing executive to the competitor. Leadership did not trust the employees and, in turn, the company had a high turnover rate. Furthermore, customers were unhappy, and many of them either had already switched or were seriously considering switching to a competitor.

After the 90 days transformation effort, ACI increased its revenue twofold in three years, and its percentage increase in revenue was 30 percent greater than that of its fastest-growing rival. In that same three-year period, net income increased threefold. Furthermore, within two years, turnover was reduced by 50 percent.

CONCLUSION

In this chapter, we introduced you in more detail to the critical success factors and the 90 days model. We looked at some case studies of companies that applied the concepts, and we analyzed why the 90 days model works.

At the end of the chapter, we looked at six companies that followed a strikingly similar path: the 90 days model. In our analysis, we recognized that companies typically don't do everything perfectly, and best-in-class practices come from many different sources. Additionally, the practices we've extracted represent instances of successful transformation efforts.

Throughout the rest of the book, keeping in mind the general framework of the model (pretransformation, the three phases, and transformation implementation) will help you follow the overall picture of the effort. Moving forward, we will now turn to the pretransformation phase, where the company recognizes it has a problem or is dissatisfied with its current situation and selects a transformation leader.

2

Pretransformation
Planting the Seeds

It may be hard for an egg to turn into a bird: it would be a jolly sight harder for it to learn to fly while remaining an egg. We are like eggs at present. And you cannot go on indefinitely being just an ordinary, decent egg. We must be hatched or go bad.

—C. S. Lewis

Have you ever tried fixing a bullet train while it's running? Transforming a company involves difficulties and complexities comparable to fixing a moving bullet train. Ailing companies cannot stop operating just because they're not performing up to par. Instead, businesses must continue with their regular operations while trying to improve those very operations and the company as a whole. Luckily, impossible as they sound, corporate transformations are not as impractical or unfeasible as fixing bullet trains in motion.

When you first find out someone isn't doing well, you're probably wondering, "What's wrong?" even before you ask the question "How can I fix it?" The same question should automatically arise when you're looking at an ailing company, and the pretransformation phase is one of the first steps in addressing this question. As a prelude to the 90 days transformation effort, this phase sets the stage for future endeavors to dig deeper into the troubles plaguing the company.

Before anything can happen, someone must first recognize that there is a problem in the company, and the organization must find the right person to lead it through the transformation effort. This designated transformation leader must immerse himself/herself[1] in all aspects of the company, intensely studying the organization from different angles while planting the seeds for the transformation effort. These seeds include creating a vision toward which the company can strive, as well as building a powerful coalition that can champion the effort.

The main goal of the pretransformation phase is to set the stage and create momentum for the 90 days effort. If the 90 days effort is creating the blueprint, or plan, for the actual transformation implementation, then the pretransformation is where you gather the necessary tools for creating this blueprint. A transformation can be visualized as rolling a ball over a hill—the ball must gain sufficient speed and momentum at the bottom of the hill before it can reach the top, after which it can roll down the hill without adding any additional energy. Likewise, a transformation effort faces a disproportionate number of obstacles and challenges at the beginning of the effort, and after reaching a critical point, the transformation will have enough momentum to carry itself through to completion. To help overcome the initial hurdles, the transformation leader must anticipate and address these obstacles and plant the appropriate seeds correctly in the pretransformation phase. Hence, a crucial part of the pretransformation phase is getting enough support and buy-in throughout the company, and various steps throughout the phase work toward this goal (see "Pretransformation Goals").

Depending on various factors such as the size of the company and the nature of its problems, the pretransformation phase can take anywhere from one to three months (though it typically spans only a month). While the pretransformation may appear as little more than a precursor to the actual 90 days effort, it is an integral part of the effort, and its importance cannot be

PRETRANSFORMATION GOALS

- Commit the organization to the transformation effort.

- Address initial resistance to the effort.

- Get support and buy-in throughout the company.

- Create momentum for the transformation effort.

- Get a high-level view of problems facing the company.

- Set the seeds for a successful effort through the use of cross-functional rapid response teams (see chapter 1).

overemphasized. Without the appropriate tools and processes in place, a blueprint cannot be created. As Nissan's transformation leader, Carlos Ghosn, acknowledged, "The most important phase in [Nissan's transformation], the aspect that cost the most time and effort, was . . . listening to people and observing conditions on the ground."[2] Understanding the root of the organization's ailments while gaining momentum and support for the transformation effort lies at the core of the pretransformation phase.

In this chapter, we outline the general steps taken by a company engaging in a transformation and give examples of how each of these steps plays out in the real world. The steps, what we also call prescriptions, are as follows:

Before the Transformation Leader

1. Recognize a need for change

2. Choose a transformation leader

After the Transformation Leader

3. Survey the grounds

4. Establish a sense of urgency

5. Create a motivational and strategic vision

6. Build a powerful coalition

7. Get some early wins

8. Create cross-functional rapid response teams

These steps are a means to get a high-level picture of the company's current situation and lay the groundwork for the 90 days effort and implementation. Hence, although steps like "survey the grounds" require that the transformation leader research the company by talking to people at all levels, the cross-functional rapid response teams developed at the end of the phase will actually be conducting the in-depth research and analysis of the situations and problems plaguing the company.

PRE–"TRANSFORMATION LEADER"

The first two prescriptions in the pretransformation phase should be applied in the company before the transformation leader is brought in. After recognizing a need for change, you must choose a suitable transformation leader.

Solid execution of the first two prescriptions results in a strong and capable transformation leader, which is extremely important for the rest of the transformation effort.

Prescription 1: Recognize a Need for Change

The first step in any transformation effort is recognizing that a transformation is needed (see figure 2-1). Though it sounds relatively simple and straightforward (and sometimes is), in many instances this diagnosis is not very clear-cut. Our research has resulted in a list of typical drivers of holistic change in companies (see "Examples: Typical Drivers of Transformations").

In any of these cases, a 90 days transformation effort is typically used when a holistic change effort is required. At the same time, the 90 days model can also be applied on a smaller scale to a particular business unit or function that is suffering from any of these problems.

In our analysis, typical financial factors, though informative, do not tell the entire story (see table 2-1 for reasons our sample companies engaged in transformation). Other major factors to consider include the organization's

EXAMPLES: TYPICAL DRIVERS OF TRANSFORMATIONS

- Revenue, profit, and/or market share are falling.

- You foresee that your competitors will dramatically pass you.

- You foresee a change in the customer base that will change the way business is done at your company.

- You foresee a major change in the market that your company is currently ill equipped to handle.

- The company is changing at such a fast rate that the old culture and style is insufficient in controlling and running the organization.

- The company is complacent with a mediocre status quo, but you want to become the industry leader.

- Any combination of the above.

FIGURE 2-1

Prescription 1

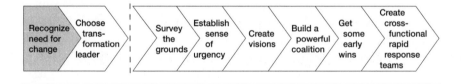

TABLE 2-1

Sample reasons companies engage in transformations

Company (year)	Reason for transformation
3M (2000)	3M suffered from a dysfunctional culture plus weak profit and growth.
ACI (2002)	There was a lack of a clear strategy, structure, and processes in the organization, which led to financial problems.
Apple (1997)	Lack of an overarching strategy, poor sales, and lack of focus on customers and its core competencies.
Bay Networks (1995)	As a result of a merger between two companies, Bay Networks faced many problems in integrating the different cultures. Hence, there was a lack of focus, and the result was a corporate culture that was not united, consistent, or efficient. Furthermore, the company had tremendous problems with the product pipeline.
Best Buy (2002)	The company was growing at a faster rate than it was prepared to handle—things were spinning out of control, and there was a lack of centralization.
General Electric (1995)	Welch foresaw that the company was not equipped to handle the future, despite current prosperity and a solid footing in the marketplace. He wasn't satisfied with the status quo.
Home Depot (2000)	The company was growing at a faster rate than it was ready to handle— it needed a cultural change, modernization, organizational restructuring, and overall, a complete transformation
IBM (1995)	The company had lost $16 billion in two years, and its stock price had plummeted.
Nissan (2000)	Management was arrogant and oblivious to customers' needs, leading to a $22 billion debt, inflated supplier costs, and standstill new product development. Nissan was on the brink of bankruptcy, and its stock price was plummeting.
VeriSign[a] (2002)	VeriSign's largest division, VeriSign Communications Services, was facing mature products with decreasing margins and a lack of innovations in the product pipeline.

[a]As mentioned in chapter 1, what we refer to as VeriSign is actually VeriSign's biggest division, VeriSign Communications Services (VCS), formerly called VeriSign Telecommunications Services (VTS).

position in the market and changes anticipated in the environment, for transformation efforts are not simply quick fixes to underlying problems but are investments for long-term growth and adaptability to change.

Transformations aren't just for companies in crises; there are many other drivers of business transformations. Desire for cultural change may be an important driver of transformation, especially when the current culture appears incapable of handling industry demands and changes in the market. Also, if you're not satisfied with the status quo, a transformation may be the ingredient that makes your company the leader of your industry. Transformations have astounding power to motivate employees behind the cause of improving the company. Employee support and morale are important for any company, and transformations can help bring an entire company to life. According to A. G. Lafley, CEO of Procter & Gamble, "You can get used to being a player without being a winner. There's a big difference between the two. So I became interested in transforming players into winners."[3]

Although some situations require a relatively deeper investigation to justify a need for change, other instances can bypass the in-depth analysis because the company's situation is so dire. For example, Nissan's market share had declined for twenty-seven years in a row, and the company had posted a deficit in seven of the eight fiscal years preceding 1999 before the company responded by bringing in Carlos Ghosn as its transformation leader.[4] In another dramatic example, IBM's loss of $16 billion in the three-year period from 1991 to 1993 resulted in a corporate crisis and the immediate decision to bring in a CEO and transformation leader, Lou Gerstner.[5] Hence, although there are often shades of gray in terms of determining a need for a transformation, there are also cases in which the decision should be clearly black or white.

When most people think of a transformation, they typically think of it as a cure for an existing problem. However, transformations can also serve as a preventative measure to address anticipated issues. This observation parallels the important role of forecasting and planning in businesses. Appropriately, Jack Welch's phrase "Change before you have to" has become a mantra for business transformations. To stay ahead in a competitive market, you and your company must always be one step ahead of your competitors. Doing so requires insight on the part of the company's leaders into both the current state of the organization and the future direction of the industry, market, and competitors. The importance of the role of anticipation of external changes and fast transformation is also reflected in Welch's argument that the rate of internal change must be greater than the rate of external change, or the company will fall behind.

There is an ambiguity inherent in recognizing a need for change. In the same way that different people can analyze the same data and come up with different results and conclusions, different people can look at the same company and have completely different perspectives about its situation and future. This difference in interpretations is exacerbated by the fact that people rarely have the same information, background, and experiences in a company. Given the natural occurrence of different perspectives, it isn't surprising that some people in a company fail to acknowledge the severity, or even the existence, of the company's problems. Inevitably, some people resist recognizing a need to transform, sometimes out of incomplete or inaccurate information, but other times out of fear. In both cases, open communication with employees, a theme throughout this book, will be crucial to the success to the transformation.

Companies that engage in transformations ultimately want a radical improvement, or even a quantum leap, in performance. They understand and internalize the costs of not changing while they embrace the benefits of changing. When the organization is finally persuaded by a cost-benefit analysis of changing versus not changing, it will see no other choice than to engage in a transformation effort.

Prescription 2: Choose a Transformation Leader

After it has been decided that a transformation is the appropriate approach to address the organization's current situation, the next step is to find a strong and suitable leader for the transformation effort (see figure 2-2). While the general criteria used in choosing company leaders hold for selection of a transformation leader, there are also specific criteria to consider. (See "Examples: Questions to Consider When Choosing a Transformation Leader" for types of questions to consider in the selection process.)

FIGURE 2-2

Prescription 2

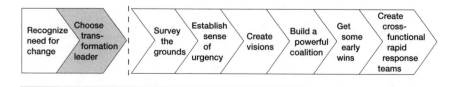

EXAMPLES: QUESTIONS TO CONSIDER WHEN CHOOSING A TRANSFORMATION LEADER

- Has he ever promoted change or led a transformation effort? If not, what skill set or toolbox does he carry that would help him in our transformation effort?

- Can he motivate the entire organization behind the change?

- Does he think holistically and strategically?

- Does he understand our corporate culture? Is he culturally aware and sensitive of his surroundings and the corporate values? How can he improve the culture?

- Is he a good listener who won't jump to conclusions? A good, strong, open, and effective communicator?

- Is he a good judge of character? Is he observant?

- Can he put together pieces of the puzzle to see the bigger picture?

- Do his goals align with those of the company?

- Does he have experience managing an organization our size?

- Does his leadership style match the needs of a company in our stage of the life cycle?

Although many leaders of successful transformations were external to the company, this is not a requirement, for some successful transformation leaders were promoted from within. One prime example is General Electric's Jack Welch, who was promoted to CEO after twenty-one years of employment with the company. During his tenure, Welch led one of the most famous and successful transformations known. Although General Electric was tremendously successful when Welch stepped in, he realized that it was not prepared to handle the future. Welch's experience highlights the finding that if the transformation leader is to be promoted from within, he should not have an institutionalized view of the company and its problems. In fact, it would behoove the company to find a leader who thinks outside the box, because a fresh perspective can speed up the transformation and prevent a stalemate. This new perspective and a fresh start are particularly important in the rare cases where the transformation leader is already at the top of the organization. Although this happens infrequently, sometimes the most qualified and appropriate person to lead the transformation is already in office and simply needs to declare, initiate, and lead the effort. Regardless of the origin of the new transformation leader, a unique and uninstitutionalized perspective on the company is a necessary driving force of change.

Looking at the Résumé and Beyond

One of the first things a transformation leader needs is experience. Does this candidate have a track record indicating he is capable of handling the job? Is he strong enough to make tough decisions and follow through with them? In some cases, the strongest candidate actually may not come from the company's industry, as in the case of IBM's Lou Gerstner. Gerstner was recruited from RJR Nabisco, never having had experience in the technology industry. Despite this lack of experience, Gerstner had an impressive set of skills and characteristics that fit the needs of the company and distinguished him from other candidates. Particularly, IBM realized that its problems weren't technical but organizational and cultural, and that it needed someone who was "a proven, effective leader—one who is skilled at generating and managing change."[6] Gerstner had demonstrated his effectiveness in this realm, having previously driven transformation efforts at American Express and RJR Nabisco.

Because the leader must be able to mobilize the entire organization around the transformation effort, he must have strong communication skills in order to articulate the need for change, as well as to create and model an environment embracing transparency, an important factor of success. From the beginning, Nissan's transformation leader, Carlos Ghosn, believed in total transparency: "The temptation to avoid the truth in public is strong, especially when times get tough. That's why Ghosn and others talked so frankly about Nissan and its problems in the beginning, pinpointing problems in sometimes painful detail for all to see."[7]

The leader should be able to reinvigorate people who are detaching themselves from the effort and the organization as a whole, and this can generally be done through open, honest communication. Gerstner claimed, "No institutional transformation takes place, I believe, without a multi-year commitment by the CEO to put himself or herself constantly in front of employees and speak in plain, simple, compelling language that drives conviction and action throughout the organization.[8]

The transformation leader must be able to use simple and compelling language to rally the company to act in support of the transformation effort. Complex messages are more likely to be misunderstood and misinterpreted, which may have important consequences down the road, making the leader lose effectiveness. Our research has demonstrated that successful transformation leaders also serve as motivators. In hindsight, Ghosn recognized, "Everything I've been able to do has been based on motivating our people. All our accomplishments start from there . . . the question was, 'How can we make the most of Nissan's human capital, how can we motivate our people?' That was the only way to start climbing out of the hole we were in. Motivating our employees was an essential step in the company's recovery. And one of our top priorities was to assess what we could do to reinforce that motivation."[9]

As a motivator, the transformation leader must be very wary of jumping to conclusions. He should be able to find data not to support his hypothesis but to develop one. In short, a successful transformation leader should neither assume a one-size-fits-all solution for the transformation effort nor have prefabricated solutions, thinking he already fully understands the company's problems without fully considering its complexities. He should also be a good judge of character, for he must form a strong, powerful coalition and choose the right people for the cross-functional rapid response teams that will drive the transformation effort (discussed in detail in the next chapter).

Cultural Sensitivity and Fit

To motivate and mobilize the entire company behind the transformation effort, the leader should be sensitive to and aware of the company's culture, even if he ultimately seeks to change and improve the current culture. Immediately trying to impose a culturally insensitive solution on a company without first assessing the situation and gaining credibility is like giving a patient medicine he is allergic to. Both actions will cause a backlash, creating more problems and potentially aggravating the situation.

So far, we have seen many CEOs serve also as the transformation leader. However, this observation leads many people to the misconception of equating the CEO with the transformation leader. While many transformation leaders are also CEOs, there certainly are some notable exceptions. (See table 2-2 for some examples of the range of the roles of various transformation leaders within their companies.) Two such examples are Carlos Ghosn, who was Nissan's COO at the time of the transformation, and Vernon Irvin, who was an executive vice president at VeriSign in charge of a business unit. However, although they were not the CEOs of their respective companies, they were

TABLE 2-2

Sample transformation leaders and their titles

Company	Transformation leader	Title
3M	James McNerney	CEO
Bay Networks	Dave House	CEO
General Electric (1995–1999)	Jack Welch	CEO
General Electric (2001–2005)	Jeff Immelt	CEO
Home Depot	Robert Nardelli	CEO
IBM	Lou Gerstner	CEO
Nissan	Carlos Ghosn	COO
VeriSign	Vernon Irvin	Executive VP

given a good amount of power, autonomy, authority, and status. Without the autonomy and ability to make decisions and carry them out, the transformation leader is extremely limited in what he can do. If he's not the CEO, the transformation leader usually takes on the role as a senior executive, empowered to make and enforce decisions and deadlines as well as lead cross-functional teams. Without status and authority, the new leader will encounter more barriers when trying to champion the transformation and get buy-in. Moreover, the non-CEO transformation leader needs support from the actual CEO. They should engage in active dialogue and maintain an open communication stream, for a CEO who does not feel informed about or involved with the changes occurring in the company may feel threatened and can easily stall or even end the effort.

Communicating a high-level goal of the transformation effort to the candidate is helpful in both the recruiting process and the transformation effort. For example, IBM wanted a strategic and cultural transformation, and for "someone . . . to grab hold of [the company] and shake it back to action."[10] These goals not only help in the selection of a suitable transformation leader but also help guide the transformation effort.

First Steps

Once the transformation leader has been selected, he will need to build a strong team to drive the effort. To assemble this team, the leader may draw on a combination of employees, both internal and external to the company. For example, if the new leader is brought in from the outside, he may want to bring with him a small coalition of his finest employees who are best suited to help transform this particular company. On entering Nissan, Ghosn brought with him a coalition of about thirty employees from Renault;[11] Dave House also brought with him several key executives on entering Bay Networks. On the flip side, Carly Fiorina failed to bring in any outside executives when she joined Hewlett-Packard, which contributed to her ineffectiveness at leading change.

Most people entering a company with the transformation leader are high-level, senior executives and managers. One position a new leader often fills is that of the CFO because it is a critical role in the company. Lou Gerstner, for example, brought into IBM Jerry York from Chrysler. Bay Networks' Dave House also brought in a new CFO. The CFO is an important position to fill prudently because the CFO serves as the transformation leader's eye in every part of the company, keeping track of all the financials and hence having a complete financial picture of the company. Often, the company will turn to the CFO to help cut costs in addition to analyzing trade-offs in key decisions. The CFO is also crucial in creating a dashboard of numbers, which makes every financial part of the company highly visible. In cases in which a new CFO is not introduced but the company is financially in trouble, the company's incumbent CFO must be able to have a unique and fresh perspective on the company's financial situation, on top of thoroughly and objectively running and analyzing the numbers.

In some cases the problem lies with the board of directors. Nevertheless, transformation leaders may not have the power to change this. Such a situation was evident in Dave House's tenure as the president of Nortel after its acquisition of Bay Networks, when the board of directors was more interested in managing the organization than in supporting the transformation effort. Because of this, and because House didn't have the power or mandate to enforce the changes, he was unable to successfully transform Nortel. However, when Steve Jobs retuned to Apple as its interim CEO in 1997, he immediately revamped the board of directors in anticipation of the potential roadblocks they would pose. In doing so, Jobs replaced all but two of the former board of directors with well-known experienced industry executives, such as Larry Ellison, chairman of Oracle Corporation, and Jerry York, former CFO of IBM.[12]

The new transformation leader should be formally identified and introduced to the company during this pre–"transformation leader" subphase. His first task should be to officially launch the transformation through an internal (and if desired, external) announcement. This can be done through various ways, including a companywide meeting and a press release. In this announcement, there is no need for the transformation leader to describe the problems of the company, since neither he nor the organization under him has conducted an analysis. After this initial announcement, however, the transformation leader should be extremely wary of leaking information to the press and the public. From this point on, until the external public relations campaign is launched after the conclusion of phase 3, all findings and plans should be kept internal to the company to prevent public scrutiny and premature assumptions and criticisms from outsiders, including investors.

When the transformation is officially announced internally, many employees will resist the announcement and the effort. Therefore, it is important to encourage all employees to be open minded about the transformation. The transformation leader needs to explain that the effort is not a cause for alarm but an opportunity to improve and prepare for a better and brighter future. At the same time, however, the transformation leader should be open to letting some employees who truly resist the transformation leave the organization of their own accord. This works to ensure that those left within the company are willing to whole-heartedly support the organization as it traverses to new territories.

POST–"TRANSFORMATION LEADER"

The following prescriptions are activities the transformation leader should engage in after his arrival. Recognizing that the situation of the company and the weight of the responsibilities may seem overwhelming to the transformation leader upon his arrival, we have prioritized the most important actions to be taken.

Prescription 3: Survey the Grounds

Transformation leaders, especially new hires, often receive both internal and external pressure to have "the answer" when they first take the helm. However, how can they have "the answer" when they don't even know exactly what "the problem" is (see figure 2-3)? (See "Dave House Finds 'The Answer.'")

FIGURE 2-3

Prescription 3

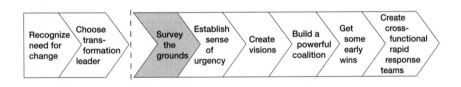

DAVE HOUSE FINDS "THE ANSWER"

When Dave House first joined Bay Networks, his initial conversation with his public relations staff and analysts alike went as follows:

"What are you going to do?"

"Well, what do you mean?"

"What is your strategy?"

"I do not know."

"You do not know?"

"No, but I can tell you how I know what it's going to be. I will talk to the customers and employees. And, from that I will know what the strategy should be."[13]

Facing the pressure of people who wanted answers, House recognized that he first needed to survey the grounds before he could make any sound conclusions about the new direction of the company.

One of the most important things the new transformation leader can do in the early stages of the transformation is to survey the grounds. Not only does it help the transformation leader become familiar with the company, it also gives him an understanding of some of the problems plaguing the company at a deeper level than in the initial stage (the initial stage was discussed in "Prescription 1: Recognize a Need for Change"). Furthermore, by surveying the grounds, the transformation leader will develop and expand his network as well as gain credibility and support for the transformation effort through communication of the need to change. By the end of this part of the pre-transformation, the transformation leader should have several high-level hypotheses about the issues that need to be resolved through the effort.

This initial assessment of the company includes a brief financial analysis to determine the feasibility of a holistic transformation, followed by a deeper analysis of the overall situation. In some cases, the initial, basic financial assessment can be done by bringing auditors into the company—this evaluation should consider the company's cash flow, for a company with heavy investments but little cash flow will find it very difficult to finance a transformation effort (see "Inaccurate Financial Assessment at ACI"). Even Nissan had severe, threatening financial problems, which Ghosn recognized: "Nissan had so much debt that it became almost impossible to invest in our future."[14] In this audit, it is extremely critical to make sure that the income statement, the balance sheet, and the cash flow are all correct and present an accurate representation of the company's financial situation.

Following this initial financial assessment, the leader himself should engage in an analysis of the overall situation of the company. The goal of this part of the pretransformation is to gain information about the company from all levels and to ultimately be able to develop an idea of the core problems creating the symptoms. By surveying the grounds, the transformation leader can develop a clearer picture of the company's situation and eventually develop a high-level vision of what issues to address and toward what direction the company should head. After surveying the grounds, VeriSign's Irvin, for example, found a lack of processes, lack of data, lack of accountability, and lack of leadership in the organization.

Surveying the grounds also has the additional benefit of helping the transformation leader assess the megatrends of the industry and market. Understanding the general direction the market is heading in will not only help both the transformation leader and the company stay ahead of the curve but also help the transformation leader develop a general idea of a vision (see prescription 5, discussed later in the chapter).

INACCURATE FINANCIAL ASSESSMENT AT ACI

ACI, an Asian company, encountered many problems that could have otherwise been avoided had the consultants conducted an accurate assessment of the financial status of the company. In later stages of the transformation, the consultants supporting the transformation found out that the company was in a more precarious financial situation than previously thought—there was a large amount of debt, and cash was running low. Because of this financial situation, the transformation effort partially focused on obtaining adequate funding. The funding was secured and the company was turned around, and through this experience the consultants learned the importance of conducting an accurate preliminary financial audit of the company before engaging in a full transformation effort.

Develop (Don't Support) a Hypothesis via Dialogue

The new leader should not have preconceived notions or stereotypes about the company and its problems, nor should he have prefabricated solutions. While the leader may in fact have a vague idea of the problems plaguing the company, he should not let those ideas color his interpretation of the data. In fact, by surveying the grounds and listening to others, the transformation leader is gaining credibility and demonstrating to the organization that he is not coming in as the company's savior but as a problem solver.

Despite being one of the most time-consuming parts of the pretransformation effort, developing this high-level analysis of the company is a fundamental step no leader should skimp on. The transformation leader's job here is to listen to what people at all reaches of the company have to say about the situation. For example, Mark Hurd spent his first month at HP listening to people and analyzing the company's situation from all levels and angles (see "How Hurd Listened at HP"). By opening a dialogue with employees through-

---

HOW HURD LISTENED AT HP

In an extensive analysis of the company, Hurd examined HP from every angle to understand how the company had reached such a dire situation.[15] Prior to his arrival, Hurd had engaged in preliminary research by looking at the books, the past and present results, and the various segments of the company. Even before his first day on the job, Hurd had submitted to HP a list of things he wanted to see and meetings he wanted to hold so he could hit the ground running. He spoke to the board and talked to employees at all levels, from those working in the sales department, R&D, consulting, and manufacturing to executives and division presidents. In his meetings, he asked people what they thought was going right, what they thought was going wrong, and what suggestions they had to improve the situation. Hurd additionally turned to external perceptions of the company, meeting with 1,000 customers in his first three months.[16]

As a result of this analysis, Hurd was able to synthesize all his data into an informed hypothesis about the problems plaguing the company. Both customers and employees were complaining that HP had gotten too complex to get anything done. While summarizing HP's problems, however, Hurd was also careful to highlight HP's strengths, which included a significant international presence and talented and dedicated employees.[17]

out the organization, Hurd took this opportunity to develop and expand his network, which was especially important given that he had just recently entered the organization. Hence, the process of surveying the grounds is not simply to get information about the company and its ailments but also to indirectly get information about its employees and leaders of the organization.

It is critical to ask employees the right questions. (See "Questions to Ask Employees to Survey the Grounds" for sample questions to ask when talking to employees.) In assessing the state of any company, remember that every company, despite its current situation, has its strengths and effective processes. Finding and recognizing a company's strengths is important because it signifies items that can be built on and enhanced. Hence, a company's strengths can be the tools the transformation leader needs to enact change, as well as a way to maintain employee morale.

In addition to listening and surveying the ground, the newly appointed transformation leader must communicate with clarity and honesty. Using various means, Ghosn communicated the need for change to both everyone involved with the company and the general public. In his first few weeks, Ghosn had initiated a series of meetings with the press, holding informal briefing sessions for small groups and making sure everyone was clear about the

QUESTIONS TO ASK EMPLOYEES TO SURVEY THE GROUNDS

- What is wrong with the company? What is currently being done to address these issues?

- What is right about the company?

- How can we improve what is wrong with the company?

- What is your role in the company? What are you contributing to the company? What about the value of your business?

- What is the company's vision? How do you fit into this vision?

- What are the roadblocks that are preventing you from achieving your goals?

- Who are the great "thought" leaders of the organization?

- What suggestions do you have for the transformation leader?

transformation effort.[18] In what Ghosn calls "total transparency," he spoke openly about the company's problems as he understood them, as painful as it was for others to hear, but he also reassured listeners that changes were going to be made to address these issues. When the company is not performing, it is transparency that will earn back some credibility. According to Ghosn, "My essential task from the beginning was to establish lines of communication with our shareholders in order to persuade them, too, to renew their faith in the company."[19] Communication about the need for change should therefore not be limited to those directly involved with the company but should extend to all reaches of the public, from employees to shareholders and even to potential investors. The key task here is to communicate the process of change versus the details of diagnosis, which will occur during phase 1 of transformation.

Gerstner's survey of the grounds also provided valuable insight into the company from all levels and angles (see "Gerstner Surveys the Grounds at IBM"). Like Hurd's, Gerstner's conversations with employees served the dual purpose of both gaining and disseminating information about the imminent change in the company. In talking to employees, Gerstner made sure to rally them behind the transformation effort, assuring each employee of his value to the company and his potential to make a tremendous difference in the transformation effort by taking on crucial tasks and roles. Additionally, Gerstner made a point to communicate with the customer base. In his dialogue and interactions with customers, Gerstner made sure they felt valued and appreciated by the company. From the beginning, Gerstner realized that "it is crucial that [he] get out into the field. [He] didn't want [his] understanding of the company to be based on the impressions of headquarters employees."[20] To get a more balanced view of the situation, Gerstner, like many other successful transformation leaders, talked to both satisfied and dissatisfied customers.

While subjective assessments of the company are very important in diagnosing the problems, objective measurements and assessments also add value to the analysis. Although numbers by themselves should not be taken at face value (there's usually a story behind the numbers), they can, in conjunction with the company's reality, add value and clarify some key issues that need to be addressed. These objective measurements can come from within the company, such as the company's finances, or extend beyond the company, such as benchmarking. For example, IBM's CFO Jerry York was asked by Gerstner to compare IBM's costs with those of its competitors. To help conduct this benchmarking study, York hired outside consultants to compare IBM's expenses in each of its business units with the average of other com-

GERSTNER SURVEYS THE GROUNDS AT IBM

One of the first meetings Gerstner called when he entered the company was a briefing of the state of the business in order to gain a high-level idea of some of the issues ailing the company. Because Gerstner had no previous experience managing a technology company, he met extensively with industry (computer and telecommunication) experts during his first few weeks on the job. Additionally, Gerstner requested that his senior executives produce two ten-page reports—the first one focusing on the business unit's customers' needs, long- and short-term key issues, and the outlook for the upcoming year, while the second was to focus on the executives' ideas about changes necessary to the transformation effort. Gerstner read each of these reports closely and spent a full day with each of his senior executives privately discussing the reports. These meetings furthermore allowed Gerstner to evaluate the executives' performance and leadership potential.

Gerstner traveled extensively outside headquarters to review the business with senior executives, hold employee meetings, and visit customers. Traveling to company sites, he not only listened to employee concerns but also informed them that change was coming and that the employees would play a key role in the transformation.

Importantly, Gerstner also met with customers and demonstrated his commitment to them. In one particular instance, he attended a customer conference at Chantilly, Virginia, where some attendees were IBM's best customers. While the IBM board members expected Gerstner to simply show up, make a speech, and leave, as previous CEOs did, Gerstner stayed for the entire two days of the conference, meeting and talking to his customers. At the conference, Gerstner reassured the customers that IBM would change and prioritize the customer first, as well as deliver the performance expected of the company. His actions spoke as loud as his words.[21]

panies in the same businesses.[22] While IBM used outside consultants to help analyze the company's situation, analysts and consultants are optional in this part of the process. Ghosn opted not to use consultants because he believed that they "would only slow [the transformation effort] down and cost too much."[23] Consultants and analysts do provide a certain amount of expertise, such as benchmarking and providing an outsider's perspective of the financial situation of the company, but they are more useful in the latter parts of the pretransformation phase, such as in the creation of a company vision and building cross-functional teams.

While this part of the pretransformation may consume tremendous time and energy, one must be patient and exhaustive in surveying the grounds (see "Review: Important Practices for Surveying the Grounds"). Some of the less successful transformation leaders end this process prematurely, sometimes because of impatience or fear of creating a crisis. Whatever the reason, failure of the leader to thoroughly complete this step of analyzing the company's situation often has dire consequences later on in the transformation effort and ultimately leads to a transformation failure.

Prescription 4: Establish a Sense of Urgency

Communication of the need for change is not enough for a 90 days transformation effort. Rather, the transformation leader needs to establish a sense of urgency (see figure 2-4). Although companies engaging in a transformation effort may have different timelines for how long they expect it to take, transformations typically take longer than expected when a sense of urgency is not communicated.

Companies that haven't established a sense of urgency tend to encounter more complications and resistance, delaying the transformation process. In fact, it is very easy and common for companies to spend the bulk of their

REVIEW: IMPORTANT PRACTICES FOR SURVEYING THE GROUNDS

- Enter without preconceptions—listen before making judgments.

- Talk to people at all levels of involvement with the company, from employees at all levels to suppliers and customers, in both small and large settings.

- Communicate the value of change to everyone you talk to, including shareholders.

- Reassure employees of their value to the company.

- Use objective measurements to support your subjective findings and conclusions.

FIGURE 2-4

Prescription 4

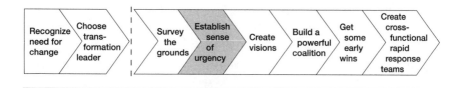

time in the planning stages without ever taking any action, because it is generally easier to speak of action than to act. This sense of complacency serves as an initial source of resistance that must be overcome before the transformation effort can even begin on a companywide scale. The sense of urgency serves as the catalyst to overcome this resistance to spark immediate action and creates the momentum necessary for a successful transformation early on in the effort (see figure 2-5). The importance of using a sense of crisis as a driving force for change is highlighted by Lou Gerstner: "The sine qua non of any successful corporate transformation is public acknowledgement of the existence of a crisis."[24] Without this sense of crisis, Gerstner believes, transformations are doomed to failure.

In many ways, a sense of urgency mobilizes the company and justifies the transformation effort. According to renowned researcher John Kotter, the

FIGURE 2-5

Changing resistance over time

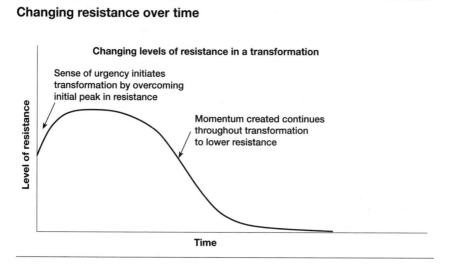

sense of urgency necessary to drive a successful transformation occurs when about 75 percent of a company's management truly believes that business-as-usual is unacceptable.[25] Once this critical mass of employees believing in the need for a transformation is reached, the transformation will essentially drive itself. This momentum is critical, especially for the later stages of the effort. The role of urgency as a driving force for change was also noted by Ghosn: "If there's a reticence about sharing the results [of a diagnosis of a failing company], there can be no shared sense of urgency. If you don't yell, 'Fire!'—if you content yourself with saying, 'Hey, it's really hot in here. Maybe something's burning somewhere'—then the flames will continue to grow. You have to identify the problem and circulate your diagnosis."[26]

The longer you take, the more severe the problem becomes and the more time it will take to remedy the situation. For the most efficient and effective effort, the problem must be recognized and addressed head-on and immediately, and this mind-set can be created by spreading a sense of urgency throughout the company.

In many failed transformations, the leader typically underestimated the difficulty of driving people out of their comfort zones in support of change. The importance of a sense of crisis in addressing this roadblock to change is reflected by Gerstner: "If employees do not believe a crisis exists, they will not make the sacrifices that are necessary to change. Nobody likes change. Whether you are a senior executive or an entry-level employee, change represents uncertainty and, potentially, pain."[27]

Some negative emotions associated with change can also be associated with an extreme sense of urgency. Hence, although a sense of urgency is critical for a successful transformation effort, it must be used and communicated carefully. Companies trying to instill a sense of urgency in their employees can often make the mistake of overcommunicating it, which can result in counterproductive emotions, including panic, anger, and frustration. While a moderate sense of urgency will inspire and ignite the passion of employees, an extreme sense of urgency will be completely demoralizing and may lead to a sense of helplessness and hopelessness throughout the company, which, in effect, ends the transformation effort before it even begins.

Spreading Urgency Like a Wildfire

So how do you create and communicate this sense of urgency without sparking counterproductive emotions such as anger and fear? Prescription 1 highlighted the importance of recognizing a need for change even before a transformation effort is undertaken. To establish the necessary sense of urgency, the transformation leader must communicate several of the core issues at the heart of the organization's problems (found in "Prescription 3: Survey the Grounds") with the rest of the organization and why these problem areas necessitate changes that can only be accomplished via a transformation effort. General Electric's former CEO Jack Welch recognized the importance of justifying and communicating the necessity and urgency of the change for the success of the effort: "How do you bring people into the change process? Start with reality. Get all the facts out. Give people the rationale for change, laying it out in the clearest, most dramatic terms. When everybody gets the same facts, they'll generally come to the same conclusion."[28]

When information and findings from the high-level analysis are clearly communicated to employees, they will see and understand the problems the company is facing and be motivated to address these issues. Welch also noted that the facts must be presented dramatically, to activate the emotional state of employees. People are more likely to remember and respond to emotions than simple facts, and when people feel emotionally driven, they are less likely to resist change. However, there is a fine line between drama and parody. Communicating the urgency too dramatically may counterproductively lighten the situation and underemphasize its importance. In an extreme scenario, overdramatizing the direness of the situation may make it comedic and the transformation effort a joke.

Another way to communicate the sense of urgency to employees in a memorable way is to create visual presentations explaining the problems and the importance of addressing them immediately. While numbers and statistics are important and help identify the company's problems, they often do not motivate employees to the level necessary to induce full-scale change. Instead, employees typically comprehend the urgency of the situation and support the transformation wholeheartedly only after they are emotionally moved and can see the organization's problems from different perspectives and in a fuller sense. For example, an effective means of communicating the sense of urgency is through a video where important customers express their frustrations with the organization. These grievances often hit on key issues of the problem and can be expressed in a direct and honest way without completely demoralizing employees.

As you can probably tell by now, there are many different channels to communicate a need for change and a sense of urgency. (See "Review: Communicating a Sense of Urgency" for examples.) Different senses can be targeted and modes of distribution can vary. While the most dramatic and memorable methods of communication are typically most effective, other

---

REVIEW: COMMUNICATING
A SENSE OF URGENCY

- Use every opportunity available to communicate the sense of urgency

- Use various channels to achieve both breadth and depth

- Target different senses:

  - Audio: speed and tone of speech, music, and so on

  - Visual: text, images, graphs, and so on

- Be emotional, logical, and so on

- Vary the modes of distribution:

  - Visual: videos, flyers, posters, and so on

  - Audio: announcements, speeches, podcasts, jingles, testimonials, and so on

  - Interactive: focus groups, informal dialogue, meetings, and so on

---

means also have their merits. On the whole, the various methods complement one another and target different types of employees, and more variety in how the sense of urgency is communicated translates to a greater portion of employees who receive the message. Furthermore, employees will be more deeply affected when the message hits them through different channels. For example, an employee to whom the sense of urgency is communicated through graphs and numbers as well as through videos expressing customer frustrations will generally remember and understand the message better than an employee to whom the urgency is communicated through either means alone. Hence, different means of communication achieve both breadth and depth in the organization's reception of the message, and the sense of urgency should be communicated at every opportunity possible.

Road shows, one-day sitewide communication meetings specifically targeted at all employees, are effective mediums for using a variety of means to communicate a sense of urgency. Not only can road shows communicate the problems plaguing the organization, they can simultaneously alleviate some fears that accompany change, especially regarding job loss and pay cuts, by examining the future opportunities that will result from the effort.

Strong and appropriate communication of the sense of urgency is critical at this stage in the transformation effort because it creates momentum and buy-in and also sets the tone for the rest of the process. As expected, the transformation leader plays a vital role in this communication effort: "It is the job of the [leader] to define and communicate [the] crisis, its magnitude, its severity, and its impact."[29]

Prescription 5: Create a Motivational and Strategic Vision

A solid, inspirational vision plays an important role in an organization, especially during a transformation effort (see figure 2-6). Morale during transformations usually deteriorates because employees fear layoffs as a result of the general approach of cost cutting. Employees also tend to become focused on the present and the diseases ailing the organization during a transformation, causing them to lose sight of the future. This present orientation and decreasing morale can be countered by the creation and communication of a strong, compelling vision. A vision not only inspires and motivates employees, it also serves as a tool for filtering and aligning all projects undertaken by the organization by ensuring that projects and key decisions are consistent with the vision. In addition, an exceptional vision will help create a sense of alliance, rather than simply compliance, within the company, motivating employees to act in accordance with the vision on their own.

"Toe-may-toe" or "Toe-mah-toe"?

When people think of a vision, they usually think of a motivational, spiritual goal toward which the company strives. In contrast, people conceptualize a strategy as more rational, down-to-earth, and focused. In this chapter, however, we will describe both notions as visions because they are both goals toward which the organization grows. Although both must be inspiring, we will

FIGURE 2-6

Prescription 5

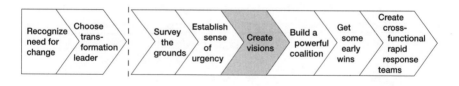

distinguish them as motivational visions and strategic visions. While the motivational vision is broad and all-encompassing, the strategic vision is more business oriented.

As an idea that will be ingrained in the culture, heart, and soul of every employee in the company, the motivational vision is crucial to the company's workforce. The motivational vision should be compelling and exciting, for it should galvanize employees and inspire them inside out. Every employee, old and new, must internalize the message, moving the company toward the desired mind-set or culture with certain values. The motivational vision is also a way to communicate the core values and goals of the company to customers in a sentence or two, and hence must be clear and articulate. For example, Apple's vision, as articulated by Steve Jobs, is "to make contributions to the world by making tools for the mind that advance humankind."[30] A motivational vision can also be more realistic and focused, such as McKinsey's: "to help leading corporations and governments to be more successful."[31] Whether the motivational vision is far-reaching or more focused, it is important in defining and guiding the direction of the strategic vision.

The company's strategic vision, however, should be more focused and supported by research, logically following the leader's analysis of the company's problems and culture. At a high level, the strategic vision should set a clear and realistic direction for the company and answer the questions Where do we want to go? How will we get there? and Why will we be successful? The vision should align the company with the market and give a general direction of where the company wants to go. As in setting the direction for a ship, the initial direction and preliminary course of action are critical—if you to not point your ship in the right direction, you may end up heading west when you actually wanted to head north, which could have disastrous consequences. A strategic vision points you in the right direction without laying out the day-to-day plan or charting the specific stars to follow. Providing this flexibility is critical, because the vision cannot change with the whims and frequent changes of the business environment.

A strong, high-level strategic vision should be responsive to various internal and external factors, from consumer and market evolution and trends in technology and competition to the company's core competencies and financial goals. Additionally, it should align the market and platform, products and services, and technology and value chain strategies. These are aspects the transformation leader should have assessed and analyzed at a high level when he surveyed the grounds (prescription 3), especially with respect to the megatrends.

One common misunderstanding people have about the strategic vision is that a plan is an important deliverable and aspect of the strategy. While planning will inevitably result from a good strategic vision, it is too early in the transformation to plan the details at this point. Vision setting, whether strategic or motivational, should be intuitive and macroscopic rather than microscopic and detailed.

The creation of a strategic vision is very important because it guides the company in its transformation and future actions and decisions. At this stage, it is not necessary to know exactly how you will achieve your vision. For example, you may know that you want to head south, but you don't need to know how you will get there—not yet. Recognize at this stage that there are various means to achieve your vision—for example, you can walk, drive, swim, or even fly. While these different methods will all help you achieve your vision (albeit at different speeds), there are many advantages and disadvantages to each of them. Don't worry about them yet. Here, it is more important that the vision be well informed and backed by the high-level analysis performed earlier. Developing a vision that tells the company it wants to head south when it should really go east can aggravate the situation, stall the transformation, or even lead to the company's demise. For that reason, you may opt to call in outside consultants to get some expert opinion, but the company should be the ultimate driving force for the development of the vision because ultimately it is the company that will be implementing it.

One example of a company's strategic vision is Apple's decision to refocus on the customer and the company's core competencies. Jobs realized that Apple was struggling partly because of lack of an overarching, unifying strategy, and so he realized that the company needed to refocus on its strengths and ignore the noise. Jobs recognized the importance of pursuing Apple's key market segments, education and creative content; however, at this point he hasn't decided to pursue specific partnerships or identified specific products to develop, although he did identify the Mac OS as a key asset to expand on.

Another example is Gerstner's decision to reverse IBM's former strategy of separating the company into independent units, creating instead a culture of unity to bring about integrated solutions to customers.[32] Another example of a high-level strategic vision can be deciding how you want your company to be organizationally structured—for example, a company can be centralized, decentralized, or divided by functions or businesses. Aligning the vision with the company, its business, and the market are all important aspects to remember.

Creating the Perfect Message

To be effective, a vision's message, whether motivational or strategic, should hit several key ideas and touch on the heart of the company. One of the key elements of a vision is anticipating and preparing the company for the future at a very high level. In doing so, a vision should not be equated with a plan or even a business model or strategy.

Additionally, an effective vision not only looks toward the future, it also recognizes the past and its successes without dwelling on it. To do so, the vision must be consistent with the past values of the organization at some level, even while changing the direction of the company. Some of the most ineffective visions dwell on past failures or simply explain business models without recognizing the emotional drivers in an organization.

Furthermore, ineffective visions tend to be either too specific or too broad. A vision that is too specific fails to have significance for the entire organization and is generally unsustainable. In contrast, a vision that is too broad or vague fails to have any real implications for the particular organization. A broad vision clouds the employees' ability to find a meaningful connection between the vision and the organization or their particular work. Ultimately, people want to do something that has meaning and makes a difference, and a strong vision will motivate and empower people to feel so. Likewise, a vision needs to be simultaneously a dream and attainable. A vision that is too much of a dream will be counterproductive, for employees will not believe in it. At the same time, people will resist making sacrifices for a vision that is not like a dream but simply based on the realities of the business and its survival.

The crux of a motivational and strategic vision is to inspire—inspire employees, managers, executives, leaders, customers, and the general public. An effective way to inspire the target audience of the vision is to illustrate how the world is a better place because of the organization's existence and work. People are typically driven and inspired when they acknowledge their impact on the world. Especially in a transformation effort where much of the employee's work is focused on the microscopic aspects of the effort, the employee also needs to see how his work contributes not only to the mission of the organization but also to the world at large. Effectively crafted and communicated, both the motivational and strategic visions make employees feel that they are part of something larger than both themselves and the organization. For example, instead of selling coffee beans, Howard Schultz, founder of Starbucks, promotes the idea of a "third place" community between work and home.

There are many different ways to approach the creation of a vision, both motivational and strategic. In some instances, the transformation leader calls in an entire team to provide input for the visions (see "Bay Networks Develops Its Vision"). In other models, the transformation leader alone, with minimal guidance and feedback from his immediate coalition, creates both the motivational and strategic visions. For example, at Nissan, Ghosn believed that "[the ideal] is your own vision of what the company wants to be . . . You have to define an ideal; you have to orient the company in such a way that every decision made tends toward that idea . . . People form an image of your idea, as they perceive it, and they reflect it back to you."[33] By having people mirror the vision back to him, Ghosn ensured that the message was not misinterpreted and that everyone shared a common understanding. Hence, visions serve the additional benefit of keeping everyone on the same page and working toward the same ideal.

Is It Still a Sound If No One Can Hear It?

Because both the motivational and strategic visions lie at the heart of every decision and action, they must be communicated and internalized at all levels of the company, from senior executives to low-level employees, and

---

BAY NETWORKS DEVELOPS ITS VISION

At Bay Networks, Dave House held a strategic planning session to discuss where the company wanted to be in the long term. In this session, House, along with his core powerful coalition (see prescription 6), identified the company's key strengths and values. At the end of the session, House had with him the company's values, a strategic plan, and a list of five-year objective goals. Hence, in a single session, House and his colleagues created both the motivational and strategic vision. Bay Networks' motivational vision was to accelerate the way the network is "revolutionizing the way people work, learn and play by eliminating the constraints of distance and time."[34] Because he realized that the company would change drastically, he waited until a later phase to clearly define the long-term strategic vision.

even to the public, including investors and customers. Communication of a vision involves several different aspects. On the most obvious level, the wording of the vision is critical. A simple, catchy phrase is sometimes, though not always, enough to embody a vision. For example, the motivational vision for The Home Depot was "To improve everything we touch," which had to be communicated to 325,000 associates.[35]

On the next level, there are different means of communicating the vision, such as speeches, presentations, and flyers. (See "Communicating the Vision at Banca Intesa.") These channels and modes of communication were discussed in "Prescription 4: Establish a Sense of Urgency." Another means of communication not discussed in the previous section is action. A vision and its importance to an organization can be implicitly communicated to employees through the actions and decisions of leaders. It is critical that the company can walk the talk—not only does that rally the employees, it also gives them confidence and trust in the organization.

These principles of communication were recognized by key leaders of successful transformations. For example, Bay Networks' leader, Dave House, communicated the vision through a wide variety of means, including posters, videos, and meetings, to access different channels of human behavior (that is, thought and emotion). At Scandinavian Airlines System (SAS), transfor-

COMMUNICATING THE VISION AT BANCA INTESA

Corrado Passera, CEO of Banca Intesa, developed a nationalistic vision he had to communicate to sixty thousand employees at Banca Intesa: "To become the top bank in Italy and one of the best in Europe." To spread the word, he wrote a book that most people could read and understand. Instead of inserting figures and graphs, he used everyday language to communicate the bank's current position, its desired destination, and the means of reaching it. Each employee got a personal copy of the book, which actually became the foundation for an extensive training program. To further disseminate the message, Passera traveled around the country, explaining the vision to both managers and employees alike. Passera believed that for his employees to follow him, he had to put himself out there and personally spread the message.[36]

mation leader and CEO Jan Carlzon created and distributed a little red book titled *Let's Get in There and Fight*. This book, distributed to all twenty thousand employees, communicated the vision and goal of the organization clearly and concisely.[37] Table 2-3 compares these two different, but equally powerful visions. Because you cannot afford to distort the message through communication, simple messages are most effective. This simple fact, what we call parsimony, is important in the creation of a vision. When phrasing and wording a vision, think simple. And when communicating this vision, think inspirational.

Prescription 6: Build a Powerful Coalition

Operating by himself, a transformation leader is minimally effective at best. For the transformation effort to be successful, there must be adequate buy-in and support from the organization, especially from the higher levels (see figure 2-7). Through the domino effect, overall support throughout the organization will increase once key people demonstrate their support for the transformation effort. Indeed, support is one of the greatest assets of the transformation leader in a transformation effort.

TABLE 2-3

A tale of two visions

A comparison: motivational versus strategic visions

	Motivational vision	**Strategic vision**
Goal	Motivate and ignite the passion of employees	Set the direction for the company; focus and guide the company
Driven by	Heart: emotion and drive	Head: logic
Message	Shares the core values of the company	Expresses the direction toward which the company is heading
Answers the questions	Why does our organization exist? How are we improving the world? What are our core values? What is the driving force of the company?	Where do we want to go? How will we get there? Why will we be successful?
Considers	Factors that drive and excite employees	Both internal and external influences on the company
Communication	• Is clear, simple, and catchy • Uses a wide variety of communication channels, including action • Inspires—highlights world impact	

FIGURE 2-7

Prescription 6

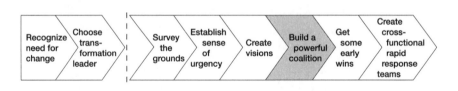

Who's In?

Developing a powerful coalition is one of the first steps toward gaining widespread support. Consisting of company employees, ideally senior-level executives and managers, members of this coalition truly believe in the necessity for change and the goals of the transformation effort and want to be on the "winning team." Convinced by the potential of the transformation, they are willing to express their convictions vocally and actively. The coalition's power stems from its powerful members, such as senior-level management, who have tremendous influence throughout the company. If middle-level managers are included in this powerful coalition, they should be highly regarded, respected, and talented, renowned throughout the company as thought leaders. Members of the coalition must be dependable and trustworthy, for the success of the transformation relies heavily on them. They are the transformation leader's core alliance and serve as his eyes, ears, and hands. As implied earlier, one of the most important people to have on the coalition is the CFO because of his oversight of the budget and his tremendous insight into all aspects of the company.

However, while many coalition members come from within the company because of their insight and understanding of the company's nuances, the transformation leader may also find himself relying on the coalition he initially brought with him into the company. Although these members from outside may not have the same insight about the company, they bring with them a unique perspective on the company and outside expertise. Despite the benefits of these members, though, the importance of having coalition members internal to the company cannot be overlooked. Not only do they have insight, they also already have connections within the company and a communication network, both of which will be tremendous assets. As noted in the advice given to Lou Gerstner in his first few weeks on the job, it was important that he "find a private cadre of advisors who have no axes to grind."[38]

There are many ways to select the members of the coalition. One important method is through the recommendations of others, for the well-known thought leaders of the company will be easily recognized by most employees. Furthermore, while meeting with senior executives and talking to employees during the process of surveying the grounds, the transformation leader has the opportunity to judge their competence and level of enthusiasm for the change. For example, while Gerstner was discussing the ten-page reports with his senior executives (described in "Prescription 3: Survey the Grounds"), he was simultaneously "sizing up [his] team, trying to understand the problems they faced and how they were dealing with them, how clearly they thought, how well they executed, and what their leadership potential really was."[39] In evaluating his team, however, the transformation leader may come across some employees who are less than enthusiastic about the changes (see "ACI's Leader Builds a Powerful Coalition").

To effectively choose a powerful coalition, the transformation leader must actively integrate himself with his employees and place himself in the center of the communication network. For example, Bay Networks' transformation leader, Dave House, never ate alone or with the same senior executives. Rather, every time he went to the cafeteria, he sat with someone new. This allowed him to talk to a wide variety of people throughout the organization and open up dialogue, making himself approachable to the employees. By building a network of contacts within the organization, House not only gained credibility but also got additional buy-in for the transformation effort.

Because building the coalition allows the leader to judge the potential of various employees, managers, and executives, he will inevitably find employees who don't fit the company and the transformation. In deciding who he wants to weed out, the transformation leader must consider interactions with a particular employee in addition to honest and trustworthy recommendations and feedback from the employee's colleagues.

According to Jack Welch, there are four types of employees and business leaders in a company. The first type of employee meets all of his commitments and fits the company's culture. The second type neither meets his commitments nor fits the company's culture. The third type misses his commitments but fits the company's culture and has internalized the company's values, while the last type meets his commitments but does not fit the culture or believe in the company's values. It is clear that the first type of employee should be kept and the second type of employee should be fired. The third type of employee has potential and may perform better in a different department. It is the decision regarding the fourth type of employee and

ACI'S LEADER BUILDS
A POWERFUL COALITION

The transformation leader of ACI individually met with every one of his key employees and direct reports to discuss both how the transformation would benefit the company and contribute to the employee's personal growth, emphasizing the potential role these key employees could play and the impact they would have. They discussed how the transformation would propel the employee's knowledge, skill set, and career. Additionally, he expressed the importance of the transformation effort and differentiated from previous attempts: not only would this be of shorter duration, it would have greater impact and would leave no stones unturned. The company would examine every aspect of the company and its processes and align the strategy throughout the company.

One senior manager in particular didn't see any benefit to the transformation effort and felt strongly about vocalizing his belief. However, upon recognizing that the transformation leader had approval and buy-in from other key players in the company, he compromised with the leader and agreed to suspend his judgment and be neither a roadblock to nor a supporter of the effort. In this way, the transformation leader removed a potential obstacle to the effort. By building a powerful coalition, the transformation leader found the additional benefit of removing a roadblock that could potentially stall the effort.

Those who expressed support to the transformation leader were extremely enthusiastic about the upcoming change. These members of the powerful coalition wanted to learn the methodology and championed the effort throughout the organization. They, in turn, built their own coalitions within their business unit or department.

business leader that is especially difficult, but Welch's conviction is to get rid of such employees.

One of the most difficult decisions the transformation leader must make is terminating people who are detrimental to the company—but it is a vital step in the process. But coach those whom you want to keep to reach for tougher jobs and more responsibility to test their potential. At this point, you should start developing an idea of which managers would work well on what teams and in what departments. The decision does not have to be finalized right away, but having a vague idea will facilitate the process of putting together cross-functional rapid response teams later.

Having built a powerful coalition, the leader needs to consider various ways to lead the coalition and keep the members involved in the transformation process. The most important thing for the transformation leader to keep in mind is to stay at the center of the communication network so that people turn to him when they have insightful comments or important corporate feedback. For the coalition to stay motivated, members need to feel that their interest is a priority of the organization and the transformation effort, and it is the role of the transformation leader to keep them informed and happy. Constantly communicating with the members will also ensure that their interests are aligned with those of the organization.

Beyond the powerful coalition, the transformation leader should informally extend his coalition to employees who are less powerful and influential, because his ultimate goal is to motivate the entire company behind the transformation effort. To do so, the leader should establish credibility and display his dedication to the employees. For example, VeriSign's Irvin stayed "in the room, at . . . 9 o'clock at night eating cold pizza and sweating the details" partly to show his devotion to and involvement with the effort.[40]

Another method VeriSign's Irvin used to get involvement and commitment from employees at all levels was to tell them that none of them had a job in the company until planning for the transformation effort was complete. Such an ultimatum created a sense of responsibility within the workforce to understand companywide issues and helped build a coalition behind Irvin.[41]

While the leader must motivate the entire workforce behind the transformation effort, ultimately the powerful core coalition should be an elite group selected especially for the transformation effort, and the members of the coalition must be responsible, dependable, enthusiastic, and powerful. (See "How Do You Build a Powerful Coalition?" which highlights some key methods.)

Prescription 7: Get Some Early Wins

Every tree has its low-hanging fruit. If you leave this fruit on the tree too long before picking it, it will overripen and rot, eventually falling off the tree. Similarly, every transformation has its opportunity for early wins, which are successes that can be achieved early on in the transformation effort (see figure 2-8). If the transformation leader waits too long before capitalizing on the potential of these early wins, they will become ineffective and the transformation effort will lose momentum. Because of the importance of a timely

HOW DO YOU BUILD A POWERFUL COALITION?

- Talk to different people within the company and get their insight about who the best worker or leader is, and so on.

- Assess the employee's or manager's capabilities and potential when talking to them directly.

- Select employees who can make a difference in the company, either because of their experience or because of their connections (i.e., they can "run the halls").

early success, the transformation leader should keep his eyes peeled and get some early wins at this point in the transformation to create momentum and energy. Early wins can come not only in the pretransformation phase, but they should begin as early as possible.

People are generally unwilling to spend time and energy on anything for a long time without seeing any results or progress. Even if people truly believe in the need for a transformation, they will be unable to maintain their enthusiasm for long without seeing their efforts bear fruit. Of course, the complete transformation and the most important and major changes accompanying the effort typically take time. Even ninety days, the length of the accelerated transformation model proposed throughout this book, is too long a period to go without any publicly acknowledged progress or success. While the transformation as a whole should be focused on more complicated long-term initiatives that take time to plan and implement, complete commitment and sole dedication to long-term initiatives will result in decreasing morale and en-

FIGURE 2-8

Prescription 7

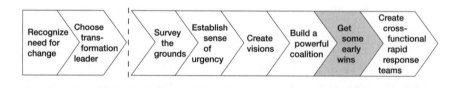

thusiasm. Therefore, it is critical that these long-term initiatives be interspersed with readily achievable short-term successes that give employees a sense of accomplishment and counter the impatience typically encountered in a transformation. As such, early wins serve to recharge and invigorate the employees.

Early successes not only reinforce the employees' role in the transformation effort, they also build credibility and create momentum. Management must gain credibility from the rank and file because of the dedication and excitement necessary for a transformation effort. By demonstrating that management initiatives in the transformation effort can succeed, the leaders of the effort have a stronger basis and more justification for encouraging further dedication, involvement, and enthusiasm from the organization. Partly because of this, momentum is maintained and even increased through early wins. Early wins also build the confidence of the company's employees, which is furthermore invaluable in the future when the company is striving to achieve more challenging, complex, long-term goals.

Picking the low-hanging fruit also has the benefit of addressing and quelling resistance within the organization, thereby increasing buy-in. This is because those who resist the transformation often do so because of fear of failure. However, by seeing the company successfully pick the low-hanging fruit, skeptics of the transformation effort will be more convinced of the value and potential effects of the effort.

A poorly chosen or sloppily implemented early win, however, can have the opposite effect of deflating morale and breeding cynicism toward the transformation effort. One particularly damaging situation occurs when the chosen early wins are actually not readily accessible and initial attempts to achieve these early wins fail. Reasons that these initial targets may not be readily attained include the occurrence of unanticipated complexities in the problem-solving and implementation processes. Such a situation not only damages morale but ruins the credibility of the transformation effort and leaders.

Picking Your Battles

Given the great potential for an appropriately chosen early win and the dire consequences of the opposite, a careful and deliberate process for choosing and communicating these wins is both critical and necessary. This is not to say, however, that choosing and executing them should become the organization's main focus. But early wins must be chosen for their feasibility and a high likelihood of success. Additionally, they must be aligned with both the company's motivational and strategic visions and the general goals of the

THINGS TO CONSIDER WHEN CHOOSING YOUR EARLY WINS

- Can it be implemented immediately and swiftly?

- Can the results be seen immediately?

- How risky is it? What is the likelihood of success?

- Does it align with the developed vision? Is it a first step in the direction we want to head?

- Can the early win be communicated effectively to motivate employees and maintain or increase momentum?

- How does this early win complement other early wins?

transformation effort. (For a list of some criteria to consider when choosing projects to symbolize early wins, see "Things to Consider When Choosing Your Early Wins.")

How do you define an early win? What kind of time frame constitutes an early win? One multinational engineering company we researched took the initiative to quantitatively categorize issues and solutions under a short-term, medium-term, and long-term time frame. (See "Time Frame Categorization" for details.) Typically, a short-term project can be recognized as low-hanging fruit, because it is short and self-contained.

These early wins should not be very complex, nor should they last indefinitely. It is important to create a timeline for the early win, as well as clear, distinct measures of success. These metrics not only help define a successful early win, they also help assess progress in longer-term projects. This planning portion, however, should not be extremely extensive or exhaustive, because the essence of an early win is the ability to act virtually immediately. (See "Documentation as an Early Win at VeriSign.") For some longer projects, early wins can be achieved through clearly defined and predetermined measures of success in the earlier stages (see "Apple Partners with a Competitor").

Early wins may also refer to winning over the employees and gaining credibility. This may not require any deliberate action, but it may just be winning credibility through nonverbal actions. For example, Irvin proved his dedication to the transformational cause by staying late at night and constantly

TIME FRAME CATEGORIZATION

- **Short term:** implement in less than thirty days
  - Minimum dependence from other groups

- **Medium term:** implement in thirty to ninety days
  - Dependence on team interfaces
  - Can be achieved without additional resources

- **Long term:** implement in more than ninety days
  - Based on gap analysis (discussed in phase 2)
  - Multiple interdependencies, may require creation of new groups, training, transfers, or new hires
  - Significant new investment to implement

communicating with people. Similarly, Ghosn put in so many hours just traveling and talking to people that he was nicknamed "Seven-Eleven," beginning his days at dawn and ending them long after sunset, like a popular convenience store chain in Japan.[42] Such dedication and motivation are acknowledged and appreciated by the workforce, and the transformation leader can hence gain credibility and support for the transformation effort.

DOCUMENTATION AS AN EARLY WIN AT VERISIGN

To achieve an early win, VeriSign called for the creation of a binder detailing information from the sales and marketing group. The team needed to deliver real-time information about the company's customers, what they planned on buying, and what the company should expect from a typical interaction. Using that information, the team put together a binder with the detailed data. Metrics were also created using that information, and these metrics were subsequently included in the binder. Furthermore, sales managers and employees were told to record their plans, which made them accountable for their public and written commitments.[43]

APPLE PARTNERS WITH A COMPETITOR

When Jobs joined Apple in 1997, the company viewed Microsoft as a fierce competitor to beat. By refocusing the company on its core competencies and its customers, Jobs recognized the potential in partnering with Microsoft. Soon after Jobs joined, Apple entered an official partnership with Microsoft, where Microsoft would buy $150 million worth of Apple stock and develop and ship future versions of Microsoft Office and Internet Explorer for Macs for at least the following five years.[44] This critical act illustrated the company's shift in focus from competitor to customer. Not only did this refocus the organization, but it also helped galvanize the employees behind a new, longer term challenge: satisfy its customers and reignite the Apple brand.

Many potential early wins are overlooked because of the common misconception that a strategy must be fully and thoroughly developed before a company can follow up with operational effectiveness or implementation. In fact, many early wins that facilitate smooth operation of future implementation efforts of these strategies can be taken immediately (see "Six Sigma at 3M"). These types of early wins include training employees on how to run effective meetings, how to make decisions effectively, and how to manage conflict. It is also important that a stage of transparency, accountability, and customercentric focus be set at this point in the transformation effort. Setting these fundamentals in place is an important early win that will prevent or moderate roadblocks in the future of the transformation effort.

Spread the Word

Documentation and communication of early successes are just as important as selection of these projects and targets. Early successes do not play a significant role in maintaining momentum and building credibility if they are not effectively communicated to employees. In fact, poor communication of early wins—typically through insincerity, exaggeration, or overstressing their importance—are counterproductive, negatively affecting the momentum of the transformation effort and detracting from the credibility of the leaders. Also, using and communicating too many early wins may give employees a false sense of progress and security and may even create a feeling of complacency, which counteracts the necessary sense of urgency created earlier.

SIX SIGMA AT 3M

Although Six Sigma was at the heart of 3M's transformation effort, James McNerney launched the initiative early in the effort, even before details had been hammered down. As part of this early win, middle-level managers were quickly identified and sent through an intensive four-week training program to become a "Black Belt," or an internal process improvement consultant. These managers worked together on cross-functional teams and focused on specific projects that were independent of the mandate of the respective function. These managers would play a key role in the change effort and in exchange were offered good jobs and promotions pending strong performance. Although the exact logistics regarding how the Black Belts would change the organization had not been set at the time, launching training for selected managers early in the change effort was important for building momentum and laying the groundwork for the rest of the initiative. Not only did this approach inspire and empower the future leaders of the company, but it also communicated the importance of Six Sigma to the rest of the organization.[45]

Sincere, open communication is the most effective way to announce the early wins. Celebrations may even be warranted for early wins deemed most important to the transformation effort. However, these celebrations must be closely monitored to ensure that they do not misconstrue the early wins as long-term, all-important wins. This can be achieved by warning against complacency in these celebrations. The key balance to strike is recognition of the impact and hard work while not overemphasizing its importance in the bigger transformation puzzle.

Because they require a delicate balance, early wins are extremely complicated and difficult to execute effectively. The first scale an effective early win must be balanced on is importance. On this scale, the early win must not be completely insignificant and insultingly simple, but it also cannot be so critical and important that it is extremely complex and may last indefinitely. The second scale lies in communication. Undercommunication of the early win trivializes the success and fails to use the early win to increase momentum and build confidence, while overcommunication results in cynicism and distrust. Given the astounding potential of an effectively selected, executed, and communicated early win, early wins cannot be overlooked in a transformation effort but must simply be carefully used.

Prescription 8: Create Cross-Functional Rapid Response Teams

The success of the transformation effort is directly related to successful organization, implementation, and leadership of cross-functional rapid response teams. These teams are responsible for all stages in the transformation effort, especially in identifying key problems and providing recommendations and implementation plans for these problems (see figure 2-9). These teams will be the focus of the next chapter.

CONCLUSION

The pretransformation is the first stage of a transformation effort and holds special importance in setting the tone for the effort. In this chapter, you learned about the general steps to plant the seeds for a successful effort, from how to select a transformation leader to how to gain buy-in and momentum. While these prescriptions are not set in stone, they have demonstrated to be logical, effective steps in a pretransformation setting. The pretransformation phase officially ends with the creation of cross-functional rapid response teams.

In the next chapter, we explore the advantages of cross-functional rapid response teams, their role in the transformation effort, and how to structure them effectively. Because of their critical role in the transformation effort, we have dedicated an entire chapter to these teams. They start with a moving ball (via a transformation that has been set in motion in the pretransformation phase) and give it a "push" to accelerate it to the top of the hill.

FIGURE 2-9

Prescription 8

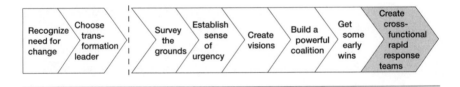

3

Cross-Functional Rapid Response Teams

Harnessing the Power

To lead the people, walk behind them.

—Lao Tzu

ross-functional rapid response teams, hereafter referred to simply as either cross-functional teams or rapid response teams, are the heart of the transformation effort, and their importance cannot be overemphasized. Not only do they accelerate the transformation effort, but rapid response teams also get employees throughout the company involved and increase the effectiveness of the transformation effort.

Traditionally, transformation efforts are organized and run by an army of external consultants that gives a recommendation but leaves the organization relatively unchanged. Rapid response teams decrease the number of consultants needed and minimize the role they play in the transformation effort by calling on the company's employees to take responsibility for their own transformation. Because they give employees a sense of ownership over the transformation, rapid response teams serve to rally employees behind the effort. Members of the teams not only identify the company's problems by gathering and analyzing data, but they also use their analysis to develop a recommendation for the company's future course of action.

Surprisingly, despite the potential impact cross-functional teams can have, many companies do not use them for either planning or implementation. Rather, they rely on outsiders to develop a recommendation and then impose this implementation proposal on executives. As a result, executives frequently either misunderstand the proposal or fail to gather the necessary support for implementation. In both cases, the transformation effort fails because key players were not involved in the transformation process but were included only as an afterthought. Cross-functional teams remedy this problem by engaging key players from the beginning of the transformation effort to ensure that (1) they understand the final recommendation, and (2) they have or can get sufficient buy-in to implement the recommendation.

In this chapter, we first introduce the concept of cross-functional teams and explain their crucial role in the overall transformation effort. Then, we highlight some important advantages to implementing rapid response teams, before we propose a general model for structuring them. Here, we draw from best-in-class examples of successful uses of rapid response teams in transformation efforts, including Nissan and VeriSign. In these examples, we highlight effective variations of our model and analyze situations in which these variations are most likely to be effective. We then delve into the specifics of structuring each team, explaining the roles of key members of each team and how you should approach the selection process. Last, we highlight some of the key meetings the rapid response teams engage in. Figure 3-1 provides an overview of the points to be discussed.

WHAT IS A CROSS-FUNCTIONAL RAPID RESPONSE TEAM?

Cross-functional rapid response teams bring together members from diverse functions and departments across the organization for a common goal (see figure 3-2). These teams break the barriers that typically prevent open communication among employees of different functions, geographies, and ranks within organizations. Encouraging cooperation and open dialogue, cross-functional teams make the organization more cohesive by allowing members to share their unique knowledge and perspectives with each other. In the transformation effort, we call them rapid response teams because they are critical to the quick speed of a 90 days transformation.

FIGURE 3-1

Chapter overview

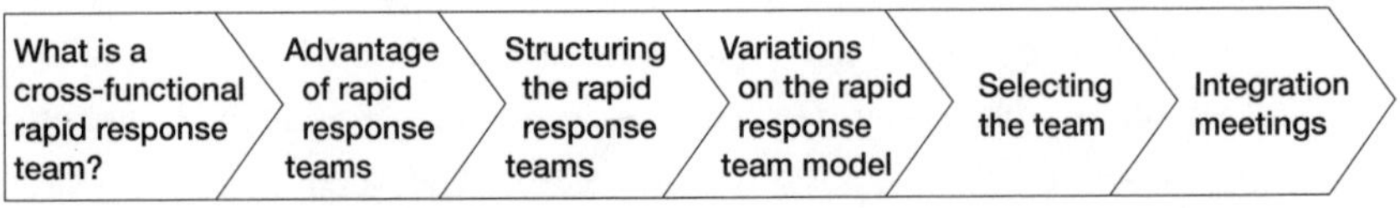

| What is a cross-functional rapid response team? | Advantage of rapid response teams | Structuring the rapid response teams | Variations on the rapid response team model | Selecting the team | Integration meetings |

FIGURE 3-2

What is a cross-functional rapid response team?

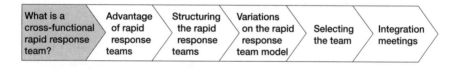

*Role of Rapid Response Teams
in the Transformation Effort*

As drivers of the entire transformation effort, rapid response teams involve many employees and get everyone on the same page working toward the same goal. Not only do they accelerate the transformation and make it more effective and efficient, but they also challenge the traditional transformation model by requiring fewer consultants than were historically required.

Typically, transformation efforts involve an entire team of consultants, from junior to senior consultants, who not only investigate the situation and the problems but also develop the plan. There are a few main problems with involving a large number of consultants in the transformation effort:

- Employees do not internalize the transformation effort and may not understand or embrace the transformation at all, leading to problems in implementation.

- Consultants do not necessarily share the same goals or have as much at stake in the transformation as employees in the company.

- Consultants are very costly in both time and money.

There is also conflict of interest between the consultants and the company, for while a fast transformation effort is beneficial to the company and increases the likelihood of the effort's success, it comes at the cost of a shorter engagement for the consultants. Hence, transformation efforts driven by consultants may take longer than otherwise necessary. Also, consultants may misunderstand the vision or strategy of the company—while a successfully implemented proposal constructed by consultants may have a positive outcome, it may not be aligned with the company's original goals or desired results. By limiting the number of consultants and restricting their role to that of a coach, the accelerated transformation effort uses the expertise of the seasoned consultants while giving the employees the steering wheel of the transformation. Not only do the employees become experts in the transformation effort and the company as a whole, they also become more involved—after all, if you're involved in making the baby, you're also in charge of taking care of the baby. According to Ava Butler, a consultant involved in the VeriSign effort, "When a company like this has to make such significant changes, it is very difficult, if not impossible, without the involvement of the employees. You could hire a bunch of consultants to make changes in a smoke-filled room, but they'll never come up with exactly the right answer, and they'll never understand all the nuances of the company. It's much better to get the employees involved in making a change."[1]

The main deliverable of the rapid response teams is developing and presenting the best recommendations after analyzing the problem in detail. Rapid response teams are often created especially for the transformation effort and are hence typically disassembled when the ninety days are over. This temporary nature of the teams adds to the sense of urgency of the transformation effort, and their unique structure helps shake up the organization and expand its comfort zone.

We mentioned in the earlier chapters the critical success factors we found necessary for a successful transformation effort. To recap, successful transformation efforts tended to be all-encompassing, integrative, and fast and also had full, passionate commitment and buy-in, especially from the top layers of the organization (see figure 1-1).

The true power of cross-functional rapid response teams is that they enable and drive these critical success factors.

- *All-encompassing.* Rapid response teams diagnose and assess various parts of the company. They look under rugs and leave no stones unturned.

- *Integrative.* That the rapid response teams work in parallel allows them to integrate their recommendations and take advantage of synergies between different teams, findings, and recommendations. Through the 90 days model, rapid response teams work together and integrate their recommendations in order to ensure that different recommendations are not redundant or in conflict with each other. Cross-functional teams engage in not only weekly conference calls but also monthly integration meetings to communicate their findings and next steps. This will be discussed further later in the chapter.

- *Fast.* The parallel nature of rapid response teams accelerates the transformation effort by addressing all aspects of the company at the same time.

- *Had full, passionate commitment and buy-in.* Rapid response teams involve key players in the transformation, which increases their commitment and buy-in, described in the next section.

ADVANTAGES OF CROSS-FUNCTIONAL
RAPID RESPONSE TEAMS

Partly because of their cross-functional nature, and partly because of their critical role in the transformation effort, rapid response teams have numerous benefits in addition to those stated above:

- The whole is greater than the sum of its parts.

- They harness the power of a boundaryless organization.

- Communication is facilitated—"There's no 'I' in team."

- Members gain a new perspective.

- Forced change is problematic.

- Involved members demonstrate the greatest commitment to change.

- Parallel initiatives reap unparalleled benefits.

- They help in evaluating future leaders

Figure 3-3 shows how this section fits into the mind-set of adopting rapid response teams.

FIGURE 3-3

Advantages of rapid response teams

| What is a cross-functional rapid response team? | Advantage of rapid response teams | Structuring the rapid response teams | Variations on the rapid response team model | Selecting the team | Integration meetings |

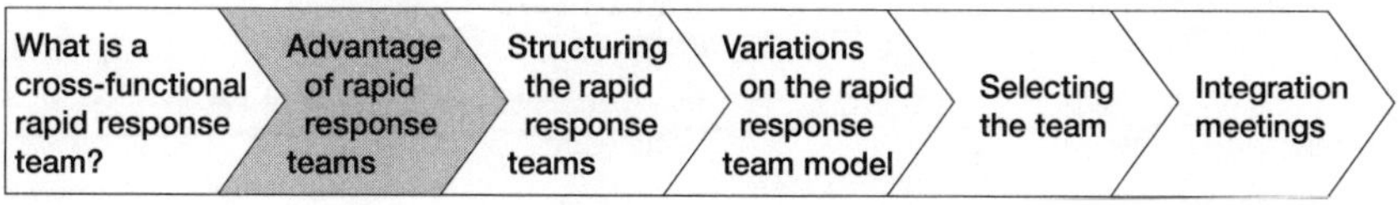

The Whole Is Greater Than the Sum of Its Parts

Rapid response teams turn a group of individuals into a true team. Let's first distinguish between a group and a team.

A group is simply a collection of individuals, resulting in individual efforts with little collaboration and interaction between members. A team, however, uses frequent interactions and communication to create a unified effort aimed toward a common goal. In this way, a team takes advantage of the differences between individuals and capitalizes on the synergies of the interactions between members (see table 3-1).

In a team, all the members are equally accountable for the team's success and failure, but in a group, only individuals are recognized and held accountable. As the Change Implementation Team at Best Buy recognized, "As a team, [members] could maintain their credibility and effectiveness. If they operated as individuals . . . they would be picked off and neutralized.[2]

Rapid response teams maximize the power harnessed by teams to analyze and address a few striking issues within the company and present the recommendations to the transformation leader. The collaborative nature of the transformation effort feeds directly into the emphasis on teamwork and joint accountability in rapid response teams. This sense of camaraderie and joint accountability can even propel the team to perform beyond its own expectations (see "Team Accountability at Nissan"). Having individuals working together in a team, rapid response teams reaffirm the old adage "The whole is greater than the sum of its parts."

TABLE 3-1

A comparison between groups and teams

Group	Team
Members work individually toward a common goal	Members work together and collaborate, creating a united effort toward a common goal
Individuals are held accountable	Team as a whole is held accountable, with members
Doesn't take advantage of the synergies available in the group	Takes advantage of the available synergies in the team
"Sum of individuals"	"The whole"

TEAM ACCOUNTABILITY AT NISSAN

In Nissan's transformation effort, Carlos Ghosn's purchasing cross-functional team provided recommendations that missed the mark. Instead of analyzing why or assigning blame to individuals, Ghosn told the team outright that its recommendation wasn't aggressive enough and immediately sent the team back to the drawing board. In doing so, Ghosn gave the team additional pressure, holding everyone responsible and accountable and making it clear that there would be no "sacred cows." In fact, Ghosn told the team that the savings had to be double the amount proposed in the recommendation, a number that the team had initially declared aggressive enough. Within two weeks, the team went back to collaborate with the engineering department and developed a more aggressive and acceptable recommendation. By holding the entire team accountable for meeting both the deadlines and the targets, Ghosn used the power of teamwork and created a sense of intense unity and solidarity within the team.

They Harness the Power of a Boundaryless Organization

According to Jack Welch, a boundaryless organization serves as the ideal toward which organizations should strive. A boundaryless organization is one that has gotten rid of the horizontal, vertical, and geographic boundaries that typically prevent open communication throughout the entire organization. Welch argues that the way to harness the power of an organization's employees is "to turn them loose, and get the management layers off their backs, the bureaucratic shackles off their feet and the functional barriers out of their way."[3] This can be done through cross-functional teams. Ghosn also recognized that cross-functional teams are powerful in getting executives to "look beyond functional and spatial boundaries of their direct responsibilities . . . , to tear down the walls . . . that reduce a collective enterprise to a congregation of groups and tribes."[4] By teaming together a diverse group of employees from many different parts of the company, rapid response teams break down not only horizontal barriers between departments but also vertical barriers. One way this is done, for example, is by allowing executive vice presidents to work directly with general managers.

With a boundaryless organization, the entire company works together as a whole, which allows it to harness the strengths and power of each employee. Rapid response teams facilitate cooperation and allow employees to work together, using their differences to complement each other and make the team and the company as a whole more effective. Hence, rapid response teams play a critical role and serve as an important first step toward reaching the ideal of a boundaryless organization.

Communication Is Facilitated—"There's No 'I' in Team"

Employees from different departments typically don't interact with each other in everyday operations. Cross-functional teams help break these departmental barriers and open up dialogue, facilitating communication between employees. This improved communication comes in conjunction with the ideal of a boundaryless organization. Because rapid response teams meet regularly and have frequent, focused discussions about the issues at hand, lines of communication are opened and team members have more opportunities to share their perspectives on the areas needing improvement, whether the perspective stems from their particular function or department or from the insight they have gained through their experiences. Rapid response teams not only create a forum for open communication, but brainstorming sessions encourage input from experienced and knowledgeable members who may not have an outlet to voice their opinions and suggestions. As recognized by Ghosn, cross-functional teams are powerful in getting executives "to compel people to talk to one another, to listen to one another, and to exchange knowledge."[5]

Furthermore, this open communication developed through rapid response teams can be carried back into the daily jobs of members throughout the organization. In this way, the teams not only temporarily facilitate open dialogue but help create sustainable communication networks, since employees have made connections to key employees outside their domain of expertise.

Members Gain a New Perspective

As a result of more open communication, team members are able to more clearly see a situation from many different perspectives, including those of members from functions other than their own. In most companies, employees don't get the opportunity to interact with employees from other functions. Overcoming the typical employee's microscopic view of the organization that is limited to his particular function or domain, rapid response teams provide members with a macroscopic view that integrates perspectives from the various functions and divisions. For example, if the goal is to create applause, just having the left and right hands recognize each other's existence is not enough. Applause, especially the best or loudest applause, requires that the left and right hands work together toward the common goal to find the best configuration. A rapid response team serves to introduce the left and right hands and facilitate their cooperation toward applause. Additionally, allowing employees from different business units, departments, and regions to compare their perspectives and progress through dialogues within rapid response teams facilitates the process of identifying and solving the problem. Finally, this new perspective gained by exposure to teams makes the company more willing to accept radical measures that overturn established practice.

Forced Change Is Problematic

Many failed transformations have been documented where a new organizational leader enters the company and tries to create and implement change from the top. By doing so, he or she is not empowering the employees or even convincing them that change is necessary. Such leaders fail to understand the human component of change—that most people innately dislike change and are satisfied with the status quo. By simply spreading change from the top, the leader fails to mobilize the company behind his or her effort and achieves superficial change at best (see "Superficial Compliance at Best Buy").

Additionally, leaders who impose top-down change tend to overestimate both their ability to spread change through the entire organization without

SUPERFICIAL COMPLIANCE AT BEST BUY

Best Buy's first attempt to change the company was developed by a premier consulting firm, and the solution appeared to be quite rational. However, rollout proved to be more difficult than anticipated—while all the stores passed the certification checklist with a score of at least 90 percent, the transformation team found only 44 percent true compliance. This was partially because the solution was developed from the outside and imposed on each store without regard to the input of store managers. Because of this, store managers knew and gave the "right" answers but didn't internalize the deeper meaning and implications of the transformation plan.[6]

getting adequate buy-in and their ability to fully assess the scope of problems plaguing the company. People at the top of an organization typically believe that they have fully identified the problem, when in fact they have identified only a portion of the problem. With top-down change, this means that either the problem may be improperly defined, or the solution may be too narrowly focused as a result of this premature diagnosis. Therefore, even if employees were committed to the transformation effort, the solution will inadequately address the organization's ailments.

Cross-functional teams, however, not only empower employees at all levels to seize the steering wheel of this transformation effort but also ensure that the problems will be more fully identified. By dedicating teams to specific functions or processes, a transformation effort using rapid response teams will be able to more fully assess the problems in the organization and recommend effective solutions based on their expertise in those particular functions or processes.

Involved Members Demonstrate the Greatest Commitment to Change

We mentioned earlier that rapid response teams contribute to the critical success factor of having full, passionate commitment and buy-in, and that many transformations fail when they fail to involve employees throughout the effort. Without widespread support throughout the organization, change cannot be successfully implemented, yet transformation leaders often underestimate employees' resistance to change. This resistance, however, can be combated by involving employees in stages throughout the transformation effort and giving them a voice in the direction of the change, which is what cross-functional rapid response teams do.

Many instances have shown that empowering people in the effort is critical to overcoming their resistance to change and ensuring their commitment to implementing and maintaining change. People who must drive and live with the change are most dedicated to change when they are influential in identifying and solving the problem. Furthermore, empowering people throughout the transformation process reassures those involved in the change that the problems being addressed are the right ones, which helps the transformation leader get buy-in from employees at all levels.

Rapid response teams are instrumental to getting employees involved throughout the entire transformation process. By holding team members responsible for identifying and recommending solutions to be implemented, rapid response teams diffuse the responsibility from a single transformation leader to the entire organization. By sharing his responsibility with the teams, the transformation leader empowers his managers and employees in decision making and equips them with tools they can carry with them and use effectively even outside the transformation effort. Additionally, should their recommendation be accepted, team members are held at least partly accountable for eventually implementing their solution, giving them more incentive to propose feasible solutions.

Furthermore, in a rapid transformation effort where the company must be prepared to react quickly to a constantly changing environment, companies often don't want decisions to be made through a departmental hand-off process. Rather, employees must work together to address the issues both quickly and efficiently. Rapid response teams allow this speedy and dependable response, for they are brought together to identify and solve a particular problem or set of problems. By getting members directly involved in this process, the recommendation will be thought through more thoroughly because there is more at stake for the members.

Finally, the use of cross-fuctional teams during transformation protects people's self-esteem and revives the spirit of employees and managers. Quite often, morale in a company plummets when change is imposed on employees without their input, because it sends the message not only that their current performance is unsatisfactory but also that the leaders of the company and the transformation have little faith that its own employees can devise a solution to turn the situation around.

Parallel Initiatives Reap Unparalleled Benefits

Projects critical to the transformation effort can be undertaken either in series or in parallel. Under a serial structure, one main team is responsible for driving the entire transformation, from identifying the problems to proposing and planning a recommended solution. For this single team to fully identify and address all the troubles ailing the company, it needs to look at the issues sequentially in a series, which would take a very long time. Furthermore, it is more than likely that the problems will not be adequately identified and addressed because of the limited resources and perspectives of this single team. However, with multiple rapid response teams and subteams, many different projects are simultaneously undertaken—hence, the amount of time required for the task is divided among the teams. Because the teams' attention and resources are more focused, the quality of the projects and recommendations will generally be better than that of a single team trying to attack all the various problems at once.

Some might fear that having multiple teams addressing the different complex issues of a company translates to chaos and lack of common direction among the teams. To ensure that the separate teams are aligned in their goals and direction, the transformation leader and a select group of leaders should guide the transformation effort and monitor the high-level progress and strategy of each team.

They Help in Evaluating Future Leaders

One of the greatest powers of cross-functional teams is that they create a level playing field on which there is nothing for employees to hide behind. Rather, they are transparent, with their actions and abilities on display. In this way, the teams help the transformation leader evaluate the future leaders of the company. Additionally, rapid response teams serve as pilot studies for their leaders and team members. This allows the leaders of the transformation and organization to assess the leadership potential of employees, as well as each member's strengths and weaknesses. Rapid response teams also give the transformation leader the opportunity to identify areas of improvement. Because many potential leaders are running the teams, the transformation leader can gauge potential and identify the future leaders and executives of the company, taking the first step toward creating a sustainable leadership pipeline.

In the evaluation of leadership potential, some team members may not perform up to par. In these cases, rapid response teams create an outlet for these underperforming employees, either by giving them another chance or by giving them the opportunity to transfer their expertise and know-how. Rapid response teams may allow these employees to train their successors in a safer manner, through an environment where collaboration is encouraged. Their presence during this transition is critical in saving time and preventing the loss of valuable information, for tremendous costs are incurred when the company has to either train a new employee from scratch or identify what information has been lost. Hence, the teams not only screen for potential leaders but also facilitate the transfer of expertise to these potential leaders.

STRUCTURING THE TEAMS—
A GENERAL FORMULA

There are essentially an infinite number of ways to arrange your organization into rapid response teams for the transformation effort. However, experience may tell you that not all possibilities are equally effective and that some work

FIGURE 3-4

Structuring the rapid response teams

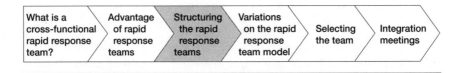

better than others. Here, we will help protect you from making fundamental mistakes as a result of trial and error by presenting the most effective generalized model developed through our research (see figure 3-4). Because there is no single cookie-cutter solution for modeling teams, this is simply a toolbox to help facilitate the process that has been found effective for many drastically different transformation efforts.

This section starts with the macroscopic structure of the rapid response teams—in particular, the important roles of integration by the executive management team (EMT) and the program management office (PMO) are highlighted. Then, the microscopic structure of each team is discussed, explaining the various roles within the team. Figure 3-5 introduces a high-level

FIGURE 3-5

General macroscopic team structure

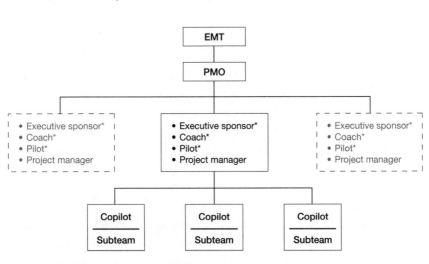

*These members also typically sit on the EMT.

structure of the rapid response teams. Many of the details will be expounded on later in the chapter.

Executive Management Team

At the macroscopic level, the overarching leadership team, called the executive management team, oversees the entire transformation effort and the overall team structure. In addition to guiding the rapid response teams toward the transformational and organizational goals, the EMT selects which recommendations presented by the teams to implement. Having the ultimate decision-making power, the EMT is also responsible for ratifying the major decisions made by rapid response teams to ensure that these decisions are reasonable and aligned with the overall transformational goals. Furthermore, the EMT is typically initiated by the transformation leader and several consultants, who lead the structuring of the teams.

Depending on the size of the company, the EMT usually consists of the transformation leader, a few senior consultants involved in the effort (called coaches), the executive sponsors for each team, and the pilots of each rapid response team (described later). While the EMT is responsible for selecting which recommendations to accept and adopt, it is the transformation leader who carries the ultimate decision-making power. The transformation leader is also responsible for leading the integration meetings (explained later) and delegating responsibility at a high level.

The consultants for the transformation sit on the EMT as a sounding board and to share their expertise, especially their knowledge of best-in-class practices. As coaches, however, they are typically not granted executive decision-making power. This is both to ensure that the consultants do not become dictators of the transformation effort and to empower executives who have the necessary expertise. Additionally, the consultants are assigned to a team as a coach in order to "sprinkle [the teams and projects] with experts in each of the categories."[7] Some instances may require a consultant to coach more than one rapid response team, but typically each coach should map to a single team. The role of consultants as coaches for individual teams will be described in the next section.

Executive sponsors, usually at the level of senior or executive vice president, are high-level leaders who bring with them extensive knowledge of the company and their function or department. Almost every high-level executive on the EMT should be assigned to sponsor a rapid response team to remove the roadblocks and obstacles faced by his team as well as to serve as a bridge between the different teams, facilitating both communication and co-operation between teams. An executive sponsor's specific role within the rapid response team will be described in a later section.

The pilot of each team is responsible for presenting the team's findings and recommendations to the EMT at the monthly integration meetings and the weekly meetings (described later).

Given the intimate relationship and interconnectedness between the rapid response teams and the EMT, a delicate balance of power must be maintained. While the teams should be empowered to make important decisions critical to their domain, certain decision-making and ratification abilities should be restricted to the transformation leader and the EMT. This is because the EMT, housing the leader (pilot) of each rapid response team, has stakeholders and experts in various sections of the organization, giving it the ability to weigh the trade-offs associated with different decisions, projects, and project mixes. Hence, while rapid response teams should be able to make key decisions involving their recommendation, their autonomy should be balanced by the EMT, who holds the right to ratify or veto major decisions.

Program Management Office

With the potentially large number of teams involved in a transformation effort, integration and coordination can get extremely messy. The program management office is in charge of addressing this need for coordination. The PMO consists of essentially one person who serves as the central nervous system of the transformation effort, making sure that things get done by the right teams at the right time. The main function of the PMO, therefore, is to manage and coordinate the teams, keeping track of all of their projects and timelines. The PMO should not tell people what to do, for it does not have the power and ability to approve or veto projects. In order to coordinate the entire transformation effort, the PMO must meet regularly with each team's project manager, whose role will be discussed later in this chapter.

The Teams

Each cross-functional team is composed of an executive sponsor, a coach, a pilot, a project manager, and team members, some who serve as copilots leading subteams. Each member or subgroup of the team has a unique role and must work together and communicate openly with the other members of the team to ensure successful functioning. Here, we will go through each member on the team and highlight his key role within the team and the transformation effort.

As a coach, the consultant serves as a sounding board but is detached from the day-to-day operations of the rapid response team. In VeriSign, for example, the consultants deliberately avoided attention during key team meetings in order to allow the pilots to creatively manage the pressures of responsibility and indirectly evaluate their leadership potential.[8] Instead of being overbearing and dictatorial, consultants should maintain a "guardian angel-like" relationship with both the pilot and the team, providing feedback and helping the pilot grow and mature. If the consultant were to dominate the team, it would become a top-down transformation vehicle, which would jeopardize the lines of communication and lead to the reemergence of organizational barriers. Hence, the consultant's expertise should be delicately sprinkled across the team, and everyone involved in the transformation effort should be wary of signs of a flood.

Executive sponsors are critical in guiding the team at the macroscopic project level, overseeing all the cross-functional projects, ensuring that resources are allocated effectively, and helping prioritize and align projects with the company's vision. With a holistic view of the projects and the transformation in general, they must keep the big picture both in mind and in focus. Hence, the executive sponsor is in charge of both deciding to do the right thing and helping the team do things right. Furthermore, executive sponsors have the authority and the responsibility to remove roadblocks and obstacles for the team. As a result of periodic updates by the pilot, an effective executive sponsor will actually anticipate some potential roadblocks the team may encounter and remove them before they get in the way, thereby increasing the efficiency and effectiveness of his team. Also, assigning an executive sponsor to each team illustrates the high importance of the transformation effort and creates a sense of accountability to carry out its necessary duties and projects.

Team pilots work in tandem with the executive sponsors who selected them to guide the direction of the team. The difference between the pilot and the executive sponsor is the level of involvement with the team and the specific projects. The executive sponsor plays a more "hands-off" role, while the pilot serves as the sponsor's eyes and ears, ensuring that the projects stay aligned with the goals predetermined by the executive sponsor. Communication must remain open and strong between the pilot and the executive sponsor in order to maximize the synergies of the duo. In particular, communication regarding the team's progress and direction is critical to ensuring that the team is on course and aligned with the overall transformation strategy. More often than not, just as in navigating a ship, minor course corrections are frequently required in order to reach the ultimate destination in a timely manner. Because the pilot of each team guides the team at a more intimate and interactive level than the executive sponsor, he provides the team with more strategic leadership and specific direction, including identifying and setting the strategy, goals, and specifications for the team and driving team meetings. He breaks down the main goals dictated by the executive sponsor into a set of smaller goals and milestones to be met by his team. The importance of team pilots to the transformation effort was not lost on Ghosn: "Pilots play the most crucial role in the [cross-functional team] concept, driving the agenda and discussions of all meetings, and strong leaders are needed to keep the focus on finding solutions rather than placing blame or posturing for selfish reasons."[9]

Because the pilot is responsible for selecting members for his team, he is also responsible for ensuring that the structure and composition of the team are appropriate for his goals. The pilot is also in charge of empowering his team, thereby improving morale. The team should be rather autonomous and empowered to make critical decisions, though the pilot should oversee major decisions and be prepared to step in as necessary. Additionally, the pilot is responsible for reporting his team's findings to the EMT at each integration meeting and championing his projects and recommendations to the rest of the organization. Hence, it is the pilot's responsibility to make sure that the goals are being met at a high level and that all the projects are contributing to the overall objective and mission of the team. The pilot must maintain a holistic view of the various projects and integrate their findings into a more holistic recommendation.

However, the pilot doesn't have to run all the projects by himself. To free himself for higher-level tasks, he relies on his project manager to carry out the day-to-day operations of the team. The project manager works intimately with the pilots to develop and run project plans, meet deadlines, budget resources, and perform other duties critical to the team's and subteams' functioning. Through regular meetings and frequent communication, project managers work closely with each other and the PMO to set project timelines and coordinate logistics with other teams. Additionally, the project manager is responsible for working with individual members to help them balance their transformation projects with their regular job duties and routines. All in all, the project manager is responsible for driving the team and making sure that deadlines and milestones are met—he is held accountable for ensuring adequate progress in the team. Because the project manager works so closely with the team pilot, he is selected by the pilot and approved by the executive sponsor.

Teams are typically composed of approximately seven to ten members of diverse expertise, although even ten members cannot analyze the situation and processes to sufficient depth. To ensure that neither breadth nor depth is sacrificed and that there is an appropriate balance between the two, each team has a coalition of subteams analyzing particular aspects of the problem in greater detail. Like the teams, subteams also consist of ten members each and are run by a copilot, who is a member of the original rapid response team. Each team should have at least one subteam responsible for the process of the particular function the team is dedicated to. On top of mobilizing forces to further gather pertinent data, subteams should rally additional troops behind the transformation effort. This serves not only to get more buy-in from employees but also to ensure that a greater portion of the organization is committed to the change effort. For example, over five hundred Nissan employees directly participated in the initial rapid response teams and subteams, with each employee contributing to the ultimate success of Nissan's transformation.

VARIATIONS ON THE RAPID RESPONSE TEAM MODEL

What we highlighted in the previous section was a general model for designing cross-functional teams that our research has shown to be extremely effective. However, there truly is no single cookie-cutter solution, and the general model can thus be adjusted to fit the particular needs of your organization. In this section, we will highlight some of the major adjustments used in some extremely successful transformation efforts, as well as summarize in what situations these adjustments are likely to be the most effective (see figure 3-6).

FIGURE 3-6

Variations on the rapid response team model

| What is a cross-functional rapid response team? | Advantage of rapid response teams | Structuring the rapid response teams | Variations on the rapid response team model | Selecting the team | Integration meetings |

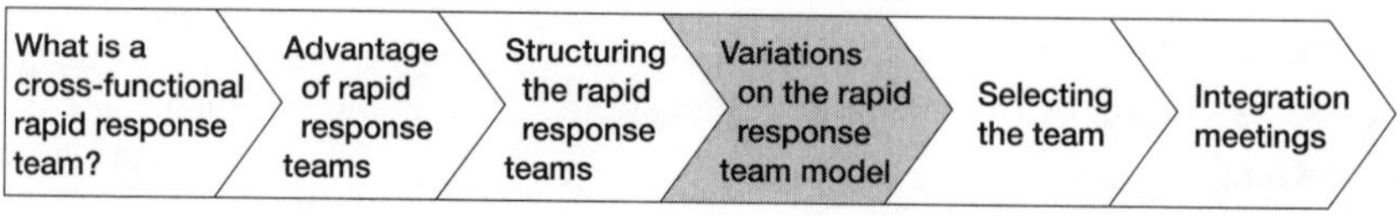

VeriSign

VeriSign's transformation, led by executive vice president Vernon Irvin, occurred within the company's largest division, VeriSign Telecommunications Services. VeriSign's main structural deviation from the general model proposed above is its use of content and process teams within each major domain (see figure 3-7).

In this model, each domain is divided into several distinct content teams and several process teams. Process teams study the processes of a certain domain or group and focus on how to make the process more efficient. Hence, these *process improvement* teams answer the question How do we do so-and-so? and try to improve on the answer to that question by answering *How* are we going to do so-and-so to make the process better? Content teams, in contrast, study the whats of a business. For example, a content team analyzes such information as the type of market the company is chasing, essentially answering the questions What are we doing in this domain? and What are we following? and searches for ways to improve on and expand the answer. After

FIGURE 3-7

VeriSign's cross-functional team structure

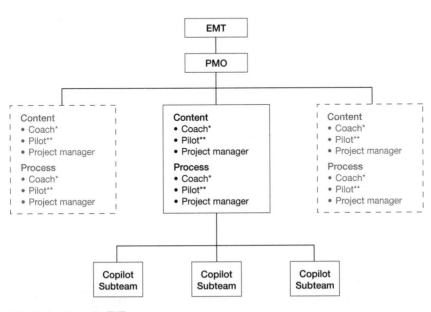

*Coach also sits on the EMT.
**Pilot sits on the EMT and serves as the executive sponsor.

looking at the present situation, the content team assesses the future of the domain: *What* do we want to do in this domain? *Where* do we want to go with this?

For example, under the domain of market teams, the process teams included sales processes, customer service processes, and engineering and operations processes, and content teams included the wireless, wireline and cable, and international teams. Each process and content team was structured as a full rapid response team, with a coach, a pilot (who served the dual role of an executive sponsor), and a project manager.

A model that uses both process and content teams within a given domain should theoretically try to balance the power and influence between the two teams. In practice, however, content teams often have more influence because they make recommendations seemingly more critical to the business, such as which markets to enter, what products to develop, and the strategy associated with these decisions.

In the VeriSign transformation effort, rapid response teams were given a tremendous amount of decision-making power and autonomy. This was possible largely because of the relatively small size of the division, which allowed Irvin to serve as a safety net, working more closely with the teams and monitoring their progress and decisions in greater detail than otherwise possible. Similarly, pilots were also given tremendous autonomy and authority to make key decisions.

This model was particularly effective because after the initial pretransformation analysis, Irvin and the EMT had developed a high-level idea of where the company should head even before they created the rapid response teams. Specifically, they developed a high-level view of their desired posttransformation organizational structure, and the team structure gave the EMT a way to pilot its design. Furthermore, this model has the additional benefit of having two pilots within a single domain, which allows the transformation leader to assess the leadership potential of each pilot and directly compare the two. Because of this additional benefit, this variation can be used when there is no clear leader to manage certain functions or areas after the transformation effort ends.

This model is also particularly effective in organizations with clearly defined and delineated content and process domains, especially in small to midsize companies. The reason this VeriSign model works well for smaller companies is because the pilot serves the dual role of both pilot and executive sponsor, which is effective because employees involved in the transformation effort typically already come from the higher rungs of the corporate ladder. Hence, there is less need for a corporate sponsor to remove the institutional roadblocks because the pilots themselves are capable. Pilots were not only in charge of decomposing the goals into a schedule of smaller goals and milestones but also given complete autonomy and authority to make key decisions. Furthermore, in this model, the subteams were not formalized but were informal teams of people helping the content and process teams gather additional information and analyze the situation in greater depth.

Nissan

One of the main differences between Nissan's structuring of rapid response teams and our generalist model is that under Nissan's model, each team had two executive sponsors in charge of removing roadblocks and anticipated obstacles for the team (see figure 3-8).[10] These two executive sponsors came from extremely different backgrounds—for example, the executive vice president of purchasing and the executive vice president of engineering were paired to lead the purchasing team. Ghosn argued that by assigning each team two executive sponsors instead of one, he was preventing the team from focusing its efforts too narrowly.

Another major difference is that the single pilot also served as the project manager, since there were two executive sponsors capable of setting the high-level strategy for the team and anticipating and removing institutional

FIGURE 3-8

Nissan's cross-functional team structure

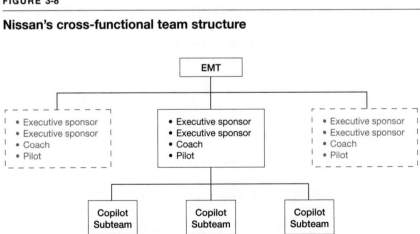

Note: From the teams, only the executive sponsors and coaches sat on the EMT.

roadblocks. While this means more work for the pilot, the model is effective in that it centralizes the management of the teams under a single person, ensuring that the strategy and overall goal will neither be lost in translation nor miscommunicated down the chain.

The Nissan model is particularly effective when the transformation leader and the EMT already have an idea of the future leaders of various functions and departments and need an opportunity to pilot these leaders and assess their potential. This differs from the VeriSign model in that the pilot test serves as a trial run rather than a means to compare two potential leaders. Additionally, the Nissan model is best for larger organizations, where more organizational barriers may be encountered by the team, for two executive sponsors may be necessary to anticipate and remove all of them.

Although the Nissan cross-functional teams were fully responsible for making recommendations to the EMT, they were not given the same amount of decision-making power as VeriSign's teams were. This is partly because of the large size of the organization, where it is more critical that all decisions made are in alignment with both previous decisions and the overall goal of the transformation effort. To ensure consistency between decisions, the EMT was given the decision-making power, with Ghosn overseeing the entire decision-making process.

At Nissan, Ghosn divided his company into nine teams dedicated to specific areas: (1) business growth, (2) purchases, (3) manufacturing and logistics, (4) R&D, (5) sales and marketing, (6) general and administrative services, (7) finance, (8) phasing out a product, equipment, and service, and (9) organization and value added. Within each of these areas, the teams analyzed and addressed key drivers of performance and made recommendations about how to return to profitability and where the potential for future growth lay.

In alignment with our general model, each team also had subteams to focus on specific issues in more depth. These subteams collaborated closely with the rapid response team and had ten members each to ensure steady progress. By involving more employees in the transformation effort, the subteams increase buy-in for the effort and help ensure that once the teams are disbanded, implementation will not fail because of lack of support and involvement.

SELECTING THE TEAM

In this section, we'll examine the process for putting together the team (see figure 3-9), including criteria for screening the people to fill each key role and the best methods to use in the selection process.

FIGURE 3-9

Selecting a team

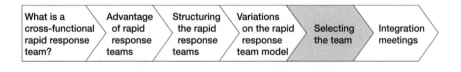

Selection Criteria

Because of the importance of the transformation effort, the executive sponsors, pilots, project managers, and copilots (pilots of the subteams) all have to be spectacular performers with a proven track record. As a general rule of thumb, those involved directly with cross-functional teams ironically "need to be the people the company can't afford to give you."[11] Since executive sponsors, pilots, and project managers have additional responsibilities allocated to their roles, they should be chosen with exceptional prudence. It is critical that the selected employees have demonstrated excellence and dedication to the organization. (See "Criteria for Selecting Teams" for a summary of some key criteria to consider in the process.)

CRITERIA FOR SELECTING TEAMS

- Dedication to the company and the transformation effort

- Willingness and ability to accept a challenge

- Willingness and readiness to work essentially two full-time jobs

- Ability to handle stress and more than one task at a time

- Teamwork ability and experience

- Leadership ability and potential (especially for pilots)

- Thought leadership and high-flying ability

- Willingness and ability to provide and receive open and honest feedback and opinions

Employees can often be screened preliminarily by their rank. In a transformation effort, recruiting high-level employees to rapid response teams speaks volumes to the level of priority given to the transformation. As mentioned earlier, executive sponsors must be at the level of senior executive in order to have the ability to effectively anticipate and remove institutional roadblocks and barriers. Without the authority and rank of senior executive, executive sponsors cannot effectively live out their roles. Pilots and project managers should also be of high rank. The reason behind this is threefold: (1) employees of high rank have demonstrated ability and expertise; (2) high-ranking employees understand the company, have established networks, and have a high-level understanding of the issues plaguing the company; and (3) assigning high-ranked employees symbolizes the importance of the transformation effort to the rest of the organization. For example, at VeriSign, "The [pilots] were almost always VP's or directors. The team members were sometimes senior managers. I don't think we had anybody below that. The key thing is this: how to make sure that you involved people who actually know what's going on. And on this level, these were the right levels."[12]

On the other hand, team and subteam members can be from middle-level management, as in the case of Nissan. Senior or middle managers are important contributors to the team because not only do they often have a more holistic view of the company than their counterparts in lower ranks, but they also work both with senior management and executives as well as employees at a more grassroots level. Hence, while senior executives may be observing the company from space, and lower-ranked employees may be observing the company from the ground, middle-level employees are viewing the company from a plane. Importantly, this balances the high-level picture with the detailed perspective. Middle managers also have the benefit of having a rather wide network of contacts, enabling them to learn a lot about the company in a relatively short time, reach the grassroots of the organization more quickly, and get honest feedback and responses.

Despite the benefits typically associated with middle-level management, some of the highly qualified employees necessary for the transformation may not be in the ranks of middle management. While the rank of an employee is often an efficient, effective, and useful way of screening potential team members, it should not be used absolutely but in conjunction with other means. Many benefits result from having employees of different ranks cooperate within a team, such as further allowing boundaries associated with rank to be broken. However, teams that contain members from different ranks should take extra pains to recognize the equality of team members in the transformation effort, despite their ranks within the company. In order to encourage collaboration and prevent conflicts associated with rank and role, such as power struggles, members should be told to leave their titles at the door.

Since it is critical that the pilots, project managers, and team members are invested in and already have some understanding of the company and its current situation, people filling these roles should ideally be selected from within the company. This internal selection serves to "ensure ownership of the process and as an incentive to see the handoff process through to its end."[13] However, in some instances, the most ideal candidates for pilots may be hired from outside the company. In the same way that the transformation leader himself may be hired from outside for his noninstitutionalized point of view on the company and its situation, pilots may also be external to the company for this very reason. However, pilots hired from outside must be extremely credible and be able to cooperate with their team members—that is, their noninstitutionalized point of view must also be compatible with those working to promote change. Unlike leaders promoted from within, leaders from outside have a steep initial learning curve to catch up to their team members in understanding the company's situation, culture, and traditions. Ghosn, for example, was successful in bringing in a team of thirty people from Nissan's partner company Renault and integrating members from the two companies. In fact, Ghosn strongly believed that his ex-Renault team was critical in driving the transformation effort.

"Thought leadership" is a particularly important characteristic of pilots, project managers, and members, as recognized by VeriSign's Vernon Irvin and Bay Networks' Dave House. Accordingly, people involved with the rapid response teams should all be "high flyers who had histories of achievement, expertise within their function, energy, and commitment."[14] As this suggests, a proven track record is very important for both pilots and team members.

Energy and commitment of members are especially critical because team members will be stretched very thin in their time and energy. Involvement in the transformation effort is not for the faint of heart—members should be capable, willing, and ready to handle intense pressure and stress. It is not a role suitable for every employee, and, undoubtedly, some qualified employees may choose not to get involved because of the level of commitment expected of and required from them. Employees are assigned to teams and projects while simultaneously carrying out their regular jobs, which translates into working two full-time jobs. Employees must hence be willing to put in extra hours, at times working through both weekends and holidays to meet deadlines for both their regular jobs and the transformation effort. The company cannot afford to sacrifice its current level of service or production for the transformation effort, for its performance should never be worse than it was before the effort began. Although the transformation effort is critical to the organization's future, the organization has no future if it cannot make it past the present.

Hence, even given these additional projects and responsibilities, team members must maintain their high level of performance and produce high-quality work in both their normal realm and the transformation realm. This point is emphasized by Ghosn: "Never skip portions of the process when given a tight deadline; learn to work faster."[15] Although the team members are putting in extra time for the transformation effort, they cannot put their regular projects on the back burner and allow their schedules to slip. There-fore, members of the cross-functional teams should have demonstrated com-petence and ability to work on multiple projects simultaneously. Everyone involved should have internalized the need for change and be willing and ready to accept the challenge.

Also, members of the rapid response teams must not overestimate their own abilities but should instead be willing to learn from others on the team, even from subordinates. While they must be credible and command respect from their colleagues and subordinates, they must also show openness to new ideas and criticism. Additionally, pilots must also be willing to absorb sugges-tions from their advisers, including the coaches and executive sponsors. They should also be open to new ideas, methods, and processes and not be so fo-cused on the end that they ignore suggestions about the journey.

Perhaps it is even more important that team members (and not just pilots) be open to suggestions and criticism. While they must be able to *accept* con-structive criticism from others, they must also be able to tactfully *provide* constructive criticism to others. Team members must therefore be honest in stating their opinions, offering feedback for all ideas, including constructive criticism for bad ideas. To do so, members should be willing and able to en-gage in active discussions and approach the transformation effort and their projects with an open and creative mind, being willing to think "outside the box."[16] Because discussions are critical junctions where members openly integrate their findings into an ultimately workable solution, the ability to ac-tively participate in these discussions is a crucial quality that must be sought in team members.

Although we have highlighted the importance of selecting the top per-formers of a company to participate directly in the transformation effort, we should also note that sometimes an effective team requires more than simply a coalition of key players. For example, at VeriSign, "The pilots tried hard to build a balanced cross-functional team. 'You kind of had a couple of criteria with each of the team's trying to get as much of a cross-location and cross-company representation on the teams.'"[17] Therefore, despite the importance of selecting the strongest candidates for a cross-functional team, diversity is also necessary. The essence of rapid response teams lies in bringing together employees from different functions and using each unique perspective to identify and solve the problem in a holistic way. Without diversity, people may come in with similar points of view, resulting in a narrow analysis of the problems.

Having examined in depth the criteria to search for when selecting key team members, we have until now ignored the selection criteria for the consultant, or coach. Although a solid, proven track record and thought leadership are both important characteristics for coaches to have, their qualifications lie mainly in their expertise and experience. The coaches should have worked in previous transformation efforts and should understand what constitutes best-in-class for transformations. Furthermore, since coaches work so closely with executive sponsors, their knowledge base should be complementary. Inevitably, there will be overlap, but coaches should be able to offer expertise not held by executive sponsors, whether that lies in experience about the process or different content knowledge.

Keeping in mind this broad overview of what to look for in candidates for these key positions in the cross-functional teams, we will now move on to how we can assess these qualities in candidates.

Selection Processes and Methods

Because cross-functional teams allow the transformation leader to evaluate future leaders of the company, the leader should be intimately involved in the selection of executive sponsors and pilots (See "House Identifies the Thought Leaders at Bay Networks," p. 98). The benefits associated with handpicking pilots were acknowledged by Ghosn: "Pilots, from the management ranks, were chosen with input from Ghosn so he could witness 'the next generation of Nissan leaders.'"[18] Additionally, the transformation leader should have input in the selection process because of the critical role of the team pilots and executive sponsors in the effort itself. Although team members also play a major role in the effort, it would be impractical and inefficient for the transformation leader to handpick team members also. In the case of Nissan, for example, Ghosn would have had to handpick approximately five hundred employees. Because of this, the transformation leader should delegate the responsibility

HOUSE IDENTIFIES THE THOUGHT LEADERS AT BAY NETWORKS

When Dave House first joined Bay Networks as the CEO and transformation leader, he had fifteen people reporting to him. In his selection of pilots, he first had the candidates interviewed, assessing things such as their strengths and weaknesses and their desire to lead a cross-functional transformation team. Through these interviews, House believed he found the "thought leaders" of the company—people who were the "real" thinkers and developed the ideas that drove the company. To choose the pilots to lead his rapid response teams from this pool of proven thought leaders, House gave each candidate a Web-based questionnaire to fill out (he told candidates that the questionnaires were confidential in order to ensure honest responses). Questions included (again) assessments about the strengths and weaknesses of the candidates, as well as some advice they would give the new CEO. According to the candidate's responses to the questionnaire, House handpicked the employees he wanted to lead a cross-functional team. By using a wide variety of methods to assess the qualifications of the team leaders, House was better able to ensure that each candidate was best suited for his position in terms of qualifications, interests, and expertise.

of selecting members to the pilot with the aid of the coach, executive sponsor, and project manager.

One typical method for selecting the pilot is to use the recommendations of others. By soliciting recommendations regarding the key criteria from the top executives of the company, the transformation leader should be able to narrow down the pool of potential candidates. However, these recommendations must be assessed carefully to weed out those affected by political or personal reasons.

With these recommendations, the candidates can then be screened further through the use of questionnaires and interviews. (See "Sample Interview or Survey Questions" for some examples.) These questionnaires and interviews should be designed to assess the candidates' qualifications—in particular, their background, track record, leadership potential, personal goals, dedication to the company, and commitment to the transformation effort.

SAMPLE INTERVIEW OR SURVEY QUESTIONS

Why do you think you'd be such a great person for this role?

What background, experiences, and qualities do you have that will assist you in this position?

If you had a choice between these groups [list several groups], what would be your first and second choices? Why?

While direct involvement in the transformation via cross-functional teams is important to the company's future and beneficial to both your personal and your professional development, it is also very time-consuming—are you ready and willing to commit to this?

The questionnaires can be designed by consultants in order to free the transformation leader for the actual assessment of candidates. In most cases, the questionnaires are a precursor to and complement the interviews, because only through interviews and in-person interactions can the dedication, commitment, and drive of candidates be clearly assessed. In some instances, however, especially in smaller companies, those directly involved with selecting pilots and members can bypass the interview process because they already know the qualifications and capabilities of the candidates personally through previous interactions. In these cases, the questionnaire can help shed light on the candidate's background and preferences (see "ACI Uses Questionnaires to Aid Its Selection Process"). Hence, the questionnaire can aid in the best possible assignment of candidates to teams, while the interview provides an interpersonal perspective of the candidate.

Selection of the best candidates also involves talking to the candidate's colleagues, both subordinates and superiors. While an interview may provide a personal form of assessment, a more objective perspective of the candidate can be gained through open dialogues with those who work closely with the candidate. Additionally, human resources can be of tremendous help in the selection process, not only with recommendations but also with the candidate's past performance reviews. Analysis of the employee's track record can prove to be critical to the selection process, since past performance is generally a strong indicator of future performance and the candidate's potential.

ACI USES QUESTIONNAIRES TO
AID ITS SELECTION PROCESS

In selecting members for their cross-functional teams, the consultants hired for the ACI transformation first used their expertise to help design a questionnaire assessing which cross-functional team the employee would ideally like to work on and why. According to the responses to this questionnaire, the CEO, who was also the transformation leader, worked with the pilots of the rapid response teams to handpick team members. Some of the responses especially considered and assessed were the candidate's background, interests, and past performance. In this way, not only were the team leaders able to select the best candidate to join the cross-functional team, they were also able to cater to the candidate's interests whenever possible to find the best fit for both the team and the candidate.

The transformation leader was able to work so closely with team leaders at ACI to select individual team members because of the relatively small size of the company and hence the ability for team members to interact frequently with the transformation leader. Therefore, the transformation leader and team leaders were already familiar with the candidates and their track records and did not need to conduct a formal interview. The questionnaires were designed mainly to assess the goals, interests, and background of candidates, as well as to give candidates an opportunity to share any additional information with the transformation leader. With the combination of knowledge of employees through paper and in person, the EMT was able to select the candidates best suited for the positions.

Second Chances

It is often very difficult to get things right the first time. In fact, the key to a successful transformation effort lies in iterations and the willingness to learn from one's mistakes and try again. Many of the most successful transformation efforts didn't get it right the first time. For example, Best Buy's initial attempt at rolling out its transformation plan flopped, for people gave the impression of implementing it without actually doing so. Although individual stores seemed to be passing the checks and tests, true compliance was lacking in the stores. From this, Best Buy learned that it needed buy-in from its employees at all levels throughout the entire process to effectively carry out the transformation effort, and as a result, its second attempt was extremely successful.[19]

Similarly, Irvin's first attempt at creating cross-functional teams was largely unsuccessful. Recommendations made by these teams were not implemented because they failed to meet Irvin's goals. In the next attempt, Irvin learned to give teams more guidelines and guidance. Additional changes he made included creating a new high-performing leadership team, giving more clearly defined structures to the teams, developing higher standards for selecting team members, ensuring that upper management sent more signals regarding the priority of the effort, and providing increased incentives for employees to make the effort a success.[20]

Given that transformations are learning processes, those involved in the transformation effort should also be given second chances. A regional manager at Best Buy, for example, realized that the "first [rapid response team] member [he] appointed was not an ace. [He] didn't understand how powerful the position could be. For the second generation of [team] members, [he] appointed someone very different and very talented."[21] People involved in the transformation effort should, within limits, be given the opportunity to learn from their mistakes, since that is ultimately how they will grow and develop as employees and leaders. A company that gets rid of employees for every mistake they make may find itself in one of two positions: either without employees or with only a conglomerate of mistakes and little progress. Letting people learn from their experiences not only helps them grow but also helps the organization as a whole improve. To facilitate the learning process, employees, managers, and executives should share important lessons learned from past mistakes with the rest of the organization to ensure that the same mistake does not happen twice.

If you do find an employee performing subpar even after being given several chances, you may have to analyze whether the poor performer is actually suitable for involvement in the effort. The decision regarding the employee's role in the effort, however, should be considered separately from his or her role in the organization. After the analysis, you can decide that either (1) this person is not suited for a role in the team or (2) is qualified but poorly matched to his or her particular team. If you decide the latter, you believe that the person is a good employee stuck in a bad position and can reassign him or her to a new position, doing either a different type of job or simply a different function. By trying to find a better match between the employee's qualifications and interests, you can save a lot of energy, time, and money necessary for hiring and training a new employee.

Even issues surrounding underperforming pilots must be addressed, despite the additional complication involved with changing pilots partway through the transformation. In these cases, the cost of maintaining the pilot must be weighed against the turmoil and lost time that may accompany the assignment of a new pilot. Before making hasty, abrupt changes in the team dynamics, you should think the decision through carefully and assess it as the best possible solution. If the ultimate decision involves finding a new pilot, open and honest communication is critical in ensuring the smoothest transition and clearest understanding by all involved parties. Through open communication, relationships may be maintained and the integrity of the team will not be sacrificed (see "Communication Saves the Team at ACI").

INTEGRATION MEETINGS

With this overview of cross-functional teams, from their role in the transformation to the details of team structure, we now discuss integration meetings, where teams touch base with one another as well as with the EMT and the PMO (see figure 3-10).

COMMUNICATION SAVES THE TEAM AT ACI

During the transformation effort, one particular rapid response team member shone in performance and potential after the teams were assigned and announced. Noticing this, the team's coach took the current pilot of that respective cross-functional team aside and noted his observations of the high potential of the team member. Additionally, the consultant asked the pilot for his thoughts about promoting her to his current position, thereby changing the pilot's role to a supporting, not leading, one. Because he understood the situation and was able to see it from an external perspective, the original team pilot agreed and supported the new pilot in her endeavors. Eventually, because they had very complementary leadership and action styles, the former pilot was promoted to colead the team with the new pilot. Hence, all parties were satisfied, and a potentially damaging situation was moderated by open communication.

FIGURE 3-10

Integration meetings

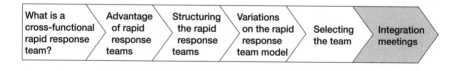

Monthly Integration Meetings

Monthly integration meetings occur at the end of each phase of the model (phase 1, phase 2, and phase 3). They are one to two full-day meetings attended by the transformation leaders, executive sponsors, coaches, and pilots. Additionally, a designated note taker records action items agreed on in the meeting, to increase accountability and to document the progress of the transformation.

At each monthly integration meeting, each team is required to give an hour-long presentation on its progress, summarizing the team's work and highlighting the key findings from the past month. Because these presentations are given in front of the other teams, the key players in the transformation effort gain a more holistic view of the organization and the effort.

Not only do these meetings give the transformation leader and the team pilots the opportunity to exchange ideas, they also allow each team to maintain an open line of communication with the transformation leader and with the other teams, ensuring integration and alignment throughout the effort. Monthly integration meetings are very useful in establishing rapport and building relationships.

Furthermore, the presentations allow the transformation leader and other teams to provide midcourse corrections by directing and redirecting the teams, as well as the opportunity to challenge the teams' assumptions and premises. Hence, these monthly integration meetings are not simply reviews conducted by the transformation leader on the overall progress of the transformation, they are also a chance to make key improvements. For example, Nissan's Ghosn gave the teams constant feedback and pressure in order to guide them to the depth he expected in their quest for answers and solutions. This push-review-push method required that the transformation leader keep pressuring his teams to provide him with aggressive answers. In fact, teams were repeatedly sent back to planning sessions, highlighting the iterative nature of problem solving and solution planning.[22]

To promote a uniform method of communication during each monthly integration meeting (also called the day 30, day 60, and day 90 meetings), PowerPoint templates, with examples of the type of information expected and required, should be distributed to each team. These templates serve as an empowerment tool for team leaders, who may have had little previous experience with integrating so much complex information. Hence, consultants should use their experience and expertise to guide the teams.

In the following chapters, we describe in further detail each integration meeting, highlighting the differences between them, as well as specific, key points to cover.

Weekly Meetings

While the monthly integration meetings are the capstone meetings for each phase, the EMT also engages in regular weekly meetings with all the teams. The meetings are informal and do not have to be conducted in person—in fact, they are typically telephone conference calls. Pilots and project managers discuss with the transformation leader and executive sponsors their progress for the week. Each team gives a ten-minute presentation updating the EMT on the team's current situation, milestones the team has met, the future direction (especially the proposed plan for the coming week), and any barriers or obstacles the team faced. To prepare for the meeting, each team should submit a short PowerPoint presentation with the information requested in the templates before the meeting. These presentations should be distributed to all the team members so everyone has a copy to follow during the presentation.

These weekly meetings not only maintain open lines of communication but also give the transformation leader the opportunity to keep the teams on the right track by redirecting and refocusing them as frequently as necessary. Without these weekly meetings, teams may not be able to meet the thirty-day deadline, or they may miss the mark with the findings presented at the monthly integration meeting. Weekly meetings help keep everyone on track, especially at the beginning of the effort. Regarding deadlines, it is acceptable to be slightly flexible with scheduling early in the effort, because that is when many unexpected obstacles are encountered. Later, as the team settles in and the members grow accustomed to working together in their particular domain, changes in schedule should not be lackadaisically tolerated. Weekly meetings are critical in controlling the pace of the transformation effort and in keeping the key players involved and on the same page. Additionally, the meetings give each group a chance to benchmark its progress against other groups' and to gain a broader view of the issues all teams are facing.

Though important, these are not the only meetings each team is expected to hold. Pilots and project managers are also expected to have several internal meetings with their team each week to make sure that everyone is clear about the progress of the team as a whole and how it fits in with the transformation effort. Logistics for these meetings are often arranged by the project manager. Additionally, the pilot and project manager should be prepared to meet with individual team members as necessary.

CONCLUSION

Cross-functional rapid response teams are often considered the heart of the transformation effort. While the pretransformation effort was focused on gaining momentum by planting the seeds of the transformation and creating the necessary conditions for growth and change, rapid response teams actively accelerate the transformation via their parallel efforts. If they are not implemented correctly, the transformation is more likely to be inefficient and ineffective, and the probability of failure increases significantly. Implemented appropriately, however, rapid response teams drive the transformation effort and improve communication throughout the organization, a benefit that extends beyond the life of the effort. Not only do they break down organizational barriers, but cross-functional teams also help the transformation leader by getting widespread support for the effort.

Now that we have examined the basics of rapid response teams, including both the macroscopic and microscopic structure and selection of members, we will explore interactions within and between teams. The next chapter, describing phase 1 of the transformation effort (the first thirty days), will highlight how the teams go about analyzing the current situation of the company and identifying the problems plaguing the company.

4

Phase 1

Diagnosing the Patient

*All truths are easy to understand once they are discovered;
the point is to discover them.*

—Galileo Galilei

After assembling the cross-functional rapid response teams, the transformation leader starts phase 1 of the transformation effort. Over the next thirty days, the leader directs the rapid response teams in identifying the major pain points of the organization.

Up to this point, the transformation leader has conducted his or her own high-level analysis of the current state of the organization. However, a more in-depth analysis by the rapid response teams is recommended and has distinct advantages. By dedicating a group of people to examining specific areas of the company, such as strategy, finance, marketing, human resources, operations, information technology (IT), and product or service offerings, the company will gain a deeper view of the pending issues within each area. Again, the power of cross-functional teams is that these areas are studied and diagnosed in parallel; attacking all areas at once is the key differentiator from reengineering efforts. Additionally, as mentioned earlier, by dedicating such a broad range of employees to the transformation effort, the organization will develop a coalition of leaders who will collectively support the transformation effort and lead in internalizing that change across the organization. Diagnosing the company is the most important phase in the transformation process.

Like an ill patient making his first visit to the doctor, the organization will undergo a series of questions and tests in this phase to diagnose the problems to be addressed and solved later. The teams will use a variety of tools and methods to gather data in order to identify the underlying issues plaguing the organization. One of the key things to remember while diagnosing the company is the difference between a symptom and a root cause. Differentiating between these two categories, although quite difficult and complicated, is necessary. If the wrong issue is categorized as a root cause, the organization will subsequently waste a lot of time, energy, and resources attacking it, most likely without seeing any results. Because the problems identified in this phase will serve as the guideline for the following phases in the transformation effort, extreme care must be taken to ensure an accurate diagnosis.

In this chapter, we outline the process and methodology for a successful diagnosis, providing the teams with tools and examples of key areas to analyze. Phase 1 can be decomposed into five main parts (see figure 4-1).

It begins informally, with a meeting called by the transformation leader to empower the leadership team. Once the full commitment of the leadership team is attained, the transformation leader leads the official launch of phase 1. In this two-day meeting for all the team members the transformation leader communicates the expectations for the transformation effort, and the teams develop their plan of attack for the next thirty days.

We then progress to the heart of phase 1—gathering the data. One of the key success factors of transformation efforts is that they are all-encompassing. In gathering the data, the various cross-functional rapid response teams must critically look at every aspect of the company. Given the tremendous amount of data available, we also discuss effective ways of organizing and analyzing the data, highlighting the use of process flowcharts. A process flowchart is an effective tool for mapping a business process and shedding light on problem areas and key issues plaguing the company.

Once the data has been gathered and analyzed, it has another use: internal and external comparisons. Benchmarking is a way of gathering more information, by comparing internal data with external data. With the key information in mind, each team also creates a set of baseline metrics by which to measure the progress and impact of the transformation effort.

Phase 1 concludes with the day 30 integration meeting, the capstone meeting wrapping up the phase.

FIGURE 4-1

Phase 1 overview

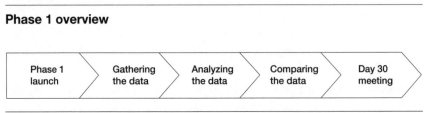

PHASE 1 LAUNCH

The phase 1 launch (see figure 4-2) has two components: an informal launch with the leadership team, followed by a formal launch, called the landmark meeting.

Empowering the Leadership Team

In the informal launch, all company managers and key contributors are invited by the transformation leader to a private meeting. In this meeting, he will have one goal: to empower the key people in the company, particularly the members of his executive management team (EMT, described in the previous chapter), and ensure that they are fully committed to the transformation effort. The transformation leader should explicitly put the company and its future into the hands of the leaders, empowering them to change for the betterment of the company. (See "Gerstner Empowers Senior Management at IBM" for an in-depth look at this meeting.) This meeting serves not only to create the critical sense of urgency discussed in the pretransformation chapter but also to reinforce the capabilities and potential of the current leaders.

Some effective ways of empowering senior management include the following:

- Provide data that shows that the company is not performing well. This could be done by comparing the organization with the marketplace and against major competitors.

- Explain that the status quo of business will lead to a company crisis and that change must happen . . . *fast*.

- Lay out the opportunities for the company and be positive that the turnaround can lead the company to success.

- Explain that people who will *commit to change* and *to internalizing change* within the organization are needed.

FIGURE 4-2

Phase 1 launch

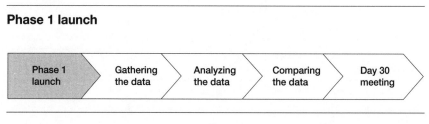

GERSTNER EMPOWERS
SENIOR MANAGEMENT AT IBM

In his first meeting with his senior management team, Lou Gerstner invited 420 employees from around the globe to New York and conveyed his major goal: "To motivate the group to focus its talents and efforts outside the company, not on one another."[1] He began the meeting by showing two charts, one for customer satisfaction and the other for market share, both of which showed very discouraging results for the company. After showing those two charts, he summarized with "We're getting our butts kicked in the marketplace!" He hoped that his message would spark a fire of anger inside all employees to take notice of the fierce marketplace and to take action against all competitors. He furthered this goal by showing pictures of CEOs from some of their competitors, including Bill Gates and Larry Ellison. He read actual quotes of them criticizing IBM, including one from Ellison, who said, "IBM? We don't even think about those guys anymore. They're not dead, but they're irrelevant."

To further convey his message, he explained that 25,000 employees had lost their jobs because of the downturn IBM had taken. "These guys came in and beat us," he said. In a call for action, he remarked, "When you have a market share like that and a customer satisfaction record like that, there isn't a lot of time for debate. We've got to get out there and start winning in the marketplace." Gerstner explained the new performance-based culture that IBM would have, where he would personally fill new key jobs in the company. He was looking for results and for "people who make things happen, not who watch and debate things happening." He wanted people who could help turn the company around, and promised that if all employees followed the recipe for change he gave them, the company would start becoming successful again. At that point, he laid out the behavioral changed required of his leaders, contrasting current leadership practices with best-in-class leadership practices that would lead to an internalization of change.

- Give all leaders positive feedback on their potential.

- Present a set of behavioral changes that will transform all members into change agents within the organization. The organization should initiate a short leadership training session to help the leaders make the new set of behavioral changes part of their daily lives.

When meeting with the leadership team, the transformation leader should develop a message that is both manageable and memorable (see "Simplifying IBM"). Before ensuring full commitment from the leadership team, the transformation leader must explicitly clarify the expectations for the effort. From this initial meeting forward, the transformation leader is expecting his leadership team to develop a new set of skills and habits, which is extremely difficult and requires deliberate thought and action. Therefore, the transformation leader needs to develop a clear way of communicating his expectations and encourage his team. One of his key messages should be the new leadership traits the leaders are expected to execute in the workplace. A clear, simple message embodying the expectations is important in not overwhelming the leadership team and ensuring that the message will be remembered and delivered consistently.

The Landmark Meeting

After the initial meeting, the transformation leader should invite the EMT and all members of the rapid response teams to a two-day convention to kick off the detailed diagnosis of the effort. If team members haven't had a chance to officially meet yet, they now get the chance. Additionally, team members also get the opportunity to meet and convene with members of the other teams, for everyone will be collaborating in the effort. In this meeting,

SIMPLIFYING IBM

In his initial meeting with his senior management, Gerstner had laid out high-level cultural behaviors for his leaders. However, he soon realized that his people were not executing the behaviors, and talked to one of his colleagues to understand the problem. His colleague responded, "Over the weekend, I counted them up, and there are about two dozen things that you want me to wake up in the morning and focus on. I can't do it. I'm not that good. What do you really want people to do?"[2] From this conversation, Gerstner realized that he "needed to take [IBM's] principles and make them come alive for all IBMers. To do that [he] needed to make them simpler and bake them into what people did every day." He then developed the phrase "Win, execute, team" to sum up the initial ideas he had conveyed earlier in his meeting with senior management, which was significantly more effective.

the transformation leader should lay down the guidelines and set the tone for the transformation effort.

The landmark meeting should cover:

Day One

   1. Establishing a shared vision

   2. Presenting the methodology

   3. Starting with a clean slate

   4. Developing a set of key values

   5. Conducting a high-level analysis of current issues

Day Two

   1. Establishing clear roles and responsibilities

   2. Working as a team

   3. Developing an effective phase 1 plan

Day One

While the transformation leader has already officially announced the transformation in the pretransformation phase, the first day of the landmark meeting marks the kickoff of the transformation effort activities and formally reconfirms the involvement and full commitment of team members. Day one of the landmark meeting highlights key aspects of the pretransformation. However, pretransformation revolves around the transformation leader, while the rapid response teams are the central part of the landmark meeting. This meeting should focus on getting everyone involved up to speed and align them to a high-level view of where the company needs to go.

1. Establishing a shared vision. At the start of day one, the transformation leader begins with a discussion of the current state of the organization. Stressing the extreme need for change that exists within the organization, the leader creates a sense of urgency, reiterating many points given in his recent meeting with his leadership team and the EMT while laying out the opportunities for the company by establishing his vision for the future. For the transformation effort to be successful, the team members themselves must be excited about the change and convinced of the need for a transformation. Hence, the sense of urgency and the need for transformation must be reinforced in this meeting.

Part of the transformation leader's most difficult tasks lies in motivating his team and aligning their understanding of this vision with his, although this can be done effectively by helping them visualize the potential results of the transformation (see "Best Buy's 'Destiny'"). This vision is important in motivating people, as Nissan's Carlos Ghosn learned after trying a variety of methods to rally his people behind him. He clearly communicated how reaching their short- and long-term goals would change the company by formulating a picture in their minds of the new company. "If we reach our goals," he said, "this is what we'll be in two years and this is what we'll be in five years."[3]

Indirectly, communicating the vision means communicating the goals of the transformation effort, since transformation effort will help the company achieve its vision. That said, the transformation leader may additionally choose to communicate a high-level vision that may be more tangible and quantitatively measured. For example, in VeriSign's transformation, a vision of a $1 billion revenue goal was communicated in its kickoff meeting. This measurable vision and goal gave team members something concrete and understandable, and represented a goal for the transformation effort as a whole. Assuming that it's not too unrealistic or too attainable, a concrete goal communicated

BEST BUY'S "DESTINY"

Consultants communicated their vision of a better Best Buy to the Change Implementation Team (CIT) by creating a mock-up of a magazine cover and article from a made-up business magazine that they called *Destiny*. On the front of the magazine were the words "How Best Buy Navigated the Waters of Change and Landed Its New Operating Platform." The title of the article was "From Chaos to Discipline: How Best Buy Changed."[4] In this article, the consultants painted a picture of Best Buy after the transformation. They highlighted "the ultimate shopping experience" and how the members of the CIT were expressing that the leadership should serve as future change agents.

The documents were highly effective in motivating the team to implement the transformation effort. One member of the CIT remarked, "For the team, the mock-ups of the *Destiny* magazine cover and article were really compelling, and what was said in the article seemed so unachievable. That had a real impact on me and the team."[5]

here helps give team members something to reach for and grasp, and can be an effective supplement to a more abstract vision.

Communication of the vision is critical because a vision has many more powerful effects than simply giving people a path to follow or a cause to fight for. First of all, it provides a framework around which to make decisions. For example, when employees are faced with a set of potential alternatives, they can eliminate some of them by asking, "Does this alternative fit with our overall vision?" If it does not, that alternative can be eliminated. This framework allows more employees to take responsibility and control of the decision-making process. Decisions can be made more quickly, which saves time and resources that can instead be dedicated to projects that support the overarching vision.

Second, a vision helps people see the value of completing short-term tasks. By motivating short-term action, a vision helps communicate to employees that their work will be rewarded in the future. In this way, a vision eases the natural resistance to change and reinvigorates team members.[6]

2. Presenting the methodology. At this point, a coach or an expert on the 90 days model, along with the transformation leader, presents the methodology for the upcoming months and the rules and expectations for the transformation. The transformation leader must facilitate the presentation to demonstrate his endorsement of the effort and illustrate that the effort will be run not by consultants but by those who have a stake in the company, including the transformation leader himself.

In presenting the methodology, the transformation leader or other expert explains the helicopter-view goals for the upcoming three months. While this is similar to the vision described earlier, it is more directly tied to the transformation effort and the greater opportunities that lie in the future. For example, the transformation leader in one company we studied used the following goal to motivate his team: to over-resource a great opportunity. In describing this goal, the transformation leader tied the goal directly to his conviction that this was the chance for the company to turn over a new leaf and break away from its competitors. Furthermore, the transformation leader of that company shared the transformation's goal of striving for a disciplined, metric-driven, commitment-oriented, and innovative culture. He expressed that not only should this new culture be the outcome of the effort, but it should also be developed and executed during the effort.

The transformation leader and the methodology expert should emphasize up front that there is no cookie-cutter solution and that the company must find and solve its own specific problems. All employees need to understand that the 90 days transformation is not a simple elixir for the company. Rather, it is a methodology that will guide the company through a quest for quantum leaps in improvement. This is also an opportunity for the transformation leader to allay the fear of layoffs, a common occurrence during most transformation efforts. The transformation effort should generate better opportunities for the organization, and the employees need to know that they will be able to reap the benefits of the improved organization.

In this presentation, the transformation leader should lay out the ground rules and expectations for the transformation effort. For example, the environment of the effort should be gossip free. Not only will this allow employees to speak their mind freely and comfortably, it will also make the effort more efficient by decreasing politics and unnecessary bickering and harsh feelings. The team members involved in the transformation are all thought leaders of the organization and extremely capable people, and gossip only wastes time and decreases their ability to carry out the necessary tasks. Similarly, the transformation leader should emphasize that there are to be no sacred cows or pet projects—every aspect of the company should be analyzed objectively in depth. There should be no boundaries that hinder performance in the transformation effort or the company as a whole.

The presentation is followed by a question-and-answer (Q&A) period, during which the transformation leader and coaches open the floor to questions from all members of the rapid response teams. They should be encouraged to ask questions and resolve any misunderstandings early on. A few of the most common questions are, Can we really do this in ninety days? How is this effort different from other turnaround efforts we have tried in the past? How do we know this will work? (See "Q&A: How Do We Know the Process Will Work?" on the next page for some sample answers.) All these questions need to be settled at this stage, and all remaining doubts should be addressed.

3. *Starting with a clean slate.* When helping employees embark on the transformation effort, the leader should point out that there will be raised stakes for all employees. To get the most out of people during the effort and beyond, the leader should give everyone a clean slate to start on. From here on out, past performance is generally irrelevant, and people who deliver measurable results will be the first in line for leadership positions after the transformation effort. This encourages all employees to prove themselves in the transformation.

At the same time, however, employees should not be afraid of making mistakes. The transformation leader needs to emphasize that the transformation is a learning experience for those involved and that, generally, mistakes—

Q&A: HOW DO WE KNOW
THE PROCESS WILL WORK?

Below, we share the ABCs of why the process will work. To prevent this question from even coming up, the transformation leader should try to clarify these points up front, whether in his presentation or in his meetings with key players in the organization. Some questions can be anticipated and should be preempted—for example, why the transformation process will work:

Accountability. Accountability and responsibilities are clear throughout the process.

Best practices. The method and process are based on best practices from a variety of industries.

Continuous. It is a living process that moves the organization toward world-class processes.

Dashboard. It will be dashboard- and metrics-driven. Baseline numbers will be captured to measure progress.

Education. Everyone, including senior management, will be trained on the process.

Focus. It is market-facing, with ownership and clear roles and responsibilities.

given that they are intelligent mistakes—are acceptable and part of the experience. The most important thing about mistakes is that the company and relevant parties, not just the particular person who made the mistake, learn from the mistake and don't make the same one in the future.

In dealing with the inevitable few employees and team members who seem skeptical of the effort, the transformation leader should first explain the severity and reality of the situation, thereby re-creating a sense of urgency. The transformation effort will not only propel the organization to a better future but also create new opportunities for these employees to ground themselves in. Despite the future opportunities, the transformation leader needs to clearly reexplain the heavy workload and potential overtime expected for involvement in and commitment to the transformation effort. While team members should have already known the extent of their commitment before joining, reiteration in this meeting gives them one last chance to leave of their own accord, and reinforces their commitment.

In addition to preparing the teams for the hard work ahead of them, this is an opportunity to reconfirm the clear belief that the team members are extremely capable individuals and the thought leaders of the organization. By doing so, the transformation leader increases the morale and confidence of the group, which is necessary to ignite the transformation effort.

4. Developing a set of key values. After the Q&A session, the transformation leader and coaches should prompt the rapid response teams to work together to develop a set of values for the transformation effort and beyond (see "ACI Develops a New Set of Values"). These should be values they hold themselves to and that will sustain the company in the long term. To encourage open group discussion and dialogue, the transformation leader and coaches should leave the room and give members very little direction on how to proceed. Once the teams have reached a consensus, they should present

ACI DEVELOPS A NEW SET OF VALUES

During the transformation at ACI, the rapid response teams engaged in hours of emotion, chaos, argument, and conflict to come up with their values. In the end, they not only came up with a set of values but were eager and excited to support them. The values were:

- Teamwork

- Creativity

- Transparency

- Honesty

- Positive thinking

- Customercentricity

- Accountability

- Punctuality

- Respect for peers

their values to the transformation leader and the group of coaches, who will aid them in gaining closure. To ensure buy-in and commitment, all members sign on the values. In the coming phases, the transformation leader will work with the values and flesh them out so they are measurable and have greater detail in specific behaviors embodied in the high-level values.

This method of developing values is highly effective for numerous reasons. First of all, it breeds a coalition of people who are excited about supporting the values and the transformation effort. This coalition will be particularly effective in the future, when execution of the effort may lead to resistance in the company. For example, if during the transformation effort one employee deviates from the set of values, other employees can jump in and remind the individual to abide by the values agreed on at the beginning of the effort. This self-regulation not only reduces the load on the executives and the transformation leader but also results in a self-perpetuating dissemination of and obedience to the values. Furthermore, forcing the teams to discuss and come to a consensus makes all of the members more comfortable working together and expressing their own viewpoints.

After the teams have developed a set of values, the transformation leader should communicate these values to the company, thereby making sure that they are stated clearly and that employees understand specifically what is and what isn't going to change (see "Setting Boundaries for Change at Procter & Gamble"). The transformation leader should restate the values in detail to the company and reemphasize them to the teams, using the communication vehicles described later.

5. *Conducting a high-level analysis of current issues.* After the rapid response teams develop the set of values, the transformation leader should give each team its first task: to conduct a high-level diagnosis of its assigned area of the company. In a two-hour brainstorming session, the group should document a list of key symptoms, although it's too early to diagnose the root cause. The discussion will be guided by the coaches, and team members should feel comfortable debating their opinions about the most important problems and symptoms.

After this two-hour period, the groups reconvene, and each team presents its initial findings and hypotheses to the transformation leader and other teams. By having each team present its findings, the transformation leader becomes more informed about his teams' beliefs about the key issues, and all participants get a preview of the problems to analyze more in depth.

SETTING BOUNDARIES FOR CHANGE AT PROCTER & GAMBLE

In looking at the values of Procter & Gamble (P&G), CEO A. G. Lafley first noted items and aspects of the company that would remain unchanged. He clearly stated that P&G's vision of improving the everyday lives of people around the world with P&G products of better performance, quality, and value would remain constant. Furthermore, Lafley announced that the six guiding principles of P&G, in addition to respect for the individual, wouldn't change with the transformation effort, nor would the high-level value system.

Lafley then progressed to addressing the items that had to change. For example, he noted that any business currently without a strategy would need to develop one, and any business with a strategy but not performing in the market either needed to change its strategy or improve its execution. By stating what needed to be changed, Lafley set clear boundaries for the transformation effort and laid out the constants. In his own words: "I was very clear about what was safe and what wasn't."[7]

The discussions and presentations also help people get on the same page about the different areas and issues surrounding the company. Furthermore, this initial session gives all members a chance to become acquainted with working as part of a team. Conflict may emerge, and appropriate coaching is critical in setting the tone for open debate and conflict—team members should not leave this initial discussion with a sour taste in their mouths because this is only the first glimpse of what the transformation effort entails.

Day Two

During the second day of the convention, teams reconvene and each team's pilot leads a discussion on a schedule and a set of milestones for the next thirty days. Each team works with its coach and executive sponsor, who will aid them in these tasks and ensure that all teams are ready to begin their actual diagnosis of the company.

1. Establishing clear roles and responsibilities. First, the coaches and executive sponsors should ensure that all members understand the overarching goals of the transformation effort as described on the previous day. Then, the coaches should ensure that each team member has a clearly defined role in his assigned team and that he understands his role and individual responsibilities. (See "Unclear Tasks at VeriSign" for an example of the importance of developing clear roles and responsibilities.) This should be accomplished not by assignment but by discussion among team members about their strengths and expertise, for the roles should complement the members' backgrounds. Not only does this lead to greater efficiency and decreased conflict, it also helps individual team members understand more concretely what will be expected of them in the coming months.

2. *Working as a team.* Throughout the convention, team members grow increasingly accustomed to working together. Team pilots, however, are responsible for running these very diverse groups of individuals from different backgrounds and with different expertise. To increase the effectiveness of members working together as a team, pilots may take this opportunity to lead a team activity. One example is to use the Myers-Briggs personality test to

UNCLEAR TASKS AT VERISIGN

In VeriSign's first attempt at creating and guiding its rapid response teams, unclear roles and responsibilities limited the impact of the teams. One of the teams created in this first attempt, the cost-savings team, was told to brainstorm ideas for a new strategy and cost-saving initiatives for its VCS division. However, when the team members first met in Denver, Colorado, they were unclear on what they were trying to accomplish. They spent their first meeting primarily trying to determine some guidelines for themselves. They were asking themselves:

Cost savings at the expense of what?

Do we need to cut people out of the organization?

Should we close down some of our offices?

What are the expectations?

In the end, they made a series of recommendations, but because they did not have a clear charter and guidelines, their recommendations missed the mark and were not implemented.

better understand, appreciate, and take advantage of the differences between team members. (See "Creating a Cohesive Team at Best Buy.")

3. *Developing an effective phase 1 plan.* With just thirty days ahead of it for diagnosing its assigned area of the company, each rapid response team must develop a methodology and a plan of attack to make the most of the limited time frame. This plan of attack should focus on what the team needs to accomplish in phase 1. Because team members are on their regular day jobs in addition to the transformation effort, it is very easy for tasks related to the transformation to be put on the back burner, and each week will pass without any significant progress. Therefore, a schedule with milestones and deadlines for phase 1 needs to be developed right off the bat. While the schedule will go through iterations and changes as new developments are made and the focus of the diagnosis shifts with the findings, high-level milestones need to be set. For instance, if a team needs to survey employees throughout the company, when should the questionnaire be completed? When should the results be analyzed? Additionally, the plan will help the team prioritize and coordinate the numerous tasks.

Also important in developing an effective phase 1 plan is how often the team will meet each week to discuss its progress and findings, as well as to

CREATING A COHESIVE TEAM AT BEST BUY

At Best Buy, becoming an individual hero was part of the company's culture. Therefore, employees were not used to working in teams. At first, the members of the Change Implementation Team had trouble working as a team, but they soon realized that only as a team could they fully maintain their credibility. To become change agents that would transform the company, they first had to transform themselves.

Initially, the team had to work through dealing with different personality types and people with differing motives. A breakthrough happened for their team when all of them took the Myers-Briggs test, which attempts to describe an individual's personality type. By looking at how they were similar to and different from each other, the team members were able to understand one another better. Additionally, they quickly learned how their differences complemented each other and how they were stronger as a team than as individuals.

address concerns and obstacles. One team may decide it needs to meet twice a week, while another team may decide to conduct individual meetings to address problems as they emerge and only meet collectively briefly once a week to get everyone up to speed.

In this phase 1 plan, the teams should develop their first action item and task. This initial task should be balanced between simple and impossible, for this is the task that will propel the team in its future direction. If it is too simple and easy, the team will not gain enough momentum to propel it to the next task. If it is too difficult, however, the team will lose motivation even before it begins. Hence, team members should leave the landmark meeting with an idea of what they need to accomplish before the next meeting.

With the development of the teams' phase 1 plans, the kickoff meeting can end officially, with some final summarizing words from the transformation leader. Now that the teams have a brief idea of the key symptoms of the problems in their area of study, know how they want to attack the next thirty days, and have their individual roles and responsibilities, they can disband and commence with their individual tasks.

GATHERING CRITICAL DATA

For each team, the heart of phase 1 lies in data gathering. During the landmark meeting, each team developed several hypotheses consisting of the key symptoms of its particular area. However, which of these key symptoms, if any, are root causes? In this phase, each team needs to distinguish between the symptoms and the root causes. For example, lack of adequate resources is a common problem in many companies. However, is this lack of resources simply a manifestation of a deeper, underlying cause, such as inefficient ad hoc processes, or is it the cause of other problems? Often, the line is extremely blurry, and these hypotheses can be tested and supported only with additional data and information (see figure 4-3).

FIGURE 4-3

Gathering the data

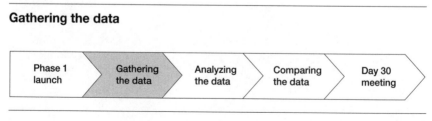

In addition to gathering data that will help diagnose the ailments troubling the company, the teams should also begin gathering data about the megatrends of the industry and the market, as the transformation leader did when he surveyed the grounds in the pretransformation phase. Beginning to study the megatrends at this point will help the teams in phase 2, when they are tasked to develop "big ideas" based on their analyses.

There are numerous ways of gathering data, each with advantages and disadvantages. The team should develop a specific set of methods based on what they would like to measure and what type of information will be most useful to them. One key to data gathering is asking the right questions to get the answers you need.

Before you begin gathering data, however, each rapid response team should discuss and develop a set of questions that need to be addressed during data gathering. From this, you can begin to determine what type of data your group needs to collect and what methods would be relevant to that cause. Often, a combination of channels is necessary, though some channels should be relied on more heavily than others. Defining the goal of the data-gathering phase is also important in giving the team something to measure itself against after it feels it has gathered sufficient information. Did the team members find answers to the questions they set out to answer? Are there any surprising findings that need to be followed up?

As when the transformation leader surveyed the grounds, note that data gathering is a tool to test your hypothesis, not support it. One of the gravest dangers for any team in this phase is to enter with preconceptions and biases and interpret the data in a way that supports its biases. Data gathering should be done objectively. Sometimes findings are surprising and counterintuitive, but those should not be immediately discounted. If anything, those findings should be further investigated to search for the truth behind that particular data.

At the same time, the teams must be prepared for the harsh realities of data gathering. Rather than brushing problems under the rug, the teams and the organization should confront them. Some of the findings may be painful to hear or discover, but those are precisely the findings the company should pay the most attention to and consider changing and improving. Sometimes, the truth hurts. But then again, no pain, no gain.

There are numerous ways to gather data. Because data gathering is often conducted to get information and honest feedback from employees and customers, most forms of data gathering have the goal of getting the opinions of these key people. The most thorough data-gathering effort is one that includes open-ended questions asked through site visits, phone calls, and interviews, as well as multiple-choice questionnaires that can be distributed to a large portion of the company. Depending on the need of the team, however, some methods may be more intuitive and useful than others.

Questionnaires

To gather a large amount of data, a company can administer an online or paper questionnaire that includes fixed-choice questions such as multiple choice or rankings rather than open-ended ones (see "Use of Questionnaires

USE OF QUESTIONNAIRES AT BAY NETWORKS

When Dave House arrived as CEO of Bay Networks, he had fifteen direct reports. After assembling fifteen teams of five people (one team per direct report), he sent the teams out on a data-gathering mission: to spend one week talking to customers. He sent group members to Europe, Asia, and South America, and each member was to visit and interview three to five customers per day. At the end of the interview, each customer was given an eight-page questionnaire, which included questions targeted at assessing their needs:

- What is your biggest technology need?

- What is your biggest business need?

- What is your greatest strength?

- What is your greatest weakness?

- What are the competitors' strengths?

- What are their weaknesses?

- What advice would you give to the new CEO?

In addition to the data gathered, a benefit was the message sent to employees and customers around the world. In the end, the teams connected with a tremendous number of customers, and their effort signaled to people that something was different—that change was imminent. By focusing on gaining customer feedback, they were communicating to employees and customers alike that from here on out, the customers would be number one.

at Bay Networks"). Fixed-choice questions allow the team to conduct a more quantitative analysis on its findings. However, open-ended questions that allow the responder to type or write in responses are also necessary to address other aspects and gather data that cannot otherwise be gathered through closed questions, such as opinions and additional thoughts. Alternatively, team members can administer questionnaires in person or conduct interviews to address the open-ended questions.

In-Person Visits

Aside from administering questionnaires, the rapid response teams can also venture out and conduct their own site visits across all geographies and functions (see "Store Visits at Nordstrom"). These in-person visits may be purely observational or either ad hoc or informal interviews.

Additionally, the teams may visit not only different company sites but also other important players, such as suppliers and customers (see "Customer Visits at IBM: Operation Bear Hug"). Data gathering does not necessitate a one-way information flow. In fact, visits with employees, suppliers, and customers make a great opportunity to communicate the imminent change to them and to let them know how important they are to the organization and any other relevant message.

STORE VISITS AT NORDSTROM

During the transformation effort at Nordstrom, chairman Bruce Nordstrom started an initiative in which he and his sons embarked on a "listening tour" of all seventy-seven existing stores. During the tour, they talked to over two thousand employees, saying, "Look, we made a lot of mistakes. What are your thoughts? What do you think is most important and how can we improve?"[8]

The stories they gathered allowed them to gain a high-level picture of the issues facing their company. At the highest level, they found that they were losing customers because they were losing the customercentric and individual-attention approach the company was known for. They were not giving customers a reason to come to them. This knowledge and understanding was a critical finding that Nordstrom knew he needed to address.

CUSTOMER VISITS AT IBM: OPERATION BEAR HUG

At the beginning of the transformation effort at IBM, Gerstner launched an effort called Operation Bear Hug to identify the causes of many of the internal problems already recognized.[9] The operation required each of the fifty executives from his corporate management board to make a "bear hug" visit to at least five of IBM's biggest customers in just three months. During each visit, the executives were instructed to listen to each customer, record their concerns, communicate IBM's commitment to customer satisfaction, and implement holding action as appropriate. Each executive was required to submit to Gerstner and relevant parties a one- to two-page report detailing the problems found. Gerstner read and addressed every report, and when people realized that he did this, there was significant improvement in responsiveness from his executives. From the beginning, Operation Bear Hug had three main goals:

- To reduce the customer perception that IBM's top executives were difficult to deal with

- To identify the top executives, according to who performed well on this assignment

- To push the new customercentric culture

Recommended Areas to Diagnose

Successful transformations are all-encompassing, and this is critical in the diagnosis phase. Teams need to look under every rock and pebble, leaving no stones unturned. Because this task may seem daunting for the transformation team to undertake, we highlight here some of the key areas that should not be overlooked. While every aspect should be analyzed, this section will help you prioritize which sections to focus on, as a result of our research (see figure 4-4).

In particular, we highlight seven key areas, some with several subareas: (1) strategy, (2) organizational excellence, (3) finance, (4) innovative product or service offerings, (5) customer care, (6) sales, and (7) information technology.

We must emphasize again that this diagnosis should be conducted by the cross-functional teams in parallel rather than serially. It may be tempting to

FIGURE 4-4

Areas to diagnose

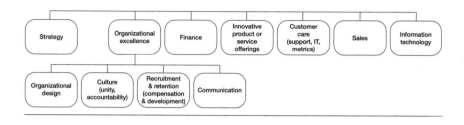

focus on one area where the company is most troubled, but the rapid response teams ensure that everything gets assessed and analyzed and that the company doesn't get derailed by certain findings. Such a massive undertaking may initially seem chaotic, given that all gears are turning at the same time, but it is ultimately this parallel processing nature of cross-functional teams that establishes order amid chaos.

Area 1: Strategy

In the context of an organization, strategy describes the set of goals and activities the organization engages in to gain a competitive advantage. It describes how a company decides to allocate its resources and details what these resources will be used to achieve. To set the strategy of an organization, management must first determine where the company is, where it is going, and finally the steps it should take to get there (see figure 4-5). Once the new strategy is selected, every other aspect of the company should be aligned with it and support it.

All organizations have a set of capabilities or strengths as well as a set of weaknesses. In weighing potential strategies, an executive should not be blind to these capabilities. In other words, given a specific set of resources and ca-

FIGURE 4-5

Diagnosing strategy

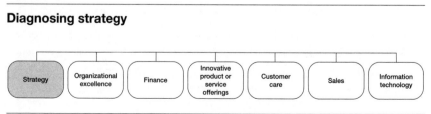

pabilities, the executive must ask, Is this strategy possible? A strategy may sound great but impossible with the given set of resources. To take this a step further, a leader should first look at the capabilities of an organization before developing potential strategic alternatives. At the same time, future resources should be considered in setting the strategy. Therefore, the following question must also be asked: Would this strategy be possible with the incoming set of resources?

To get started, you may use the following questions as a guide:

- Who are the competitors? What is their share in each market?

- What's the business like (commodity/high-value)? What are some drivers for profitability?

- What are the strengths and weaknesses of competitors?

- What is the current strategy of the company? What are our core competencies? Are we leveraging them?

You should have a good sense of the competitors, the market, and your organization in setting the strategy (see "Setting the Strategy at SAS"). Benchmarking, described later in the chapter, is particularly important here, although you should also not lose sight of the company's inherent capabilities.

Area 2: Organizational Excellence

Organizational excellence, very similar to human resources, includes various "fuzzier" aspects of the company, all of which need to be aligned with the strategy and direction of the company. Once the strategy is set, the organizational excellence team should analyze its domain to make sure everything is aligned with the new strategy. Many processes and aspects falling under the umbrella of organizational excellence should be addressed in the transformation effort. In particular, the four main subareas we will discuss in this section are (1) organizational design, (2) culture, (3) recruitment and retention, and (4) communication (see figure 4-6).

Subarea of Organizational Excellence: Organizational Design

Different organizational structures arise in response to the activities they guide within an organization. Management constantly reorganizes its structures in response to many factors, such as growth, changes in the marketplace, and technological innovation.

SETTING THE STRATEGY AT SAS

When Jan Carlzon took over SAS, the market for airline operations was experiencing zero growth, and Carlzon was determined to figure out how to make SAS profitable. Up to this point, the company had, in rough times, used what Carlzon called the "standard weapon," or the cheese-slicer approach, which "cuts costs equally from all activities and all departments," with little regard for market demands.[10] Although this method had succeeded in cutting costs, it often did not focus on cutting the right things, cutting value-adding services while retaining some non-value-adding ones. In effect, the company was "slicing away its own competitive strengths." Carlzon realized, however, that further cutting costs would have been like "hitting the brakes of a car already standing still. You might push your foot through the floor of the car and cause permanent damage." The only solution was to increase revenues by analyzing the current strategy and setting a new one.

The first thing SAS did was to survey the outside world and determine its position within it. Then the company determined a goal—to become the "best airline in the world for the frequent business traveler"—and the steps necessary to achieve this goal. Therefore, by developing service programs to meet its specific needs, it hoped to gain the business of these reliable business travelers.

FIGURE 4-6

Diagnosing organizational excellence

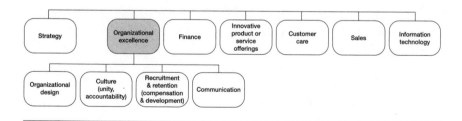

The typical trends of reorganization are toward the opposite poles of centralization and decentralization. Both have their merits and demerits, and are effective in different types of situations (see "Organizational Design Analysis at VeriSign"). In our research, we found that companies that constantly evolved and underwent piecemeal, incremental change often naturally drifted to a more decentralized structure that failed to take advantage of the synergies of the company. These companies were hence often composed of fiefdoms that undermined rather than cooperated with each other (see "Decentralization at IBM" and "Decentralization at Home Depot"). Such organizations typically need centralization as part of their transformation effort. This centralization is important in creating a galvanized organization through revolution.

To get you started, the following questions may serve as a guide:

- How is the organization structured? (Consider function, business units, geography, customer segments, etc.)

- How does the structure *really* work? For example, regardless of how the organization looks on paper, does one person informally wield all the power because of his personality, and so on?

- What are the strengths and weaknesses of this current structure?

- How does this organizational structure contribute to the strategy of the company?

ORGANIZATIONAL DESIGN ANALYSIS AT VERISIGN

While evaluating the current structure of the organization, the organizational design team at VeriSign found that the relationship between markets and products was not being managed very well, with the link weak and the connection not apparent. Hence, the products were not being tied to the market and the strategy.

The organizational design team hoped that the division would maintain a centralized sales organization with a strategic marketing group that dedicated resources to the market segments. The team also anticipated a need to establish clear accountabilities, a decision-making process, and an aligned rewards system.

DECENTRALIZATION AT IBM

At the beginning of the transformation effort, IBM consisted of regional fiefdoms that concentrated only on their specific customers and did not bother to align themselves with the company's overall goals. Because of this regional divide, IBM's individual units had a very difficult time following the work of other units and spent excessive amounts of time reinventing business processes. Furthermore, decentralization resulted in salespeople who severely lacked product knowledge. As a result, instead of focusing on delivering the right product for the customer, salespeople for any given business unit often concentrated on delivering profit for that particular unit, even if it meant not supplying the customer with the right product.

Through its experience, IBM has learned to ask itself the following key questions to make sure the organization has the appropriate design and structure:

- Are the business units aligned with company goals?

- Do the individual business units spend a significant amount of time developing their own business processes and redundant services?

- Is there a lot of parallel work between different units?

- Do salespeople have sufficient cross-product knowledge?

Subarea of Organizational Excellence: Culture

The second major subarea the organizational excellence team is responsible for is the company's culture.[11] An organization's culture is often directly tied to the organizational design and the company's strategy. Culture is the voice and personality of the organization. It is the set of behaviors, attitudes, values, and types of social interactions characteristic of an organization. According to Dave House, "Culture is what people fall back on when there are no instructions. It gives you rules for when there are no rules. It provides a common language for moving forward."[12] Cultures are live entities.

When looking at your own culture, consider two of the goals toward which most companies strive: a united culture of unity and a culture of accountability. Companies need to look at their own culture and ask themselves some of the following questions:

DECENTRALIZATION AT THE HOME DEPOT

At the beginning of The Home Depot's transformation effort, "every store was a separate fiefdom."[13] The do-it-yourself philosophy embraced by the customers extended to the management style promoted by the company's two founders. According to CEO Robert Nardelli, "The company's co-founders used to tell store managers to ignore messages from headquarters and do what they each thought best." Such a decentralized structure led merchants and store managers to write their own rules and to devise their own methods for evaluating employees, leading to the use of over 140 different appraisal forms. Furthermore, this loose structure and lack of centralized procedures fed into the culture, which was known for its unstructured, entrepreneurial character and independent-minded managers.

With the growing size of the organization, this cowboy culture was becoming a problem and was deemed incapable of carrying the company to the next level. From 2000 to 2005, The Home Depot's earnings per share increased by approximately 150 percent with revenue doubling from $45.7 billion in 2000 to $81.5 billion in 2005. Nevertheless, because of high market anticipation in 2000, The Home Depot stock never appreciated, which ultimately led to Nardelli's resignation in 2006.

- Is this the culture that will propel us to where we want to be?

- What are the merits and demerits of our particular culture?

- What attitudes and behaviors are rewarded in our culture? Are these the ones we want to foster?

- Who gets promoted and how?

- What type of person seems to fit in, and what type of person doesn't fit in?

Create a united culture of unity. Even when companies have an overarching culture, they also often have subcultures. While these subcultures may be a natural result of the organizational structure, a united culture throughout the company is important, for it aligns the entire organization to the strategy and symbolizes cooperation. A united culture of unity means one overarching culture that promotes cooperation rather than internal competition (see

INTERNAL COMPETITION AT IBM

When Gerstner arrived at IBM, he found a company that was completely focused on its internal rules and conflicts. "Units competed with each other, hid things from each other. Huge staffs spent countless hours debating and managing transfer pricing terms between IBM units instead of facilitating a seamless transfer of products to customers."[14] Hence, this culture of internal competition significantly weakened the company and negatively affected the customer.

"Internal Competition at IBM"). Often, companies that have undergone mergers and acquisitions need to reconcile two different cultures, as in the case of Bay Networks (see "Two Cultures Under One Roof at Bay Networks").

Create a culture of accountability. Every company needs to be able to hold its people accountable. Without a culture of accountability, employees do not have a sense of ownership, and processes are extremely inefficient (see "Frequent Task Allocation at IBM"). Accountability ensures that people will do what they say they're going to do, and also provides a mechanism for tracking tasks. A culture of accountability feeds into a culture of discipline, which is extremely important in creating a self-sufficient and efficient organization.

TWO CULTURES UNDER ONE ROOF
AT BAY NETWORKS

When House arrived, Bay Networks had a very divided culture after its merger. It had two main offices—one on the West Coast and one on the East Coast—and the geographic distance between the two locations, along with their associated cultural differences, created tremendous conflict between the two offices. This whole situation led to internal competition among employees and eventually spiraled into people focusing on competing with people from the other office for jobs. As a result, they were blind to the competition outside.

FREQUENT TASK ALLOCATION AT IBM

In his research phase, Gerstner told one of his senior executives to conduct a detailed analysis of a major money-losing business in IBM. When he checked up on the executive's progress, he kept getting the response "I'll check with the team and get back to you." In other words, Gerstner noted that the senior executive understood the task at hand, allocated the task, and then waited for it to get done.

Gerstner noticed that top executives often acted this way throughout the company. Current senior executives were "acting the roles that the long-established interior culture asked them to perform."[15] They typically presided over others and allocated tasks. Hence, when tasks didn't get completed on time or correctly, the executives could push the blame downward. Instead, Gerstner wanted executives who would "dig into the details, work the problems day to day, and lead by example, not title. He wanted executives to take ownership and responsibility for end results and to be drivers rather than boxes high on the organization chart."

Subarea of Organizational Excellence: Recruitment and Retention

A company's most important assets are its people. To succeed, an organization needs to attract, retain, and develop the right people. In terms of recruitment and retention, two particular areas should be analyzed in the transformation effort: (1) employees' compensation and benefits and (2) talent development.

Employees' compensation and benefits. Very few people will work for free, but that doesn't mean you have to pay an exorbitant amount to get the best people for your organization on board. Therefore, the appropriate compensation package needs to be assessed to attract the best talent for the company.

Additionally, in considering employee compensation, you need to analyze how employees—and executives—are rewarded and what they are rewarded for. Compensation and benefits often affect employees' goals and motives because they will perform acts that they are compensated for more than those that they aren't (see "Employee Retention at 3M").

EMPLOYEE RETENTION AT 3M

On joining 3M, James McNerney quickly found that employees had become complacent and didn't fear losing their jobs. Promotions from within
were common, and layoffs were very rare. In fact, many employees had
worked only at 3M for over 30 years.[16] As a result, management was satisfied with the status quo, cut corners, and delivered mediocre performance.
Additionally, because management had been averse to layoffs, performance
reports, metrics, and benchmarks were neither valued nor well-defined.

An appropriate compensation system is critical in supporting the organization and all its decisions (see "Revising the Compensation System at
Nissan"). Additionally, compensation based on performance is important in
aligning employees with the company's strategy.

Talent development. Recruitment and retention of employees also depends on career and personal development. Employees need to know that

REVISING THE COMPENSATION
SYSTEM AT NISSAN

Nissan, like many traditional Japanese companies, was formerly based on a
culture of seniority rather than meritocracy.[17] Regardless of their performance, Nissan employees were promoted according to their age and time
spent at Nissan. This system led to complacency among managers and those
in power in an era when customers were demanding high-performance,
high-quality, well-designed cars. Therefore, Nissan employees needed to deliver high-quality products with the right features on time, though the culture of seniority was undermining their ability to do so.

Furthermore, in Nissan's compensation system, employees did not receive
incentives and rewards for performance, and few bonuses were included in
compensation packages. Hence, employees who were involved in the most
influential decisions of the company did not have an incentive to focus their
time and energies on these decisions.

they will grow and develop by working at the organization. Talent development is also important in growing leaders for tomorrow, and can happen at many levels, from classes to formal and informal mentorships. Some companies may not dedicate enough resources to talent development, while others may have forms of development that are inappropriate for their desired goals. Talent development may be an effective way to address some other underlying issues of the company, as recognized by Dave House of Bay Networks (see "House Training at Bay Networks").

Subarea of Organizational Excellence: Communication

The organizational excellence team should also assess the level and means of communication within the organization. Communication is particularly important because that is how information gets passed around. Some questions to consider are:

- Does information get to the right people in a timely manner?

- Do people who should communicate with each other have a convenient means to do so?

- Are employees encouraged to openly and honestly communicate with one another and share information?

HOUSE TRAINING AT BAY NETWORKS

In his analysis of the company, House concluded that the core issues involved fundamentals such as decision making, managing conflict, running effective meetings, and prioritizing tasks. To address these issues, House decided to initiate a series of classes that would teach the company's employees these fundamentals. Because he felt extremely strongly about implementing this training effectively, he refused to delegate the task to human resources or the consultants involved in the transformation effort. For this "House training," House developed a unique methodology for trickling the training down to the depths of the organization. With 6,000 employees, he figured out that if he trained 4 classes of 30 people, or 120 of his highest executives, they would in turn teach the same course to everyone else in the organization. Every thirty days, he taught a new class, meaning his executives had thirty days to reach the rest of the organization.

Communication is closely intertwined with culture. Organizations with a culture of competition and blame tend to stifle communication, whereas organizations with collaborative cultures encourage open communication. Sometimes, vertical communication between ranks is the major problem, whereas other times, horizontal communication between functions or groups is the problem.

Area 3: Finance

In any transformation effort, the financials should be analyzed. In some efforts, however, the company may realize that its finance processes, such as budgeting, are inefficient or inappropriate for its needs and may need to make some adjustments (see "Too Many Budgets at IBM"). Figure 4-7 shows how this next step fits into the process.

In addition, all the areas of finance and accounting should be diagnosed during the transformation. The accounts payable and accounts receivable cycles, the debt ratios, the cashflow, revenue, net profit and balance sheets should be diagnosed for past, current, and future projections. The ability of the firm to provide real-time financial data to the senior executives should also be examined. Finally, transformation often requires investment in new

FIGURE 4-7

Diagnosing finance

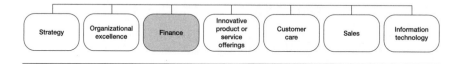

TOO MANY BUDGETS AT IBM

When Gerstner arrived at IBM, he realized that there was no single, consolidated budget. Each element of the "organization matrix," including the various geographic and product divisions, had its own budget. Therefore, there were at least two or three different budgets at any given time. To make matters worse, budget allocations were constantly debated and altered, making accountability very difficult to identify.[18]

resources, technology, and markets, and the finance team should ensure that there are adequate budget left aside for this.

Area 4: Innovative Product or Service Offerings

For a company to stay ahead in the market, it needs to develop innovative product or service offerings (see figure 4-8). Some companies struggle to take advantage of the creative juices flowing through the organization (see "Poor Innovation at 3M"), while others fail to prioritize projects and stretch themselves too thin by taking on everything that comes along (see "Lack of Product Birth Control at Bay Networks"). Along the same lines, some companies also fail to develop innovative offerings because of inappropriate allocation of resources and indiscriminate cost cutting (see "Product Development Issues at VeriSign"). Additionally, some companies have innovative offerings but fail to deliver on quality.

FIGURE 4-8

Diagnosing innovative product or service offerings

POOR INNOVATION AT 3M

For a company known for and dependent on innovation, 3M had a haphazard innovation process when McNerney joined the company. Although 3M implemented the "15% rule" whereby employees were allowed to spend 15 percent of their time on pet projects, product development relied on a simple, outdated structure. Regardless of their performance, profitability, and potential, business units all received uniform increases in funding.[19] This laissez-faire attitude toward innovation was reflected by one of 3M's first presidents, William McKnight, who said that running an innovative company "requires considerable tolerance. Those men and women to whom we delegate responsibility . . . are going to want to do their jobs in their own way."[20] However, given increasing customer demands and shorter cycles of innovation, 3M could no longer carry this laissez-faire attitude and stay competitive.

LACK OF PRODUCT BIRTH CONTROL
AT BAY NETWORKS

When House arrived at Bay Networks, there was what he called a "lack of prod-uct development birth control."[21] Projects were not being prioritized, and every project was starving to death because no projects were being killed. Products came out late, and they often had bugs and were missing features. House was hence determined to staff only the projects they could staff at 100 percent.

To address this problem, House first asked all employees in product de-velopment to submit the name of the project they were currently working on. To his surprise, people sabotaged the process because they didn't want to be identified. In response to this, he announced to the company that whoever wasn't on the list wouldn't have a job. When the list was returned the second time, it was full. House then held a two- to three-day convention during which every product development manager presented his project to all employees in product development. Each presentation included the fol-lowing: a description of the project, its key advantages and disadvantages, how competitive the project was against existing products, the project's cur-rent level of development, the current level of resources available, the level of requested resources, and the scheduled deadline.

After these presentations, House created a prioritized list of the projects to weed out those that were not adding value to the company. He took a red pen and drew a line, and explained that everything below the line would be canceled. He then reallocated resources, both human and capital, and an-nounced the next day, "Good news, everybody in engineering has a job. Bad news, it may not be the job you have now."

Area 5: Customer Care

Customer care (see figure 4-9) is critical and needs to be assessed, ei-ther formally or informally, during the transformation. The goal of customer care is to drive customer loyalty through quality and timely support. An im-proved customer experience leads to improved customer morale, which will aid a company in growing and maintaining its business. In fact, a positive customer experience can have the following benefits:

- A short-term improvement in customer retention

PRODUCT DEVELOPMENT ISSUES AT VERISIGN

Upon analysis of product development at VeriSign, the product development group found that VCS was too busy managing existing product offerings and had insufficient resources invested in new offerings. In fact, over 95 percent of VCS's revenue came from maintaining old products and services. Furthermore, the group was focused more on short-term hits than on long-term strategy and had therefore missed out on several market opportunities.

Further probing revealed that the root cause of VeriSign's strategic disadvantages was poor governance. There was no accountability throughout the life of a product or service. Postproject reviews did not exist, and hence processes remained static. Resource management was not efficient, the pipeline was overloaded, and there was no bandwidth for research and development.

Process issues were another concern. Exit and entrance criteria between phases were very subjective, which caused inconsistencies and complicated hand-off. There was no way to amend the concept and/or business case documents when more information became available. Additionally, VeriSign didn't have any prioritization process; every product received top priority. There were no criteria for determining when existing products became obsolete or when new products should be introduced to keep up with the fast-changing market.

Customers were not involved intimately in the product development process and spoke only to the account managers. There was no consistent way to get continuous customer input and feedback before problems were encountered.

FIGURE 4-9

Diagnosing customer care

- A long-term improvement in customer loyalty

- The creation of competitive differentiation

Every company has numerous opportunities to make an impact on the customer's image of the company. SAS's CEO Jan Carlzon calls the moments when the employee comes in contact with the customer "moments of truth," and, together, these moments will determine whether a company succeeds or fails. (For several examples of how companies have handled their moments of truth, see "Gaining a Customer-Focused Organization at IBM," "Customer Care at VeriSign," and "Lack of Customer Focus at Nissan.")

Area 6: Sales

Many companies encounter sales-related issues. These issues are often interwoven with other issues and areas mentioned in this section (see figure 4-10) and highlight further inefficiencies of the organization (see "Sales Issues at Anonymous Telecommunications Company").

GAINING A CUSTOMER-FOCUSED ORGANIZATION AT IBM

Gerstner realized that at IBM the customer came second.[22] When he arrived, there was little focus on the customer and very little competitor information or disciplined marketing capability. Instead, focused on their internal status in the organization. Gerstner realized that they could "no longer run [their] business like the Roman Empire, confident in [their] hegemony, certain that those barbarians massing on the borders were no real threat." He wanted people to begin focusing on the customer and not on their own internal status. He said, "We needed to open the window to the outside world."

FIGURE 4-10

Diagnosing sales

CUSTOMER CARE AT VERISIGN

After a careful examination of the customer care group at VeriSign, the customer care rapid response team identified a set of key problem areas: customer support, information technology, and metrics.[23]

Customer Support

The quality of customer support was extremely poor. Because of nonintegrated and undefined processes, tools, and metrics, VeriSign's customer care group struggled to provide a consistent and timely customer experience. For example, the level of service a customer received depended largely on the time of a service call, the representative, and the product in question. The problem was exacerbated by the outsourcing of after-hours support.

To make matters worse, instead of dedicating time and resources to improving the quality of care provided, existing care groups were spending a significant effort on activities outside of the realm of customer care, primarily in finance and other development functions. Criticisms from other internal teams regarding their lack of a customer focus were intensifying, which had a negative impact on employee morale and further decreased the quality of customer support.

Appropriate expertise to answer technical questions was also lacking in the customer care group. Most of the inquiries they received were about the performance of their products. Resolving these inquiries often required detailed technical knowledge, which customer care representatives did not always have; therefore they had to waste time directing customer inquiries to other representatives. At times, customers were forced to wait over an hour for a helpful answer.

Finally, although established processes were relatively effective, they were often inconsistently applied across the organization, which significantly affected the customer experience. For instance, the process for determining the number of resources to be dedicated to customer support, including after hours, varied widely.

Information Technology

Because of the lack of integration among systems and applications dedicated to supporting customers, VeriSign was unable to provide a single view of all customers across the organization. In fact, applications were not even integrated across departments in one location, let alone across the five customer care centers. Furthermore, VeriSign was unable to accurately track and report on customer contacts because it lacked an e-mail-monitoring application. These circumstances all led to inefficiencies across the organization and poor customer care.

Metrics

Among the five customer care centers, metrics—such as customer satisfaction, job performance, resource planning, and personal accountability—were inconsistently defined, measured, and managed. The lack of standardized metrics often left VeriSign unable to compile measures corporatewide.

LACK OF CUSTOMER FOCUS AT NISSAN

At Nissan, there was a lot of talk about the customer, but customers had little merit in the company.[24] Employees didn't know the user base for a product or even why a customer would choose Nissan. There was no product planning process that involved the customer and the market, and there was a tendency to copy the competition or to repeat existing models rather than come up with new ideas. In other words, Nissan didn't really know what the customer wanted, nor did the company take the time to investigate and find out.

SALES ISSUES AT ANONYMOUS
TELECOMMUNICATIONS COMPANY

With Anonymous Telecommunications Company's (ATC's) history of multiple acquisitions, the sales group was faced with operating inefficiencies and information breakdowns that were mainly caused by nonintegrated information systems and processes. Sales representatives often had to spend a significant amount of time dealing with non-sales-related issues.

For example, in order management, a sales representative could find himself spending time researching multiple databases to answer a customer order inquiry. Orders were printed, hand-carried, and then reentered when moving to the billing system. In addition, orders could not be entered until a contract was completed, and the delay in contracts resulted in either lost business or dissatisfied customers.

Invoicing mistakes were common. It was estimated that well over $1 million in annual revenue was lost as a result of these errors. An internal audit was set up to gather more specific information on the impact and root causes of this problem.

Contract management was another area of concern. Sales representatives needed an approval to send even a standard contract to a customer. This request process took as long as three weeks for a standard contract. Lack of legal resources to assist in timely negotiations compounded the problem, and sales representatives often ended up carrying messages back and forth during negotiations.

Approvals were required for all pricing-related issues. Neither sales representatives nor sales management had any authority to approve pricing. They did not have access to cost structures or profit-and-loss information. As many as six layers of approval for pricing were required. Moreover, it was difficult to price bundles because the company's incentive structure focused on maintaining and growing margin on individual products. The entire pricing process was very slow and cumbersome.

Finally, the ATC sales group was not adequately integrated with the product development group. As a result, sales representatives could not inform customers about the full ATC product road maps, and thus customers felt that they made uninformed purchase decisions. Conversely, without a formal mechanism to gather the sales representatives' knowledge about customer needs and ATC competitiveness, the product development team would often launch new products without characteristics desired by the customers and on a timeline that was out of sync with the market direction.

Area 7: Information Technology

Information technology (IT), the subject of this section (see figure 4-11), has become increasingly important. In today's market, successful companies use IT as a source of competitive strategy. Poor use of or ignoring IT can have dire consequences (see "Cleaning Up IT at The Home Depot").

For more information on the important role of IT in the organization's transformation, read *Becoming a Real-Time Enterprise*.[25]

ANALYZING THE DATA

In the preceding section, we detailed the most important areas to diagnose. Once the data has been gathered, the next major step in phase 1 is to understand the implications of the data (see figure 4-12). There are numerous

FIGURE 4-11

Diagnosing information technology

CLEANING UP IT AT THE HOME DEPOT

When Nardelli arrived at The Home Depot, he found that the company was drastically behind the times in the technology revolution. He remembered that "the first thing I wanted to do was send an e-mail companywide, and I was told by an administrative person that, no, I couldn't do that. I said, 'What do you mean?' and it turned out I literally couldn't send an e-mail companywide because we didn't have the infrastructure set up to do it."[26]

Beyond the lack of an electronic link between stores and the company's headquarters, the antiquated computer systems and technology gap led to very manual, labor-intensive processes. In walking around the stores, Nardelli found a lot of human intervention and manual payroll. Furthermore, he saw people manually doing inventory and counting boxes, for there was no bar coding. Nardelli also saw employees doing "data entry [and processing] bills of lading and invoices."[27] In fact, as late as 2000, each new shipment to stores was still being logged with pencil and clipboard.

FIGURE 4-12

Analyzing the data

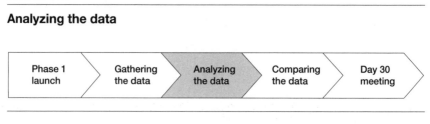

ways to analyze the tremendous amount of data the teams gather, and process flowcharts are one useful tool.

Before explaining process flowcharts, we need to highlight a key failure
of many analyses: failure to distinguish symptoms from root causes. This appeared in the data-gathering section too, but it's a critical distinction to make
in the analysis.

Distinguish Symptoms from Root Causes

A thorough data-gathering effort is important. Just as important, if not more
so, is how you look at the data. Data can be interpreted in numerous ways,
often at the discretion of the analyzers. Therefore, you must look at the data
objectively, without any preconceived notions or biases.

Keeping that in mind, you need to take further steps to make the data
useful for the company. In particular, the rapid response teams need to distinguish the symptoms from the root causes of the problems because the
company ultimately wants to address the root causes, not simply the symptoms,
of its issues. For example, a child visits the doctor with a cold, manifested as
a cough. Do you treat the cold or the cough? Often, you need to do both.
Treating the cough results in immediate relief for the patient, but treating the
cold results in extended relief and prevents additional symptoms from arising.
Treating each symptom without regard to the other would be careless of the
doctor. If the doctor simply treats the symptom, the root cause will ultimately increase the damage. On the other hand, jumping into treatment of
the root cause may result in a patient who has died from the symptoms. Therefore, a good doctor tries to treat both but focuses more on root causes than
on symptoms.

Similarly, an organization needs to treat both symptoms and root causes
of problems. Addressing the symptoms means that different issues may still
arise, but attacking the root causes hits the heart of the issue. Fixing the symptoms may lead to minor improvements here and there, but only by address-

ing the root causes can you get the quantum leaps in improvement sought after in the transformation effort.

Despite the importance of making this distinction, however, there is no foolproof, surefire way of grouping findings into these two categories. In our research, we found that the most effective way of accomplishing this is by engaging in a lot of discussion and Socratic dialogue. Only by challenging each other can teams and team members gain important, relevant insights and get to the heart of the issue.

Process Flowcharts

The data-gathering effort may result in an overwhelming amount of data. While there are many ways to analyze the data, one common way is to create a process flowchart. A process flowchart graphically displays either a high-level or detailed business process within an organization.[28] The diagram follows a process from start to finish, displaying all inputs and outputs and all decision points. It details who is doing what with whom and when, and illuminates the sequence of events in a process and any wait times or delays inherent in the process, such as bottlenecks. Through this graphical representation, employees can better analyze the business process and work on optimizing and improving it.

Why Create a Process Flowchart?

During this phase of the transformation effort, members of the rapid response teams are working hard to fully diagnose the company. One of the main benefits of drawing process flowcharts is that it illuminates an entire business function or process, thereby enabling analysis and optimization of that process at *each step*.[29] Each team can use process flowcharting to identify and improve on the key problem areas within a specific business process or function. The key benefits of creating a flowchart include:

- *Encouraging understanding.* Employees may be unclear about how a process currently works. By graphically representing the process, you illuminate all of its steps and hence encourage discussion of how a process is, and should be, working. This also helps with the gap analysis of where you currently are versus where you need to be, segueing to the next phase.

- *Analysis and process improvement.* Graphically representing a process helps problem areas become more visible. Drawing a process flowchart enables employees to identify and eliminate steps in the process that do not add value to the end product and to identify ways the process can be optimized and streamlined.

- *Generating a tool to train employees.* The flowchart can later be presented to new employees to give them a deeper understanding of the process as a set of standardized steps.

How Do I Create a Flowchart?

To initiate process flowcharting, the leaders of the rapid response teams should schedule a one- to two-day meeting with their team members and any key experts in the specific process being studied. During a series of meetings, the participants should use the following steps as a guide:[30]

1. *Conducting the effort.* After explaining the general definition and purpose of flowcharting, the pilot should:

   - Identify the process their team will flowchart

   - Identify who will use the flowchart and how it will be analyzed

   - Establish the level of detail required

   - Educate all group members in reading flowcharts and in flowchart symbols

2. *Identifying the process.* The team members should work together to identify the steps in the specific business process. First, identify the start and end of the process. Then, on a whiteboard or an overhead projector, work on filling in the chart from start to finish with flowchart symbols. To do this, the group should ask questions such as these: At what points are decisions made in the process? When are approvals required to move on to the next step? When are measurements taken in the process?

3. *Analyzing the flowchart.* In a later section, we detail how to analyze a flowchart.

What Should I Watch Out For?

You should involve many individuals in the initial effort to identify and accurately depict the process on the chart. They may not want to depict the process as it really is, because they are afraid that they will be singled out to explain why the process works as it does. To address these potential obstacles, the leader must communicate to the people that everyone is part of the solution and that there is to be no finger-pointing. To motivate the team, the leader should emphasize that the flowcharting process is to help improve everyone's lives, and the team members should feel empowered to play a role in this improvement process.

How Do We Analyze the Flowchart?

After creating the process flowchart, the team is ready to analyze it and identify key problem areas. Employees should start by searching for areas where the process breaks down. Here are some sample characteristics to look for.

Process issues. Some common process issues are these:

- *Bottlenecks.* Bottlenecks occur where the process is slowed and may be caused by a lack of capacity or unnecessary steps.

- *Weak links.* A weak link may occur where equipment needs to be repaired or replaced or where employees are inadequately trained to most efficiently perform their process function.

- *Poorly defined events.* If steps are not well defined, they may be interpreted and performed differently by different employees. This could lead to process variation.

- *Non-value-adding steps.* These events add only cost and no real value to the process.

- *Duplication.* Document duplicated tasks.

- *Unclear roles and responsibilities.*[31] This may lead to miscommunication, duplicate efforts, or skipped steps.

- *Cycle time.* Document and attempt to decrease the time per event.

- *Sources of delay.* Similar to bottlenecks, these are items that tend to delay the process.

- *Error prevention versus error correction:* Bigger proportion of time, energy, and resources should be dedicated to preventative rather than corrective measures, though correction may be necessary as a final check in the process.

Decision nodes. You should ask questions such as, Is a decision needed at this point? Look for places where you can eliminate the need for a decision, such as a trend or pattern in the answer to the decision at a certain point. You should also ask, Is it clear who is making the decision?

After completing these process flowcharts, the team should use them later to develop a new flowchart detailing an improved process.

COMPARING THE DATA

So you've gathered all the data, and you've begun to analyze it. What's next? As shown in figure 4-13, the data gathered can be used to generate additional data, since comparing the data and analysis with other internal and external measures can result in more data and further the analysis. The data can be compared externally through benchmarking or internally through creating baseline metrics.

Benchmarking

Benchmarking is particularly important in the diagnosis phase because a company's performance is often measured on a relative, not absolute, scale. Finding where the company lies on this continuum in different areas can be done through benchmarking.

Benchmarking is the process of improving company performance by identifying and incorporating external best-in-class business practices into an organization.[32] Your organization may be asking, Who provides the best customer service? or even, Who has the most efficient manufacturing process? Benchmarking will help you to find the answer to these questions and aid you in incorporating best practices into your business.

Most companies already use benchmarking in one way or another because of the powerful results such efforts can bring. Traditional methods, however, are lengthy and costly, taking an average of six to twelve months. In typical efforts, results are presented to senior managers who relegate the solutions to their bottom drawers and never consider their implementation.

FIGURE 4-13

Comparing the data

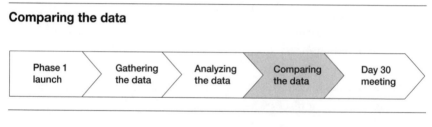

Because of this, the company's benchmarking process and methodology may be some of the first things that are revamped in the transformation effort (see "Benchmarking at Hewlett-Packard").

Here, we share with you a proven, effective approach to benchmarking that will aid your company in identifying and executing processes that will lead to a competitive advantage. In this benchmarking effort, getting the few consultants who are already involved in the transformation effort is important, for they have outside expertise and can provide valuable input throughout the process. We start by explaining some basic benchmarking rules and then describe the process of benchmarking.

Know Your Own Processes First

Before conducting a benchmarking effort, you need to identify what you are benchmarking, why this is a valuable measure, how to measure strength in this area, and how your company currently measures up.

BENCHMARKING AT HEWLETT-PACKARD

Before transformation leader Mark Hurd joined Hewlett-Packard (HP), the company benchmarked mainly against IBM, using only one metric: costs as a percentage of revenue. In revamping the benchmarking effort, Hurd first decided to change the strategy. As a result, HP now breaks down its business units and functions, compares them with those of several competitors in the industry, such as Dell and Sun Microsystems, and uses that information to try to become the best-in-class in all areas.

To make such comparisons, HP uses a spreadsheet to analyze its figures. With business units aligned in a column and functions in a row, HP then fills in the cells with benchmarks. In completing the table, HP researches the benchmarked company and makes extremely educated guesses about the competitor's situation in those specific domains. The company uses numerous variables, such as operating expenses as a percentage of gross margin, to develop the benchmarks.

Furthermore, these benchmarks are taken to help the company not only become best-in-class but also cut costs and become more efficient. With a goal to save $3 billion by 2008, the company is already under way, having saved $385 million in 2005 as operating expenses as a percentage of gross margin fell by 2 percent.[33]

Internally First, Externally Second

A rule of thumb is "Benchmark internally first."[34] Through an internal benchmarking effort, your company can identify the best practices of a specific business process and then apply those practices to similar processes throughout the organization. Once a company has analyzed its own internal processes, it can look externally for fresh ideas.

The Value in Benchmarking Outside Industry

In external benchmarking, many companies choose to compare themselves with the best in their industry. Although this yields its benefits, by not looking outside of its industry, a company may overlook innovative practices that could lead to a competitive advantage. It is here that a consultant can add tremendous value, with his outside expertise. An article titled "Fast-Cycle Benchmarking" highlights an example of a cement company that had difficulty in getting the cement to the construction sites on time. Instead of studying companies in its industry, it looked to Domino's Pizza, known for its fast delivery service. After studying and incorporating Domino's techniques into its own business, its level of timely support increased by 95 percent in just two years.[35]

Boosting Financial Results Through Benchmarking

Benchmarking can be particularly effective in areas with quantitative measures and metrics. For example, a company can benchmark its costs against those of other companies in its industry, as Nissan did (see "Nissan Uses Benchmarking to Cut Costs"). Benchmarking can also be done at a higher level, such as comparing market share and revenue with those of the industry leaders and subsequently findings ways to reach and surpass the leaders.

The Importance of Reality

Reality can be harsh. In fact, it can be so harsh that it can be hard to face. Benchmarking can enlighten the company's realities in comparison with other companies'. However, benchmarking efforts can be effective only if the company is willing to accept its findings and make use of the new insight it has gained. (See "Self-Deception at AlliedSignal" for an example of how a company can be blind to reality.)

How to Conduct a Benchmarking Effort

Use the following guidelines to conduct a benchmarking effort:

1. *Determine what to benchmark.* Be wary of vague and overly generalistic benchmarking. Identify the important items that will lead to specific and important insights.

NISSAN USES BENCHMARKING TO CUT COSTS

When Ghosn arrived at Nissan, the company was paying suppliers high premiums for their auto parts, which was significantly cutting into the company's operating budget. In an effort to cut costs and boost financial results, Ghosn relied heavily on benchmarking—he compared the prices they paid for parts with those paid by other companies in the industry.[36] From his experience, Ghosn knew that asking his managers, Are we making good purchasing decisions? would only yield the predicted response: We think so. He knew that Nissan managers and executives needed "black-and-white proof that they were paying way too much."

Ghosn initiated an extensive benchmarking effort that would produce the fact-based information needed to drive change. He said that "full-scale, up-to-date benchmarks are the only way a company can know if good buys are being made." During the turnaround, the members of the purchasing rapid response team had access to Renault's purchasing information. Ghosn therefore encouraged the team to compare the Renault purchasing documents with its own on hundreds of parts. These studies revealed that Nissan was paying a premium of 25–40 percent on almost every part it bought.

SELF-DECEPTION AT ALLIEDSIGNAL

When Larry Bossidy arrived at AlliedSignal, he immediately noticed the tendency of people to avoid confronting issues realistically. While performing his high-level analysis of the company, he realized that employees and customers tended to portray their success from two perspectives. When he asked his employees about their order-fill rate, they answered 98 percent, while customers answered only 60 percent. "The irony was," Bossidy said, "instead of trying to address the customer's complaints, we seemed to think we had to show that we were right and they were wrong."[37]

2. *Identify benchmarking partners.* Look for the best companies both inside and outside your industry. Consult suppliers, customers, analysts, magazines, and other resources to determine which companies to study.[38]

3. *Determine what to measure.* Some metrics are more obvious than others. Try to measure variables that will lead to important and concrete conclusions rather than circumstantial conclusions.

4. *Execute.* This is the most important part of benchmarking. It involves incorporating the best business practices you have identified into your organization. During the first three steps, you plan how to collect data on best practices, but nothing will happen if you don't execute. At this stage, communication, setting measurable goals, and monitoring the results are only some of the factors that will lead to success.[39]

Performing a Capabilities Audit

A capabilities audit is a benchmarking effort that captures the "intangibles" of a company. While these capabilities are more difficult to quantify, the audit can be extremely beneficial for numerous reasons. Performing a capabilities audit will not only help you identify strengths and weaknesses in your company but also highlight several capabilities that will give the company a competitive edge and aid it in executing its strategy. To perform an audit, take the following steps:

1. Identify the business division or unit to be assessed.

2. Identify the two or three capabilities most essential to carrying out your strategy.

3. Survey and gather the data.

4. Using the data, identify two or three capabilities that are critical to success; focus on weaknesses only when they are critical to success. These steps will help you find gaps between actual and desired performance in your two or three areas.

5. Develop an action plan for improving these capabilities.

Creating a Set of Baseline Metrics

In addition to benchmarking, another important internal use of the data gathered is the creation of a set of baseline metrics against which to compare and measure the results of the transformation effort and beyond. Besides measuring the performance of the teams, baseline metrics send powerful messages to employees about how they should fulfill their role within the company, and aid participants in measuring their contribution to the effort. Furthermore, baseline metrics:

- Send messages to the company of what you want to change—which behaviors to start, stop, or adjust

- Provide executives with a way to track their progress through the transformation effort

- Continually give employees an indication of what they need to adjust

- Clarify the expectations of all employees

- Align employee performance and behavior with important business results

- Provide all employees with feedback on their progress

- Provide accountability for changing by communicating the expectations to employees

Often, the set of baseline metrics against which the future state of the company will be measured results directly from the findings from the diagnosis phase. The baseline metrics are frequently represented by the current state of the company. Sometimes, however, the qualitative factors should be quantified to give a more objective and measurable metric. In such instances, the teams should work together to develop a way to convert the qualitative data and status into a quantitative metric. Once this process is developed, the same conversion should be conducted whenever progress or status needs to be measured against the baseline.

With the baseline metrics identified and in place, the organization knows where it currently stands and is ready to wrap up the diagnosis phase.

THE DAY 30 INTEGRATION MEETING

At the end of phase 1, each rapid response team should have completed its diagnosis of its particular area, which includes both data gathering and analysis. The teams should have identified not only the symptoms but also the root causes to be addressed in the next phase.

With this information in mind, teams will be presenting their findings to each other and the EMT in the day 30 integration meeting (see figure 4-14). This is a monthly integration meeting, as described earlier in the chapter, and lasts from one to two days. In this meeting, teams summarize their

FIGURE 4-14

Day 30 integration meeting

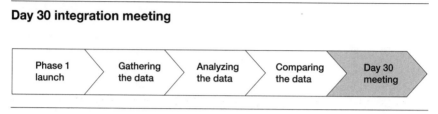

experience with the transformation effort in the past month, from the data-gathering process to the analysis of the data and finally their findings of the key pain points.

Before any presentations take place, the day should begin with an overview of the agenda and a brief presentation on the "rules of engagement" for the meeting (see figure 4-15). The rules of engagement lay out the rules for the presentation and the day, as well as guidelines for the presentations. The role of the transformation leader and the coaches is to enforce the rules of engagement throughout the presentations. As noted in figure 4-15, a note taker should jot down the action items that result from the presentations and discussion, along with the owner and deadline.

At the conclusion of the day 30 integration meeting, the transformation leader should emphasize the progress that has been made in the past month and thank the teams for all their hard work. The transformation leader should also lay out the next thirty days at a high level for the teams. In particular, he should let the rapid response teams know that now that they know the key

FIGURE 4-15

Rules of engagement

The "rules of engagement"

- 30 min/pres. with only light clarifying questions
- 30 min for questions
- No derailing into oblivion
- No definition or turf battling
- Data drive/facts driven
- Pareto: 20% of problems resolved lead to 80% positive impact
- Discuss what will be operational Monday and who is the owner
- Action items will be captured with responsible people and due date

problems of the company, they will need to determine at a high level what the company wants to (and can feasibly) achieve.

CONCLUSION

While there are many different factors in the diagnosis phase of the company, the heart of phase 1 lies in data gathering, analysis, and benchmarking. Phase 1 unofficially starts with a meeting aimed at empowering the leadership team, officially starts with the kickoff landmark meeting, and ends with the day 30 integration meeting. Companies typically analyze many areas in their transformation effort, including strategy, organizational design, finance, product or service offerings, customer care, sales issues, and information technology. The organization should now have a solid understanding of its key pain points, which include not only the symptoms but also, more importantly, the root causes. No stones should have been left unturned through the efforts of the rapid response teams. From here on out, the teams should find no more major surprises related to the company's diagnoses.

Up to this point, teams have also developed a set of baseline metrics to guide the success of their business group. Additionally, they have conducted a benchmarking analysis to determine best practices inside and outside of industry that they could incorporate into their specific business group.

With an accurate diagnosis in place, the key now is to figure out what to do with the information to improve the company and propel it into a brighter future. In the next phase, teams will develop and prioritize a list of "big ideas," which are high-impact recommendations that address the pain points identified in phase 1. Additionally, the teams can then conduct a gap analysis to assess and identify the steps that need to be taken to get from their current state to their desired state.

5

Phase 2

Envisioning the Future

*If we can really understand the problem, the answer will come
out of it, because the answer is not separate from the problem.*

—Jiddu Krishnamurti

During phase 1, the rapid response teams played the role of a doctor in identifying the major pain points within their particular area, collectively diagnosing the overall "health" of the company. Now, it is time for the teams to shift their focus and start looking at solutions for these problems. Over the next thirty days, with these pain points in mind, the teams will work on identifying various alternatives for treatment and remedy (see figure 5-1). Each rapid response team, therefore, will envision the future in its own way.

This future that the teams envision and define starts with a rationalization process whereby the company tries to assess which products or customers make rational sense to keep and which do not. Along with this process comes resource allocation; when some items are cut, those resources can be reallocated to the projects that survived.

In the next step, the teams look for a set of creative solutions to the problems identified in phase 1. In developing what we call "big ideas," rapid response teams search for innovative solutions to the organization's problems, indirectly creating a high-level vision of where the organization is heading in the future.

Knowing where the organization is heading, the teams then undertake a gap analysis, which integrates the current state of the organization with the desired future state. Through this analysis, the rapid response teams identify not only the differences between these two states but also the steps necessary to achieve the future state, given the current situation of the company.

FIGURE 5-1

Chapter overview

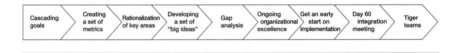

Part of the gap analysis is conducted on the competency gap within the organization. Through the findings of this competency gap analysis, the organizational excellence team will have a set of tasks to carry out by the end of the phase. For example, the team should expand on the values determined by the transformation team in the landmark meeting, decide on an organizational structure to support the new organization, and develop hiring and training practices, as well as a performance review and compensation package process.

Once the gaps are identified, the rapid response teams need to know what their specific goal is. For example, teams know that an organization needs to focus on the customer. But what does that mean for individual teams and functions? To answer this question, teams must create cascading goals, after which teams need to identify metrics against which to measure progress. The metrics hence symbolize the important criteria against which the company or team is measuring itself.

Throughout the phase, team members should keep an eye out for early wins (described in the pretransformation chapter). Often, items on the agenda do not need to wait until the implementation phase to be executed. Ironically, early execution may be beneficial for the progress of the transformation effort and the company as a whole.

Just as phase 1 ended with a day 30 integration meeting, phase 2 ends with a day 60 integration meeting. Run similarly to the phase 1 meeting, the phase 2 meeting differs in the content being presented by the rapid response teams.

Before the end of the phase, the company may find that new rapid response teams are necessary to cover areas that have been overlooked or ignored. These so-called tiger teams will need to make up for lost ground but will be supported by the rest of the transformation team.

Remember that in every step along the way, all the rapid response teams should take into consideration the new strategy of the organization. This not only keeps everyone focused and on track but also ensures that all decisions are aligned with the core strategic vision of the company.

We will now take you through all these parts of phase 2, starting with developing and identifying cascading goals.

RATIONALIZATION OF KEY AREAS

Early on in phase 2, the Executive Management Team (EMT) should work with some of the relevant teams to jumpstart the rationalization process (see figure 5-2). Rationalization here refers to the process of debating and discussing a particular area or aspect of the organization in order to prioritize elements and decide what to keep and what to toss out, given the strategic vision of the company. Hence, rationalization can be considered as the process of trying to find which elements are rational, or make sense, for the company to maintain and dedicate resources to and which elements are irrational for the company to maintain. Inevitably, some elements fall in-between these categories and represent trade-offs between different criteria, but the debate and discussion should lead to an ultimate decision.

Rationalization most often occurs with the company's offerings, whether services or products, and customers. At the end of the rationalization process, all the items should be in one of these categories: expand, maintain, withdraw, or cut. These categories should help guide resource reallocation; items that are cut should no longer get additional resources, meaning those resources can be reallocated to the other items. (See table 5-1 for details about reallocation for all four categories.)

Since companies don't have unlimited resources, the point of rationalization is to withdraw items that are not making significant contributions to

FIGURE 5-2

Rationalization of key areas

TABLE 5-1

Resource allocation after rationalization

Category	Resources
Expand	Provide increased and additional resources to help the item grow.
Maintain	Allocate sufficient but minimal resources to maintain the item at its current state.
Withdraw	Phase out current resources so the item will gradually either reach a "maintain" or "cut" status.
Cut	Drop all resources currently dedicated to the item immediately.

your bottom line or helping you attain your goals. These items are sometimes detrimental, pulling you in a direction opposite to your goal. For instance, many companies dedicate a tremendous amount of resources to customers who don't contribute much to the company's bottom line, if at all. Other companies try to court customers indiscriminately, wasting resources on customers who would never be interested in their products or services. In terms of products or services, some companies dedicate vast resources to try to fix products that are already losing the company money when they would be better off cutting those products entirely.

Before you decide how to categorize the various items, however, one of the first tasks in the rationalization process is to select the criteria to consider. (See "Customer Rationalization at Hewlett-Packard.") For example, some common criteria to consider and make trade-offs with include how much the items currently cost the company (that is, how much of your resources are currently dedicated to them), how much revenue they generate, and what their future growth prospects are. Some customers might not generate much revenue now but may generate tremendous amounts of revenue in the future.

For each item, such as customer, product, or service, individual trade-offs must be made, and there is no uniform set of trade-offs that can be applied across the board. For instance, a future growth opportunity may outweigh

CUSTOMER RATIONALIZATION
AT HEWLETT-PACKARD

To rationalize its customer base, Hewlett-Packard (HP), under the leadership of Mark Hurd, looked at its top two thousand customer accounts, chosen according to how much they spent on IT. In its analysis, the team looked at thirty parameters, such as how attractive the account was, how the IT spending broke down by business unit, the percentage of innovation that drove additional IT spending, how much HP was willing to share the customer with other companies, and how much impact adding resources would have on the customer's spending. As a result of its analysis, HP decided which customers it wanted to invest in, which customers it wanted to pull back from, and which it wanted to maintain. Through its rationalization of its customer base, HP was able to focus on targeting customers that would benefit the company the most.

current revenue generated for one customer but not another. Part of the reason is because of the team's confidence in the future projections. Even if two customers have the same numbers on the board, the team's confidence in the accuracy in the numbers of one company versus the other can play an important role in swaying the decision.

The key to rationalization is to find the whale in addition to the small fish. What do we mean by that? Whales are big and can grow tremendously. Though they dominate the sea, they are also rare and hard to find. Small fish, however, don't have much potential to grow but are plentiful in the ocean. Because of their size, whales inevitably eat more than small fish but are worth a lot more. In the rationalization process, one must try to identify the whales, which in terms of customers means those who either dominate their market or have the potential to do so. They might be more demanding and cost more to maintain than smaller customers, but they're also significantly more valuable. In terms of products, they are the ones that the company cannot operate without. Once you find a whale, hold on to it, keep feeding it, and don't let it go.

DEVELOPING A SET OF BIG IDEAS

Now that teams have analyzed the company's existing portfolio, the next step is to analyze the company's potential portfolio. The most important step in phase 2 of transformation is developing a list of big ideas (see figure 5-3) that will:

- Address existing problems identified during the diagnostic phase 1 analysis

- Improve current processes

- Create new sources of revenue and shareholder value

- Create a strategic platform and lay the groundwork for future growth

FIGURE 5-3

Developing a set of "big ideas"

| Cascading goals | Creating a set of metrics | Rationalization of key areas | Developing a set of "big ideas" | Gap analysis | Ongoing organizational excellence | Get an early start on implementation | Day 60 integration meeting | Tiger teams |

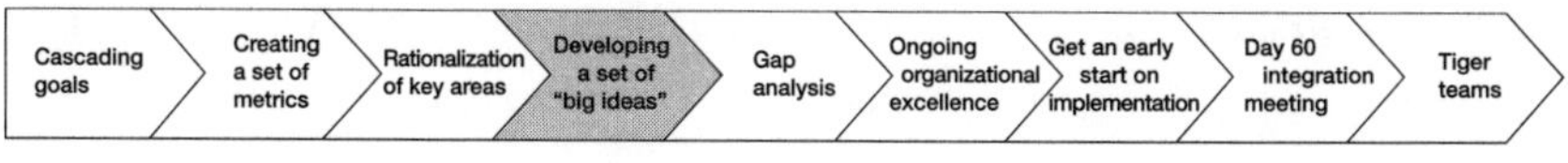

The big ideas are developed by the strategy team in parallel with the rationalization efforts. A big idea is similar to the concept of the whale. It is the thing that gives you, for lack of a better phrase, the biggest bang for your buck. A big idea is a big thing to attack that will have enormous impact and will add significant value to the company (see "Apple's Big Idea: The iPod."). At this point, it should be defined at a very high level. For instance, a big idea may involve considering an acquisition for some companies. It may also include entry into new markets or business partnerships, investment in a new technology, or even termination of product lines (which may also have been a result of the rationalization process).

When identifying big ideas to be investigated and analyzed, the rapid response teams should first look at the megatrends in the industry. Megatrends are major trends that identify, at a very high level, where the industry is heading. Although no company should follow every megatrend out there, there certainly are some that the company cannot, and should not, ignore. Once the teams identify which megatrends the company should jump on, they should make sure that the big ideas they develop are aligned with the megatrends.

APPLE'S BIG IDEA: THE IPOD

Around 2001, Apple's CEO Steve Jobs recognized an opportunity for the company and decided to enter a new market and capitalize on the growing popularity of digital music. This big idea resulted from the observation that a major customer need for a digital music player was currently not being met in the market. In line with this big idea, Apple first introduced iTunes, which was followed shortly after by the revolutionary iPod, arguably the company's most successful product ever. Interestingly, the iPod was developed in only ten months and relied heavily on partnerships, and its development was shrouded in mystery. Once Apple had decided to enter the digital music industry, a subsection of its big idea involved decisions regarding these partnerships for the iPod. In assessing the market, Apple recognized that in the growing idea of digital music playing devices, "the products stank,"[1] and the market was plagued by clunky devices with very limited memory space, failing batteries, and slow uploading of songs to the players. By collaborating with companies such as Pixo, which provided the software foundation, Apple quickly introduced the revolutionary iPod into the market in 2001.

According to Hewlett-Packard's CEO and transformation leader, Mark Hurd, "We need to try to guess what the answer looks like five years from now so that when we make a decision today, we are making a wise decision. Either in the way we take out costs or in the way we invest to grow."[2] Megatrends should guide the teams' decisions about which big ideas make the most sense for the organization in the long term.

Sometimes, in discussions about either the megatrends or the big ideas, a team member may realize that there is an "elephant in the room"—something that is big but being overlooked or ignored, such as major market or customer trends and/or an innovation in technology. Sometimes, surprisingly, people fail to see an elephant in the room because they are looking at the small things. For example, they may see a tail and a trunk, but they fail to put everything together and see the elephant. Other times, people may see the elephant but write it off, either because they don't want to deal with it or because they don't think it's important because no one else sees it. The elephant usually represents something major that, once noticed, should not be overlooked. In their discussions, team members should be aware and conscious of elephants in the room, sometimes even deliberately looking for them. Ask yourself, Is there an elephant in the room that none of us have seen?

With that in mind, you are now ready to develop and decide on a set of big ideas. At this stage, each team should take the following approach:

1. Brainstorm potential big ideas.

2. Assess each big idea according to a set of criteria.

3. Prioritize the list of big ideas.

Step 1: Brainstorm Potential Big Ideas

To develop a list of potential big ideas, the rapid response team pilots should lead each team in a brainstorming session. During this session, team members work together under the guidance of the pilot to develop creative solutions to address the problems identified during the phase 1 diagnosis.

The purpose of the brainstorming session is to come up with as many potential ideas as possible. Sometimes, the teams will need more than just one meeting because time runs out before they finish generating their ideas. Other times, teams may run dry of ideas early on, so the pilot should try different methods to spur creativity. For example, the leader could try reading through the list of documented ideas or go over each idea, briefly discussing

PUSH-REVIEW-PUSH AT NISSAN

Carlos Ghosn implemented a particularly effective method for generating creative ideas known as the push-review-push method. In this method, he looked at the solutions generated by the teams and pushed back when the solutions weren't aggressive enough. When pushing back, Ghosn gave the teams some guidance as to how far and deep to look for the answers. Through this push-review-push method, the nine rapid response teams driving Nissan's transformation generated over two thousand ideas and gained a 360-degree view of each one.[3]

their benefits and costs, in hopes of sparking additional ideas. (See "Push-Review-Push at Nissan" for an example of a particularly effective method of generating creative solutions.) Additionally, in preparation for the meeting, the leader should develop a set of fallback ideas for these creatively dry moments. If the pilot fails to generate further creativity, he should end the meeting and encourage everyone to brainstorm individually.

As mentioned earlier, there are many different types of big ideas teams can generate, depending on the diagnosed problem and the team's goal. Before a final decision is made about which of these to adopt, further investigation is required. To get an idea of some sample big ideas that were later adopted, see "Big Ideas at VeriSign."

Step 2: Assess Each Big Idea According to a Set of Criteria

Once the team and its pilot are satisfied with their list of big ideas, the team needs to categorize the ideas into those with great potential and that warrant further investigation, those that may have potential, and those that should not even be considered. This effort is similar to the rationalization process and is best undertaken through discussion and debate, although deeper analysis is required during this step to gather the data necessary to assess each big idea.

Before any assessment can be made, however, the team first needs to identify the criteria to be considered in the analysis and assessment of the ideas. Some common criteria are (1) value to the company, (2) feasibility, (3) potential challenges, (4) market readiness, and (5) implementation time.

BIG IDEAS AT VERISIGN

All the following big ideas were slated to be put in place after the conclusion of the 90 days effort.

- **Entry into new markets.** VeriSign was to become the first company to offer billing solutions that integrated prepaid and postpaid payment billing solutions. This move positioned VeriSign well in the market to seize new opportunities and partner with market-leading companies.

- **Acquisitions.** VeriSign planned to acquire Jamba!, a German company that was a leader in providing Internet mobile content and billing services to thirteen European carriers. Stratton Sclavos, the CEO of VeriSign, strongly believed that Jamba! would expand VeriSign's presence in the European market.[4] By integrating Jamba!'s offerings with the communication services platforms offered by VCS, VeriSign hoped to "be able to offer carriers a comprehensive wireless data utility that covers all aspects of the mobile content value chain."[5] During the second half of 2004, VeriSign predicted that Jamba! would generate $70 million in net incremental revenues.[6]

Value to the Company

Value to the company can be measured in numerous ways. In addition to contributing to the company's bottom line, good big ideas also use and build on the organization's core competencies and are aligned with both the company's and the team's strategic visions.

Ensure that the idea leverages your core competencies. According to Lou Gerstner, "Lack of focus is the most common cause of corporate mediocrity."[7] Too often executives would rather throw in the towel and jump on another bandwagon than put up a fight. Time, effort, and energy have to be dedicated to an organization's core competencies to develop and strengthen them further, and many executives fail to realize this. Some companies that are not doing well, however, consider entering a new business because the grass looks greener on the other side.

However, companies should be wary of entering a business completely out of its industry. A "technology company can't just become an airline manufacturer," so to speak. In other words, "Don't jump into new pools where [you] have no sense of the depth or temperature of the water."[8] Companies must try to stick with their core competencies because once they stray from them, they could potentially sink into a deeper hole and, in the meantime, give competitors time to catch up. Therefore, it's especially important to make sure that the big ideas that may be implemented use the company's core competencies.

Alignment with strategic vision. Just as the big ideas should build off the organization's core competencies, they should also be aligned with the overall strategic vision of the company. Since the overall strategic vision is the guiding beacon toward which all decisions should focus and align, the big ideas analyzed and assessed should be considered in light of the vision. IBM's transformation leader, Lou Gerstner, stressed the importance of keeping sight of the strategic vision of the company. "Every business, if it is to be successful, must have a sense of direction and mission, so that no matter who you are and what you are doing, you know how you fit in and that what you are doing is important."[9]

Projected contribution to revenue. The teams should conduct a high-level financial analysis of each big idea, including a projection of its costs and future cash flows. This is the most objective measure of value added to the company by the big idea. Do the financial benefits outweigh the costs? Furthermore, the team's confidence level in these projections must be accounted for. How much of a buffer do these numbers get to still make the project desirable?

Feasibility

To determine the feasibility of an idea, the team must consider whether the company has enough resources to implement it. Looking at the cost projections from the project, can the company reasonably cover those costs? What if the project runs over budget? How much can the project run over budget and still be feasible?

Furthermore, the team should determine whether the company currently has the infrastructure, knowledge, and expertise to properly implement the idea. How complicated is the idea? What are some of the intricacies involved in executing it? What is the likelihood that the big idea can be implemented flawlessly and seamlessly? These are all extremely important questions for the team and organization to ask. For example, in developing the Nissan Revival Plan, Ghosn stressed the importance of being realistic and understanding the capabilities of the team and the organization. He advised teams to establish a goal based on objective data and informed estimates, in addition to identifying the boundary between ambition and realism. According to Ghosn, teams should be able to answer the "question of distinguishing between the possible and the impossible, of knowing how far to go without going too far."[10]

Potential Challenges

Any new and major idea is associated with risks and challenges. For each big idea, the teams should anticipate any potential obstacles in implementing it and determine to what extent these obstacles could be mitigated. Will the team or company be able to execute this big idea flawlessly, or do the obstacles have the potential to be showstoppers? Do the rewards justify the risks? Whether the answers to these questions affect the team's or company's decision to carry out the big idea depends partly on how risk averse the company is as well as how critical this idea is to the future of the organization.

Market Readiness

Some big ideas may seem great and perfect for the company, but the timing might be off. Historically, many great ideas and products have been rejected because the market was not ready for them, only to succeed later. Therefore, even if the idea has the potential to add significant value to a market or an industry, it may have a low chance of success if the market is not ready for it or if it does not solve a particular consumer need at a given time. For each big idea, teams should identify the relevant customer and analyze the surrounding market.

Implementation Time

The teams should estimate the implementation time for each big idea in terms of when it will start generating a positive cash flow for the company. Some great ideas take years to execute; will the idea still have as great an impact by the time it is fully implemented? Is the time frame so long that this project or idea becomes extremely risky? Does the company have the resources necessary given the implementation time? Can the organization wait this long until the idea generates a positive cash flow?

Step 3: Prioritize the List of Big Ideas

Once the teams have assessed each big idea, they are ready to create a final, prioritized list of ideas (see "Prioritizing for the Future at Hewlett-Packard"). To do so, the teams should look at the set of predefined factors and determine

PRIORITIZING FOR THE FUTURE
AT HEWLETT-PACKARD

For one of its big ideas, Mark Hurd was looking into developing and identifying a growth plan. To do so, the company collected a variety of information about numerous factors, such as product pricing and market share, to gain an idea of where it stood relative to the market and its competitors. With this data, which was gathered both internally and externally, the teams developed approximately three hundred spreadsheets of information and models.[11]

From this analysis, HP decided to generate growth from its high-potential existing products. These products and domains were identified and prioritized through heavy analysis. As a result, HP identified three clusters of focus in research and development in the future: digital printing, mobile computing, and software and equipment for a new generation of corporate data systems.[12]

which are the most important. In many cases, however, each big idea needs to be analyzed and assessed individually, for relevant trade-offs can't be made across the board. Hence, extensive dialogue and discussion need to take place in order to prioritize the list of big ideas.

After the teams have created a prioritized list of the big ideas, they should prepare to present their top three to five ideas at the day 60 integration meeting. These top big ideas become the high-level recommendations each rapid response team makes to the EMT. Details about what should be presented are given at the end of the chapter, in the section titled "Day 60 Integration Meeting."

GAP ANALYSIS

Now that the company knows where it is (as a result of its phase 1 analysis) and has an idea of where it wants to go (the big ideas developed in this phase), the next step is for the rapid response teams to conduct a gap analysis (see figure 5-4). Namely, what is the difference between the current state and the desired state? What steps can the team or organization take to decrease this difference or eliminate this gap altogether?

A gap analysis can be especially enlightening with quantitative data and information. Particularly common are gap analyses of revenue or sales num-

FIGURE 5-4

Gap analysis

bers. Often, the transformation leader announces a companywide revenue or sales goal at the beginning of the effort. While that initial number is based on the transformation leader's understanding of the business at the time, new information uncovered during the diagnosis may require that the initial target be adjusted to remain realistic and achievable. These adjustments, however, should be made only after an appropriate gap analysis is conducted and the original goal is absolutely unattainable, even after taking advantage of synergies within the company.

The gap analysis for revenue or sale numbers should be conducted using two methods simultaneously: top-down and bottom-up. The bottom-up analysis should be conducted by the sales team (or a coalition of top employees in sales), and the top-down analysis should be conducted by both the marketing and strategy teams (see "Convergence of Gap Analysis at an Engineering Company"). By using two different methods, the gap analyses will show either a convergence or a divergence in the final numbers. Converging numbers reflect a highly achievable and realistic target, given that the assumptions are correct. Diverging numbers, in contrast, reflect differing assumptions and further analysis. This further analysis should include an extensive discussion on the confidence levels about the different assumptions, inputs, and outputs (target numbers). It may turn out that those who conducted the analysis using one method may be significantly more confident about the accuracy of their numbers than the other team, which used the other type of analysis. Hence, the relative confidence levels behind the different numbers should be taken into account when making adjustments to the final, overall target.

Gap analyses can also be conducted using more qualitative data. In particular, a competency gap in the organization should be assessed, often by the organizational excellence team, in parallel with the other gap analyses being conducted. The team should first assess the current structure of the organization and how it supports the company's strategy. Then, it should analyze the new structure and look at ways to transform from the current structure to the new one. In particular, what are some positions that the organization

CONVERGENCE OF GAP ANALYSIS
AT AN ENGINEERING COMPANY

In this semiconductor company, the transformation leader conducted a gap analysis of the revenue projections for the upcoming two years, focusing on the near future. He had his sales team conduct a bottom-up analysis, and worked with the marketing and strategy team to conduct a top-down analysis. In the bottom-up analysis, the team used information and assumptions from the grassroots level to generate the new target number. In the top-down analysis, the team first looked at the industry and then calculated the organization's market share in various submarkets in the industry. These calculations also resulted in a new revenue projection.

Interestingly, the two teams converged on the same number, despite having different assumptions. The two teams held a meeting and compared their notes, assumptions, and calculations and found that the differences were accounted for by varying confidence levels in the current products as compared with the future products, as well as in their faith in the company's ability to generate revenue in different geographies. As a result of this gap analysis, the transformation leader adjusted his original target revenue for the upcoming year and emphasized the importance of trying to take advantage of the synergies in the organization, which would allow the company to surpass both estimates.

may need to add? Are there key roles that need to be filled first? Are there competency gaps in the organization? Given the current employees of the organization, what are some levels of expertise that are currently lacking but necessary for the future? In all its decisions and analysis, the team should look at the new strategy of the company and develop ideas that will help the company grow in the long term.

A gap analysis hence serves numerous functions. On the one hand, it can be considered a calculated reality check. Throughout the transformation effort, in particular during this phase, you're reassessing the feasibility of your goals, in addition to continually analyzing the situation. On the other hand, a gap analysis also gives both the rapid response teams and the organization a general idea of what needs to be done to reach the desired goal, according to the current situation of the company. All the rapid response teams should conduct a gap analysis to illuminate the disparity between the real and ideal states, as well as to facilitate exploration of steps to mediate this disparity.

CASCADING GOALS

While results from rationalization, big ideas, and gap analysis represent important goals toward which the organization can strive, they are by themselves overwhelming, unmanageable, and not very useful for generating specific behaviors within the rapid response teams. Rather, these high-level goals need to be decomposed by the rapid response teams into appropriate goals and given to the relevant teams (see figure 5-5). For instance, decisions made via the rationalization process can first be broken down into functional-level goals, which can be further broken down as necessary. In this way, the major decisions cascade downward throughout the organization, representing something manageable and attainable at each level (see "Cascading Goals at Bay Networks").

The cascading goals at each level represent a contribution toward the overarching goals. At its respective level, however, the goal may not seem like

FIGURE 5-5

Cascading goals

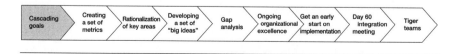

CASCADING GOALS AT BAY NETWORKS

At Bay Networks, Dave House worked with his direct reports to develop a set of corporate goals. Once these were finalized, he asked the direct reports to use them in working with the members of their respective staffs to create their own goals and objectives. In this way, setting goals trickled down to the lower levels of the organization, with each individual receiving a half-page list of five to ten measurable things to be completed by the end of the quarter. Once these goals were developed, the staff was reviewed monthly and graded quarterly.

a major contributor. Yet when all the cascading goals are combined, they roll up and build toward the original goal in amazing ways, because the various goals leverage off each other. Once again, we see that the whole is greater than the sum of its parts.

For example, if a company wants to increase the sales of a specific product, different functions across the company have to coordinate tasks to ensure that this goal is met. Marketing may have to increase a specific activity that targets the customer for that particular product, and product development may have to investigate and identify additional user needs to be designed and incorporated into the product. Hence, marketing, product development, and other relevant functions need to both cooperate and work toward their own goals before the overall goal of increased sales is achieved. However, other functions, such as human resources, may have no contribution to that specific goal.

Anytime you break something into smaller parts with tasks, there's a potential for overlap. With cascading goals, the countless interdependencies between various functions touch on the potential for conflict and redundancies among teams and team members. To avoid and overcome these potential problems, clear roles and responsibilities for each team need to be established with the help and guidance of the EMT. The role of the EMT is to make sure that the finalized set of specific functional goals and the action plan of each team are coordinated with those of the other teams. Furthermore, the EMT needs to keep track of the different goals and ensure that the cascading goals are aligned with the overall goal and vision.

Decomposing the overall goal and vision into more concrete goals and actions that are more relevant to specific teams is also related to an effective tool called management by objectives. Once the smaller-scale, clearer, and more manageable goals are understood, team pilots should work with their respective team members to identify a specific set of action items with deadlines that will help the team achieve the goals. The pilots can then use the action items, or objectives, to track the progress of the team. Not only does this increase accountability, it also promotes understanding among team members within the team.

In developing these goals, the team members should ensure that the goals are clear, specific, and easily understood (see "Clear Objectives at Telefónica de España"). People are more motivated to contribute to a goal when it is easier to understand and envision, and the goal is more likely to be achieved when it is understood. Additionally, a clear goal is easier to measure, track, and assess than a convoluted goal.

CLEAR OBJECTIVES AT TELEFÓNICA DE ESPAÑA

Julio Linares, executive chairman of Telefónica de España, once said, "If the objective is clear, then everybody has a very good view of the progress made against it." For example, in 2000, during the planning phase of its transformation effort, Telefónica de España set a clear overall objective of having one million Asymmetric Digital Subscriber Line (ADSL) subscribers by 2003. Because the objective was clear and simple, everyone understood it. Furthermore, it was easy to track at all times and therefore report to the entire organization. This overall objective also cascaded down the various levels of the organization, so different functions knew and understood how they could contribute to this overall goal.[13]

In this phase, cascading goals are important in representing a high-level vision for each team in addition to the previously established vision.

CREATING A SET OF METRICS

Once the teams have developed functional goals, they should develop a set of metrics for measuring progress toward these goals (see figure 5-6). Similar to the baseline metrics that were developed in the last phase to measure progress against an initial state, metrics developed here are to identify the particular items with which to measure progress. Furthermore, the types of metrics used depend on the particular team and the determined cascading goals. For example, some questions that address key metrics include:

- How is the leadership and morale of the rapid response teams?

- What percentage of the work of the organization is not being done due to transformation?

- Are the rapid response teams on track with their commitments?

Metrics such as these not only help measure progress but also send important signals, both positive and negative, to the teams. By closely monitoring these measurements, teams not only are quick to spot and remedy problems related to their specific goals, but are also the first to see future opportunities.

FIGURE 5-6

Creating a set of metrics

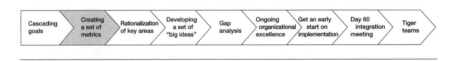

Clearly defined, valuable metrics can help businesses become more responsive to the changes happening in their surrounding environment.

Once the rapid response teams have developed a set of metrics, they should determine how frequently these metrics will be monitored. For instance, cash flow metrics may require daily monitoring, while a collection rate may require weekly monitoring. Additionally, the teams should lay out plans for how analysis of these metrics will be translated to specific adjustments and changes within the organization. Because metrics give you some important information, the next logical question would be, What are you going to do with the information now that you have it? Such decisions require tremendous discussion and dialogue within the teams, among teams, and between the teams and the EMT.

ONGOING ORGANIZATIONAL EXCELLENCE

As with conducting reality checks on your goals and targets, a set of tasks specific to the organizational excellence rapid response team—most logically after the competency gap analysis conducted earlier—should be ongoing throughout phase 2. While there is no specific time at which these tasks should be carried out, they should be completed by the end of the phase. Examples of these tasks are (1) defining the new values for the organization, (2) developing the structure of the new organization, (3) hiring, (4) developing a training program, (5) defining the performance review process, (6) developing compensation packages, and (7) implementing team incentives.

Many of these areas were analyzed and diagnosed in phase 1. Here, the organizational excellence team should use the gap analysis to start creating a vision for the future. Although all the rapid response teams should follow a similar process and use their gap analysis to lay out the next steps for the organization, we have dedicated a section of the chapter to these elements related to organizational excellence because they are generalizable across organizations and ultimately play a critical role in the success of the transformation effort (see figure 5-7).

FIGURE 5-7

Ongoing organizational excellence

Defining the New Values for the Organization

During the kickoff meeting in phase 1, the transformation team was given the opportunity to develop a set of values for the transformation effort and beyond. During phase 2, the organizational excellence team needs to look at the values and translate them into understandable and measurable terms. For example, teamwork is a common value embraced by organizations. However, what constitutes teamwork? How do you know whether an employee is being a team player? (See "Subvalues at an Engineering Company" for an example of how you can build on the value of teamwork.) A company that wants its employees to live its values needs to explicitly explain the values and give some sample actions that exemplify the values, which in turn allows employees to understand the values better and therefore live by them. In this phase, therefore, the company should not only define the values but also expand on them to make them tangible and understandable for employees. The most effective way to identify these "subvalues" is through active discussion, for developing values is an iterative process that requires feedback from many different people.

SUBVALUES AT AN ENGINEERING COMPANY

This engineering company identified teamwork as one of its values and identified the following set of subvalues:

- Work as a team with respect and trust for each other

- Achieve the team goals

- Leverage the abilities of all team members

- Find ways to contribute, learn, and support

- Recognize and support whoever owns the final decision

Sometimes, these new values in the organization feed directly into a new culture the organizational excellence team, as well as the transformation team as a whole, is trying to promote. This new culture often is directly tied to and supports the new strategy of the company. When creating the values, therefore, the company should keep in mind the goal of the transformation effort and the strategy of the new organization. The values the organization commits to should be a tangible, concrete representation of the company's culture.

Developing the Structure of the New Organization

At the beginning of phase 2, the organizational excellence team should start analyzing the organizational structure of the company and possible options for restructuring, given the pain points identified in phase 1. (See "Hewlett-Packard Addresses Its Key Pain Points.") Although some minor adjustments and updates will be made to the new structure until the official unveiling in the day 90 integration meeting after phase 3, the major changes should be decided on as early as possible to facilitate the other processes and decisions in both the transformation effort and the organization. For example, the organizational excellence team at VeriSign noted that if it had done anything differently, it would have finalized the new organizational structure more quickly, because the decisions other rapid response teams faced hinged on the final organizational design of the company.

On top of developing the new organizational structure, the team should at this point define specific positions in the new structure, along with their respective roles. While specific employees don't have to be identified to fill those roles yet (that comes next), the job description and responsibilities for those positions, especially the critical positions, should be identified here.

Often, the question facing the organizational excellence team with respect to the new structure is whether to move toward increased centralization or increased decentralization. Sometimes, layers of management are eliminated altogether, while other times new layers and increased bureaucracy are introduced. While there are advantages and disadvantages to both centralization and decentralization, depending on the company's needs, the most important thing to consider in making this decision (as well as other decisions with respect to organizational excellence) is its alignment with the company's new strategy.

In some cases, the organization may find that no major changes are necessary to support the new strategy. Rather, the current organizational struc-

HEWLETT-PACKARD ADDRESSES ITS KEY PAIN POINTS

One of the major problems hindering efficiency and customer service at HP was its organizational structure, particularly its sales structure. For example, eleven layers of management stood between the CEO (Mark Hurd) and the customer, and salespeople spent a third of their time on administrative tasks rather than working with the customer. Hurd also found that of the seventeen thousand employees working in corporate sales, only ten thousand of them directly sold to the customers, the others being either support staff or management. Customers complained that they didn't know who to contact for sales issues, and employees complained that getting a price quote or sample product to the customer was a huge ordeal.

To address these issues, Hurd looked into revamping the corporate sales force and, indirectly, the organizational structure of HP. Doing away with three layers of management by cutting underperforming workers, the company reduced the distance between the CEO and the corporate customer to eight layers. To address customer concerns, HP assigned only one salesperson to the top two thousand corporate customer accounts to serve as the point person for that customer. To help focus the salespeople, HP decreased the number of accounts each salesperson was responsible for, and narrowed the focus of products each person would sell, which would help salespeople develop expertise in specific products and product areas. Furthermore, the salespeople were placed under the business units in the new organizational structure so business units could control the sales process. By decreasing the bureaucracy of the company, HP hoped to increase the productivity of its sales force by twofold.[14]

ture is effective and should be kept intact, maybe with only minor changes. In these instances, the important task is to analyze the structure at a more microscopic level, assessing the key positions and identifying the employees who fit best in those roles.

Hiring

With the new organizational structure in place (or in development), the team should use the competency gap assessed earlier. In doing so, the team needs to ensure that the right people are in the right positions to drive the execution of plans developed in the 90 days effort, as well as carry out their daily job functions. Although sometimes a company is overpopulated with competent people, more often than not it lacks the right talent. In addressing this competency gap, there are typically two solutions: hire the people you need for the right job, or train the current people so they can perform the necessary jobs or tasks. In this section, we will talk about hiring.

Hiring in phase 2 has two different goals. First, certain hires are immediately necessary to fill critical voids in the organization. Second, the organizational excellence team also needs to look ahead and try to fill in the new organizational structure with the right people. In particular, the top two tiers of the organization should be filled by the end of this phase so the handoff process can begin in the next phase. These new hires are a direct reflection of the reorganization of the company and therefore do not need to be announced yet. Although the hiring process begins in phase 2, the following should be completed by the end of the phase:

- Hiring of people to fill critical voids in the organization as assessed in the competency gap analysis.

- Assignment of employees, managers, and executives in the new organizational structure. Even if not everyone has been reassigned, the top two tiers of the new organization should, at the very least, be determined by the end of phase 2 so the handoff process can begin in phase 3.

As early as possible, the company should hire the new employees who will fill critical competency gaps. Efficiency and speed are necessary because these new hires will play an important role in the transformation effort, especially in implementation. By hiring them early, the organization gives the new hires a chance to build an informal network as well as understand both the organization and the transformation effort. Additionally, because these new hires ideally will contribute to the development of the final recommendations and implementation plans (described in the chapter on phase 3), they will be more likely to buy in to the new plans if they had a voice in creating them.

At the same time, however, even though there is time pressure to hire people to fill the critical voids as early as possible, the organization should not settle for someone who is less than perfect. If necessary, the company can hold off as long as it takes to find the ideal candidate. It is the job of the organizational excellence team to make sure the right people fill the right positions, and the right people will get up to speed even if hired in the later stages of the transformation. Hence, much care should be dedicated to defining the capabilities and skills required of each management position and recruiting the appropriate individuals. The team and the transformation leader should ensure that quality of the candidate is not compromised for speed in hiring.

When searching for the appropriate candidate, the company can look at either internal or external hires, and there are advantages and disadvantages to both. On the one hand, new blood in an organization adds energy and introduces a new perspective. On the other hand, new hires don't necessarily understand the culture and vision of the organization and need to be trained and gotten up to speed. In filling positions in the new organization, the company should generally first look internally to reassign employees before looking externally to hire, in order to ensure that the organization fully utilizes the skills and capabilities within it. As Corrado Passera, the leader of the transformation effort at Banca Intesa, argued, "It is a big mistake to change people for the sake of change. In any organization, there is a pride, a culture, an accumulated set of things that you have to understand and respect before changing."[15] At Banca Intesa, Passera recruited colleagues from his former organization, Poste, only after "making sure that the required capabilities and experience were not already available in the bank."

Hiring is a highly variable and individualized process. Despite that, however, the goal is always the same: to find the right person for the right job. Whether the team is trying to find the perfect candidate for a current void or a future opening, team members should always make sure that their decisions are aligned with their cascading goals, the transformation's goals, and the company's goals and new strategy.

Developing a Training Program

Aside from hiring, the organization may also develop a training program to address the competency gap assessed in the gap analysis. A training program should be used to train and develop employees for the position they are placed in, whether they are new to the position or not.

The organizational excellence team should use its findings from the competency gap analysis to identify the voids a training program can fill. Using these findings, the team can then design the structure and content of a training program to develop the specific skills and capabilities necessary for employees to succeed in their jobs.

The training programs developed do not need to be extremely advanced or elaborate. In some cases, the competency gaps in the company are at the most basic level. For example, as mentioned in the previous chapter, Bay Networks' Dave House found that the core issues of the company lay in problems with the fundamentals. As a result, House implemented training programs that addressed these basic skills, such as decision making, managing conflict, running effective meetings, and prioritizing tasks. These skills are obviously relevant to a greater audience than, say, a course focused on project management. Both types of courses and training programs are necessary for the company, however, and hence should be developed.

The training programs, however, should not only focus on the immediate needs of the organization. Rather, the organizational excellence team should anticipate future needs also. For example, leadership development is an important and common training program that should be developed.

Training programs are not static or frozen in time. The development process is ongoing, and the programs should be dynamic, fluctuating with the evolving needs of the company. Developing training programs is an iterative process that requires constant feedback and evaluation of their effectiveness. Even after an effective program is established, it will need to be adjusted for various reasons, such as to account for the growth and development of employees as a whole.

Not only do the programs react to changes in the organization, however; they can also instigate and propagate change. Training programs are effective levers for change, for they provide the company with an opportunity to internalize certain skills, habits, and behaviors into its culture. The organization needs to reconcile the dual paradoxical roles of the training programs by using them for different purposes as necessary.

Defining the Performance Review Process

With the new organizational structure identified and candidates being assessed, the next step for the organizational excellence team is to identify how employees and executives will be assessed and reviewed (see "Performance Reviews at Bay Networks"). In designing this performance review process, the team should first ensure standardization across the company to make sure that the review process is fair for all employees. In addition to deciding the specifics of how individuals will be reviewed, the organizational excellence team needs to prepare the necessary documents for the process, as well as develop and manage the database that will keep the information on file and up to date. Hence, standardization refers to both the process and the content of performance reviews.

PERFORMANCE REVIEWS AT BAY NETWORKS

At Bay Networks, House had a unique way of conducting performance reviews. At the end of each year, he would give his direct reports copies of their last four quarterly objectives and goals. Then, both he and the employee would write a separate performance review with two key accomplishments, two key strengths, two key areas of improvement, and what needed to be completed in the year to come. Both House and the employee would give a representative from human resources their completed reviews.

The performance review process should also be aligned with the new strategy of the organization, as in the case of The Home Depot (see "Standardizing Performance Reviews at The Home Depot"). Additionally, consider the impact of the decisions on the organization, since how employees are reviewed ultimately affects their actions, behaviors, and decisions. For example, if employees know they are being reviewed according to how they live the company's values, they will incorporate them into their daily behaviors more so than if they were not being reviewed on such criteria. Therefore, performance review decisions are extremely relevant to the transformation effort and play a critical role in the success of implementation.

STANDARDIZING PERFORMANCE REVIEWS
AT THE HOME DEPOT

In alignment with the new strategy and direction of the organization, The Home Depot standardized its employee evaluation process. This helped create a new, more disciplined, and more organized culture, in contrast to the former cowboy culture of the organization. In doing so, 157 different employee appraisal forms were collapsed into 2. Additionally, salaried employees, from the CEO to store-level employees, are now given 360-degree reviews by employees both above and below them on identical criteria. This overall performance rating then helps determine their salary.[16]

Developing Compensation Packages

With the performance review criteria and process defined, the organizational excellence team needs to develop the compensation packages, at least at a high level, for both old and new positions in the new organizational structure. Often, individual compensation packages will have to be identified when performance reviews are conducted, for the packages depend on how well the employees do in their performance reviews. However, a method and process for determining the specific compensation packages should be developed here (see "Compensation Packages at Bay Networks").

Even though individual compensation packages cannot be identified and generalized across employees, the process developed should stipulate a range of possible compensation plans for employees filling the different positions in the new organizational structure. For example, an employee in one position should be limited to a specific range of compensation packages, according to the roles and responsibilities previously identified.

Implementing Team Incentives

While organizational excellence should be looking toward the future, it can't forget the present. In the present, team members are simultaneously working two full-time jobs, and without the appropriate incentives, they will burn out and turn bitter. The rapid response teams are working around the clock and deserve to be recognized.

In this context, organizational excellence has a responsibility to identify and implement team incentives (see "Team Incentives at VeriSign"). They not only reinforce what team members are doing well but also help propel the team into a more effective future. Phase 2 is a good time to use incen-

---

COMPENSATION PACKAGES AT BAY NETWORKS

To determine the compensation package for the individual employee, House and the employee would sit down after the performance review with both of their documents (see the previous section on performance reviews) and discuss the similarities and differences between them. From this meeting, they would determine the overall salary increase and future stock options for the employee.

TEAM INCENTIVES AT VERISIGN

To further motivate its transformation team, the executive management team at VeriSign set aside a pool of money just for its rapid response teams. To determine how the bonus would be distributed, the EMT ranked each team member on several variables, including creativity and inter- and intrateamwork. Team members were paid according to their ranking and performance, and the bonuses were paid over the long term, according to performances over the ninety days, six months, and a year afterward. Such incentives encouraged team members to work not only with their own team but with other teams.

tives because teams are halfway through the 90 days effort and often appreciate the additional push.

GET AN EARLY START ON IMPLEMENTATION

Implementation officially begins at the conclusion of phase 3. However, as mentioned in the pretransformation chapter, it is important to get early wins to create momentum for the transformation effort and improve the morale of both the transformation team and the company as a whole. At this stage, implementation can and should start early for certain projects deemed as low-hanging fruit (see figure 5-8). Implementation of the fundamentals in this phase will get the ball rolling and lay the groundwork for implementation of future plans and projects.

For example, two items described in the previous section can be implementable early wins at this stage. First, the organizational excellence team should have defined and expanded on the organizational values. Once these expanded values are finalized and given the green light by the EMT, the

FIGURE 5-8

Get an early start on implementation

transformation leader, and the CEO of the company, the values can be rolled out to the organization at large. The transformation leader can work with his executives to share and explain the new corporate values to employees throughout the organization. While performance reviews may not immediately be tied to the values, rolling out the values early gives employees at the very least time to internalize them and practice them in their everyday activities.

The second organizational excellence item that can be addressed early on is initial implementation and trials of the training programs. This is especially important if the team decides that the company is missing some key fundamentals. For example, one company we researched realized that meetings were extremely ineffective and inefficient, and hence very costly. As a result, it decided to immediately develop and launch a training program on running effective meetings. By doing so, it enabled employees to implement their new skills during the transformation effort, which facilitated the effort itself. By not waiting until the implementation phase to execute this new training program, the team saved the company a lot of money and set the stage for future training programs.

DAY 60 INTEGRATION MEETING

Like the conclusion of phase 1, the official end of phase 2 is marked by an integration meeting: the day 60 integration meeting (see figure 5-9). This meeting should be run just like the day 30 meeting, although the content will be different.

In its presentation, each team should do the following:

1. Reiterate the pain points found in phase 1, plus any additional ones discovered during phase 2.

2. Present the top three to five big ideas, including the costs and benefits of each idea, the potential risks and mitigations associated with each idea, how they ranked the big ideas, and why these were the top recommendations.

FIGURE 5-9

Day 60 integration meeting

3. Provide high-impact solutions for low-hanging fruit, with details. These solutions should include:

   – When the solution will be operational

   – Who will own the solution

   – How it will be enforced

   – How it will be measured and updated as necessary

   – How it will impact the current plan or situation as it becomes operational

   – How the team will ensure sustainability of the solution

4. Present detailed plans for phase 3 and high-level plans for after phase 3. The high-level plans can be tied to the big ideas introduced.

As in phase 1, each presentation should take approximately thirty minutes, and an additional thirty minutes should be allotted for questions. After this integration meeting, the EMT will convene to discuss the big ideas presented and will give teams either a red, yellow, or green light. Those with a green light have received approval from the EMT and can continue with their ideas in the next phase. The ideas with a yellow light require more research and data gathering, and the ideas with a red light are to be dropped altogether. All final decisions need to be signed off on by the transformation leader.

In making these decisions, the EMT should look at the entire portfolio of big ideas. Not only must they all be aligned with the new strategy of the organization, but together they should create a portfolio of solutions and recommendations that not only address the current pain points of the organization but also prepare the company for future growth opportunities. Companies can't simply say, "There will be a time for cost reduction and then a time for growth." Rather, both tasks need to be undertaken simultaneously, and the portfolio of big ideas that is officially approved should reflect the dual needs of the company.

TIGER TEAMS

Sometimes, in discussion, the transformation team may realize that some key areas are not being addressed because of the specific structures of the teams. This discussion may occur in the day 60 integration meeting, or it may occur beforehand. The particular gaps in analysis may occur because of over-laps between two teams, because some aspects aren't explicitly in the do-main of any team, or because some areas have been ignored or forgotten altogether. When there is an overlap between the domains of distinct rapid response teams and neither team is analyzing the relevant area, the transfor-mation leader may decide to either delegate the area to one particular team or create a new rapid response team to address the gap (see figure 5-10). For example, Ghosn added a tenth team after the transformation was underway to cover investment costs and efficiency at Nissan.[17]

These new tiger teams should ideally include members already involved in the transformation effort who have the relevant expertise, but sometimes new members or members from subteams may be asked to join these tiger teams. The tiger teams should be formed in time for phase 3 and should start with a diagnosis of their domain.

CONCLUSION

In the previous phase, the rapid response teams analyzed and diagnosed the pain points of the organization. In this phase, the teams rationalized and streamlined their portfolio of products and services and used gap analysis of revenue projections. Teams also developed their big ideas, which were the recommendations shared with the EMT at the day 60 integration meeting. In some cases, new rapid response teams, called tiger teams, need to be created to address areas that have previously been ignored or overlooked.

Now that the teams have their big ideas in place and have conducted an appropriate gap analysis, teams should take their big ideas to the next level and create business and implementation plans. In the next phase, the rapid response teams will work out the details of their recommendations as well as wrap up any loose ends in their domain.

FIGURE 5-10

Tiger teams

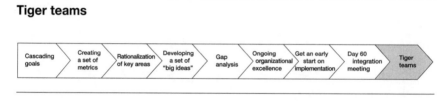

6

Phase 3

Paving the Road

*Let your plans be dark and as impenetrable as night,
and when you move, fall like a thunderbolt.*

—Sun Tzu

There are two sides to every coin, and this rings especially true when we look at phase 3. On the one hand, phase 3 represents the official end of the 90 days transformation effort. On the other hand, it represents the first step toward implementation, a new beginning for the organization. Hence, phase 3 represents the tipping point between past and future, beginning and end.

In this phase, the rapid response teams must first tie up the loose ends and continue to move forward toward the conclusion of the planning stage in the transformation effort. At the same time, however, the teams must plant the seeds and pave the road for a successful implementation effort. In creating the detailed plans for the future, the rapid response teams must remember what ailments brought the organization to its current state in the first place. They must make sure that everything is aligned and that the new plans will work and can be enforced.

Phase 3 begins with planning the external public relations (PR) campaign, should the organization decide it wants to announce its changes to the public and to investors (see figure 6-1). Planning this campaign will continue throughout the phase, and the campaign itself will officially be launched on the 91st day, which will be explained further in the next chapter. Because the recommendations will continue to change and evolve in this phase, the campaign itself should be dynamic and change iteratively with the recommendations.

FIGURE 6-1

Chapter overview

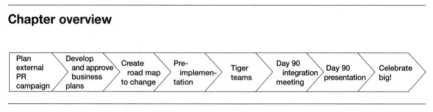

The first task for the individual rapid response teams is to use all the big ideas that were given a green light in the previous phase to develop business plans for those ideas that involve exploring new worlds, such as entering a new market, creating a new product, developing a new service, or acquiring another company. These business plans should be supported by extensive research on the markets and the customer base, and with the necessary resources to carry them out.

Once the business plan is completed and approved by the EMT, the rapid response teams need to create a "road map," better known as an implementation plan. This road map to change delves deeper into how the business plan will implemented, such as who will be responsible for what tasks and by when. Road maps to change need to be created for all the big ideas to be implemented, not only for the ones that required a business plan. All the road maps created by the rapid response teams need to be integrated by the program management office (PMO) into an overall "transformation implementation plan."

Throughout this phase, the tiger teams created in the previous phase will be running in high gear to develop appropriate recommendations by the day 90 integration meeting. In the meantime, all members of the rapid response teams should also be planting the seeds for a successful implementation in their daily jobs. For example, this can be done by talking about the importance of the transformation effort in informal, everyday conversation.

The day 90 integration meeting marks the official end of the 90 days transformation effort. However, it is followed by the day 90 presentation by the transformation leader, which details the transformation effort and the final transformation implementation plan internally to employees throughout the company. In this presentation, the entire company is finally mobilized behind the transformation effort and prepared for implementation. Before the transformation team members take that first step, however, they need to take a breather and celebrate their accomplishments and progress thus far.

PLAN THE EXTERNAL PUBLIC
RELATIONS CAMPAIGN

As mentioned in the pretransformation chapter, details of the transformation effort and its progress should be kept confidential and protected from press and media coverage throughout the transformation. Now that the organization is nearing the end of the 90 days transformation, it is even more important that the information be kept confidential, for any information leak could be very demoralizing to the company and devastating to the transformation effort. With limited information, the public is likely to unfairly scrutinize any information given to it without having a full view of the situation at hand.

For example, most transformation plans include cost-cutting efforts such as layoffs, but these decisions can easily be misconstrued without the complete explanation of the logistics of the layoffs and how the company plans on helping its employees transition from their jobs or how this is a strategically beneficial move in the long term. Cost cutting is usually only half the story, focused on addressing problems in the current state. Organizations that are transforming, however, also have long-term strategies that involve growth and overall increased and improved opportunities. Without this complete view, criticism of specific points of the effort sparks a negative reaction against the transformation and often leads to overreaction. Because the transformation leader is not given a chance to explain these particular aspects of the plan before they are scrutinized in public, the transformation effort never gets a fair trial, and the organization will have to overcome more barriers in implementation and in regaining the public's faith than it otherwise would have had to do.

However, even though information should still be kept strictly confidential at this point, it doesn't mean that this will be the case for the duration of the organization's life. Often, an organization will want to share with the public its findings and the recommendations made during the transformation after the effort is officially completed and the company has moved into the implementation phase. Furthermore, it may want to build commitment to the goals and plans created internally, and this can also be achieved by communicating to others internally and externally the goals and plans of the effort. To do this, it will want to officially launch a PR campaign at the end of phase 3, on what we will refer to as the 91st day.

Before any decisions are made about the PR campaign in terms of what to announce and how, the leaders of the transformation effort and the organization as a whole must first decide whether or not they want to go public with the transformation effort at all. In some cases, the organization may not want to go public with its findings because of the detrimental effects of doing so. For example, if the company is not a public company, sharing the pain points of the organization may lead to a negative reputation and image. Additionally, such an announcement may lead to customers losing confidence in the company, despite the fact that the organization is taking active steps to correct its mistakes. Even if the organization is a public company, it may still want to be wary of going public with the details of the effort. For example, the organization may keep the findings and big ideas proprietary to gain a competitive advantage.

If the organization decides it does want to publicly detail the transformation effort or parts of it, it should start planning the PR campaign in this phase (see figure 6-2), because of the logistics and the need for coordination among many different factors. Since the official announcement of the transformation effort in the pretransformation, the public should not have received more than occasional glimpses into the effort and its progress. The PR campaign finally gives the public, including customers and investors, the opportunity to assess the progress the company has made and see the new direction of the company. The PR campaign should especially involve analysts, since this is the first time they will be exposed to the transformation plan.

Given the number of important audience members who will be tuned in to the PR campaign, the organization should make sure that it communicates a fair and holistic picture of the transformation effort and the findings and recommendations that resulted from it. Although they may not immediately jump onto the transformational bandwagon, the public should, at the very least, gain from the PR campaign a new understanding of the organization and everything it went through before, during, and after the 90 days effort.

Goals of the Public Relations Campaign

One of the goals of the PR campaign is to restore the public's faith in the company. Hence, the transformation leader must carefully craft a message that

FIGURE 6-2

Plan external PR campaign

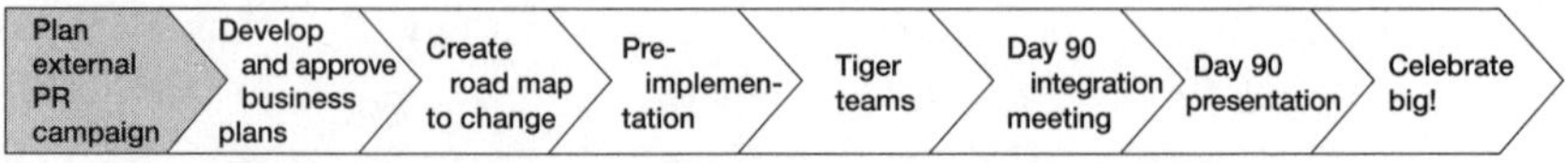

will be communicated openly and honestly. This message, however, will change via an iterative process throughout phase 3 because of the tremendous changes the ideas and recommendations undergo as they're being finalized in this phase. Given the time and effort that has been dedicated to developing a message that embodies the transformation effort, this message should also be used in the internal PR campaign, which is highlighted by the day 90 presentation (discussed later).

While the gist of the message should be the same for both the internal and the external PR campaigns, the goals communicated within the company should be set higher than those announced externally. It is especially important that the company meet its publicly declared goals because this is the critical time when the organization is trying to reestablish itself. Missing goals and underperforming now will have devastating effects on the company and communicate to the public that the organization is still not performing, causing it to further lose faith in the company. Hence, by following the motto "Promise less, deliver more," the company gives itself some leeway and flexibility in case unanticipated obstacles arise, thereby minimizing the possibility of ruining its new image and reputation.

Another goal of the external PR campaign should be to communicate to the public the new brand image, including new products and markets the company plans on entering, with the goal of restoring the public's faith in the company. As such, branding and rebranding are important facets of the external PR campaign. However, branding does take time, and the PR campaign is only the first step. According to Nissan's transformation leader, Carlos Ghosn, only after the entire company fully orients itself toward a defined ideal will the company have a brand image through which the public forms an image of that ideal, perceives it, and reflects it back to the company.[1] Hence, to be effective, the communicated image and goals should be consistent with the company's strategies and actions (see "A Message of Unity at VeriSign"). It is not enough that a message be communicated internally—a company must fully align itself with the message in all respects, or the integrity of the message will be questioned (see "Message Alignment at IBM").

There are several steps to planning a PR campaign. We do not discuss most of these items in depth, but the process should seem logical and intuitive. In the following sections, we focus on the campaign message and various communication media. The steps are these:

1. *Set a high-level budget.* The relative amount depends on how important it is that outsiders understand the transformation effort.

A MESSAGE OF UNITY AT VERISIGN

As part of VeriSign's new market strategy, the company decided to integrate its legacy organizations into one entity, which VeriSign formally communicated to external customers and shareholders in the first quarter of 2004. This official announcement communicated not only the new solutions that resulted from this integration but also VeriSign's new product offerings. Furthermore, this message of the importance of integration in VeriSign's new market strategy was clearly visible in the level of resources and effort dedicated to the effort. As a result, a consistent message was clearly communicated and more easily understood and accepted by its intended recipients.

MESSAGE ALIGNMENT AT IBM

One of the core goals of IBM's transformation effort was to build a culture of unity. Within the company, the message of unity was effectively communicated throughout the transformation effort, both verbally and nonverbally. However, the message communicated to those external to the company was very mixed. After researching IBM's branding, marketing executive Abby Kohnstamm found that IBM's brand message was overly disparate and completely disorganized because of the decentralized structure of the company. Because each product manager hired his own advertising agency, IBM was actually working with seventy agencies, leading to a wide variety of messages and no clear or consistent statement. As a result, the internal culture of unity was not being communicated externally. Therefore, Kohnstamm unified all IBM's brand messages and combined all advertising efforts under one agency. This led to a new advertising campaign that clearly communicated the important message that although IBM is a global company, it is creating integrated, total solutions under the culture of unity.[2]

2. *Identify the target audience.* You may want to communicate with investors, stockholders, customers, suppliers, and so on.

3. *Design the campaign message.* What's the message you want to communicate? Is it simple, easy to communicate, and easy to understand?

4. *Determine the appropriate communication medium.* Examples include traditional media, press releases, newspaper coverage, and road shows.

5. *Allocate the budget accordingly.* Depending on the target audience and the chosen modes of deployment, you can determine how to allocate the high-level budget across these individual marketing activities.

6. *Develop a plan of deployment.* For each marketing activity, develop an execution plan and communicate that plan to everyone who will be involved in the deployment. Ensure that roles and responsibilities are clear and that each marketing activity is assigned the appropriate set of resources. Also, ensure that the plan laid out is sustainable over a specific period of time and that the business has the proper resources in place to launch the plan in parallel with other marketing efforts.

7. *Measure results.* The organization should lay out a system for measuring the results of these marketing activities, such as in stock price or the number of new customers, so that the benefits can be later weighed against the cost of these activities.

Campaign Message

Up to this point, we have discussed the goals of the PR campaign and the high-level content that should be covered, such as a holistic view of the company and the transformation effort. We've talked about the importance of developing a message that embodies the transformation effort, but exactly what should this message cover? A thorough PR campaign should include the following aspects:

- Explanation of the transformation

- Key findings

- Key recommendations

- New organization

- Expression of confidence

Even more important than the content itself, the campaign should integrate these aspects into an overall message that is coherent. Hence, these aspects should all be tied to and aligned with the new strategy of the organization.

Explanation of the Transformation

Before the transformation leader jumps into what has happened in the past three months, he or she should first explain the background of the transformation effort, illustrate why the transformation was necessary, and give an overview of what the transformation team experienced during the 90 days of the effort. What made this transformation different from other turnarounds the organization has tried, if any? Why is this effort going to be successful and effective?

Key Findings

Before the transformation leader moves on, he should explain the new corporate vision that resulted from the transformation effort. This should be the motivational vision, not the strategic vision, which will be shared later.

After this, he can describe and explain the key findings from the diagnosis phase of the transformation. What were the key pain points identified by the teams? What was particularly surprising or enlightening? What were the core issues plaguing the company? The transformation leader can take this opportunity to highlight and distinguish between the symptoms and the root causes.

This information may be the most difficult for the transformation leader to share, and may even seem counterintuitive, given the organization's goals of building a new image and brand and restoring the public's faith. However, being honest about the company's weaknesses helps restore the public's faith, given that the company plans to fix the problems. Masking the problems and covering up the issues will only increase suspicion about the problems the company is facing and breed distrust among external customers and investors. In talking about the issues honestly and openly, the transformation leader is creating a layer of transparency that is extremely comforting to the public.

While it is natural to want to show your good side, it is only fair to the company and investors to paint a balanced picture. Therefore, in addition to confronting the ailments of the organization, the transformation leader should also share with the public the strengths of the company. What aspects were going well, amid all the problems the company was facing? What strengths can the company leverage through the transformation and beyond? Why does this company have the potential to be the best in its industry?

Regardless of how the strengths and weaknesses are organized, the most important thing is to be open, honest, and up front in communicating the issues. If the organization can't muster the courage to face and attack its problems, what will make the public think it has the strength to fix things and improve its situation?

Key Recommendations

With the problems out on the table for everyone to analyze and assess, the next step is for the transformation leader to explain the steps the organization plans on taking to address them. Knowing the problems is useful only if you plan to fix them, and information is useful only if you need it and can apply it.

First, however, the company needs to explain the new strategy that will guide its direction into the future. Because this is the overarching goal and vision with which other aspects will be aligned, the transformation leader must explain it clearly and directly. To make sure that people understand the rationale behind the new strategy, he should also explain how the new strategy came to be and justify why it will be effective. Furthermore, the transformation leader should share the goals and target numbers of the transformation effort, as well as some high-level cascaded goals as necessary.

After the strategy is laid out, the recommendations will make more sense. In explaining the recommendations of the teams, the transformation leader should turn to a high-level view of the overall implementation plan (described later in this chapter) and some of the key big ideas developed in the previous phase, which can include new products and services or plans for an acquisition or a partnership. The objective recommendations should be made in conjunction with how the company's problems and how the organization will enure that implementation goes smoothly. How will the changes be sustained? Why were these recommendations chosen? What value do these products, services, or ideas add to the organization and its customers?

Laying out recommendations that represent a balance between the present and the future is important for creating a holistic view of the transformation. Cost-cutting efforts can be shocking and demoralizing, especially if they include layoffs. However, recommendations that address the present state of the company need to be counterbalanced with decisions that affect the future growth opportunities of the company, such as investment in research and development. Furthermore, since the company underwent an all-encompassing transformation, the recommendations shared should reflect the various functions, though they can be weighted toward certain functions as necessary.

This is the opportunity to give the public a holistic view of the transformation effort and the recommendations that were developed. The transformation leader should make sure that this view does the effort and the organization justice.

New Organization

The transformation leader may also choose to announce the new organization, developed in phase 2, in the PR campaign. Of course, only the most major changes should be mentioned, such as a new structure or the movement of high-level executives. For example, Nissan's external PR campaign explained that the transformation team consolidated senior executive positions that were redundant in the global structure.[3] Those changes especially relevant to the new strategy, such as centralization or decentralization, should be explained and justified.

Expression of Confidence

The transformation leader should take some active steps to restore the public's confidence. Why should the public believe you? He can do this by explaining again why the effort will be successful and how changes will be sustained. He can demonstrate that he has a stake in the company and is truly invested in its growth. He can give some examples of early wins and use actions and results to demonstrate the progress the company has already made. And in some cases, he may even make bold claims and dramatic ultimatums (see "Ghosn's Ultimatum at Nissan").

GHOSN'S ULTIMATUM AT NISSAN

On October 18, 1999, Carlos Ghosn stepped up to the podium to unveil the Nissan Revival Plan, to which many employees had dedicated their time and hard work for three full months. This long-awaited public announcement summarized the implementation plan as having three main goals for Nissan: (1) return to profitability in fiscal year 2000, (2) reach a profit margin in excess of 4.5 percent of sales by fiscal year 2002, and (3) have a 50 percent reduction in the current level of debt by 2002. While these announcements weren't surprising to his employees and staff, his next statement shocked the organization: Ghosn announced that he and his executive committee would all resign if any one of the goals mentioned was not met within the time frame at the declared level. Surprisingly, he declared this bold ultimatum without consulting even his executive staff. However, Ghosn's commitment to Nissan's transformation effort and his determination helped rebuild the public's confidence in the company and demonstrated Nissan's new performance culture and increased accountability.[4]

Communication Media

Most external PR campaigns are launched with a heavily publicized presentation by the transformation leader. However, the campaign can also be communicated through various media, including externally focused road shows, press releases, meetings, advertisements in business publications, and media appearances.

In communicating the new message, you should keep the audience in mind. In particular, the public may not speak the same language as employees, especially regarding terminologies, processes, tools, and strategies. Hence, when an external message is crafted, the language used should be understood by customers, investors, and the general public alike. Simplicity and clarity are a must.

Furthermore, the communication medium should also be tailored for the audience. For example, if the customer base and audience are both extremely tech-savvy groups, it may make sense for the organization to use blogs and online ads. While an organization can spend an exorbitant amount of money on the communication medium, the key is to find the most effective ways to reach the relevant people. Just as in advertising, tailored messages are more effective than a message targeted at the masses. It would be impractical to try to reach everybody, so the organization should instead try to reach just the right people.

This external PR campaign should not be considered a one-time campaign (see "Rebranding Apple"). Although the initial presentation is critical in communicating the main message and getting support and buy-in from

REBRANDING APPLE

When Steve Jobs joined Apple in 1997, he identified one of Apple's key underutilized assets to be its brand. To this end, Jobs sought to strengthen its brand through a rebranding campaign that conveyed important aspects of the company's transformation. In late 1997, Apple launched its "Think Different" campaign with a television commercial, followed by print, television, poster, billboard, and wall sign advertisements for the various Apple products. In this campaign, Apple used a number of different communication media to clean and reinvigorate its tarnished brand and stress its emphasis on fostering creativity.

external customers and investors, an external PR campaign is actually a series of communications through different media, and it continues well beyond the 91st day. For example, white papers are an important means of communicating the overarching message and overall transformation implementation plan, and they can be released on the company Web site on the 91st day along with the launching of the external PR campaign. While these later stages of communication are difficult to plan at this point, the company and the transformation leader should be prepared for these future campaign efforts, as they will take up company time and resources.

The transformation leader should be ready for public scrutiny and skepticism at the main presentation and in subsequent interviews with the media. After all, the goal of the transformation effort was to improve performance, and the organization had most likely promised on a number of plans previously but never delivered. This skepticism may last for some time, and the transformation leader must be prepared to manage it. According to Banca Intesa's transformation leader, Corrado Passera, "You shouldn't expect people's mind to change until you have some facts to persuade them . . . which will . . . demonstrate that you are delivering on your promises."[5] The key is patience, for the public generally has to "see to believe."

DEVELOP AND APPROVE THE BUSINESS PLANS

Rapid response teams that have big ideas or recommendations involving entering new markets or developing new products need to develop a business plan to assess the feasibility of these ideas (see figure 6-3). A single business plan should be written for each big idea—therefore, the plan should be portfoliocentric rather than productcentric.

The business plan plays the important role of providing a built-in check on the proposed solution by forcing the team to think critically about its recommendation and hence challenging the feasibility and desirability of the plan. An idea that cannot pass this business plan approval checkpoint sends

FIGURE 6-3

Develop and approve business plans

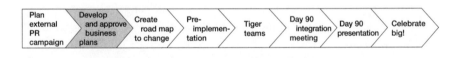

up a red flag and signals to the team that something is not right, either with its solution or its approach to the solution. The recommendation cannot continue until the business plan is approved.

Furthermore, in this stage, a solid business plan is important in getting funding for the project. A business plan that makes a strong case for the project's existence is more likely to have priority and receive the necessary funding to carry out the project. Poorly written business plans put teams back on the drawing board and force them to rethink the solution and finances for the project. A strong business plan therefore justifies investment in the project, and places the solution farther down the pipeline and clearly explain the value added.

Because a business plan is based on a big idea for creating new products, entering new markets, engaging in an acquisition, and the like, it is based on a megatrend that the company has identified. Looked at from a different perspective, this megatrend is the justification for this particular business plan. For example, a telecommunications company may want to acquire an Internet company because the Internet is the thing of the future and can add to the telecommunications offerings. The business plan and the big ideas therefore hinge on a conviction about the megatrends. The company should be convinced about the megatrends before creating a business plan.

Business Plan Defined

A business plan is, at the most generic level, a written plan detailing what the company or project plans on accomplishing and how it plans accomplishing these things. Therefore, it's a road map of the project and communicates not only where the project or business is planning on going, but also how it expects to get there. In that sense, it resembles the strategic vision, but a business plan is in fact more specific and details important aspects of carrying out the projects and solutions.

While there are many different perspectives on the ideal scope of a business plan, all business plans will answer the same core questions (see "Typical Questions Answered by Business Plans"). In the next section, we will describe the actual sections of a business plan in further depth.

Developing the Business Plan

Because the business plan is critical in critiquing and prioritizing projects, all business plans developed by the cross-functional teams should follow a

TYPICAL QUESTIONS ANSWERED BY BUSINESS PLANS

What? What is the problem? What is the solution or plan, and how does this solve the problem? What is the objective of the project? What results do we desire from the project? What can it add to the company? What are the risks and uncertainties of this solution?

Why? Why is this plan necessary? Why is it the best possible solution? Why should dedicate resources to this project? Why should we absorb the risks involved in undertaking this project?

When? When will this solution be implemented? How long will it take to implement it? What is the time scope of the project? How long will it take before we break even?

Who? Who is our target for the project? Who is our market? Who are our customers? Who are our competitors? Who will be in charge or carrying out the plan? Who will manage or oversee the project? How many people do we need to involve? Who will play the supporting role?

How? How will we achieve our objective and implement the solution? How will we finance the project? How will the project be managed? (Note: This "how" is a high-level how in terms of actual implementation—details should be saved for implementation plan.)

standardized format in order to allow for comparison between projects. To that end, the EMT should develop a business plan template for the teams, similar to the way the EMT developed a template for slides for the integration meetings. This template is simply a framework around which teams construct and explain their project. Importantly, teams should know that sections can be expanded or even cut, depending on the solution. Despite these alterations, however, the basic format of the business plan should remain the same. On the flip side, these basic elements are not comprehensive, and other sections should be added as necessary. (See "Business Plan in a Nutshell" for typical elements of a business plan.)

Business plans should typically be kept to twenty pages or less, and the quality of the content is significantly more important than the number of pages. In fact, for the sake of time and efficiency, the EMT should limit the

BUSINESS PLAN IN A NUTSHELL

- Executive summary (a summary of the entire business plan, highlighting key parts of the plan; written after all other parts are completed, and limited to two pages)

- Problem/opportunity description

- Product definition/architecture

- Market segmentation and size, and market forecast

- Selling channels/sales plan

- Product development plan/operations plan

- Financial operations/profit and loss/business model

- Risks/mitigation

- Fund-raising plan, expected ROI, capital structure

Note: A business plan written for an acquisition will differ from these sections. It must include analyses such as how the acquisition fits with the company's existing strategy (that is, whether it will bring new customers, technology, capabilities, expertise), plans for integrating the two companies (culturally, strategically, logistically, and so on), how a return on investment will be generated, and what the company plans to do with the new employees.

length of the business plan to ensure that the teams are not tempted to fill the pages with fluff.

Because of the cross-functional nature of the business plan, writing and developing it often requires collaboration across the rapid response teams, especially since a critical success factor of transformations is that they are integrative. Even with the involvement of more than one team, the development of each business plan should be owned by a single driving team. Collaboration across the teams is, in essence, more of a consultation than an equal collaboration. The main team becomes the central hub, seeking input and advice from other groups while holding the ultimate decision-making power.

The collaboration among teams should be organized, arranged, and managed by the PMO. Remember, the PMO coordinates all the efforts of the numerous rapid response teams and keeps track of their logistical aspects (refer to chapter 3; Program Management Office). In this instance, the PMO should organize and arrange meetings across teams, as well as coordinate deadlines and timelines.

Business Plan Approval Process

The business plan development and approval process is iterative. A good business plan demonstrates a solid understanding of the market, customer, financial model, risks, and resources necessary for a successful implementation. Since approval is a prerequisite for implementation, business plans that are not approved must be modified iteratively until they are approved, though teams should be given a limited amount of time until the business plan needs to be resubmitted to encourage productive dialogue and discussion.

Just as the EMT and the transformation leader are responsible for making key decisions in the transformation effort, they are also in charge of reviewing and approving the business plans. Additionally, the EMT and the transformation leader have to prioritize these key projects and allocate resources appropriately. (See "Typical Criteria Used for Prioritization" for some common aspects considered in the prioritization decisions.) Ironically, perhaps the most important aspect of prioritizing is not the criteria but the discussion that is generated and the subsequent knowledge shared as part of the review process. In the discussion about prioritizing the projects, the

---

TYPICAL CRITERIA USED FOR PRIORITIZATION

- Feasibility

- Forecasted profit (immediate and long-term)

- Necessary investment and available resources

- Risk analysis—size and means of mitigation

- Fit with existing business or strategic model

- Implementation schedule

- Market readiness

- How the recommendation addresses customer needs

EMT and the transformation leader are able to critically think about the project, the value the project adds to both the transformation and the company, as well as how well it fits with the other initiatives.

Additionally, although the EMT is critical in the review process, the transformation leader has the ultimate decision-making power. In prioritizing business plans and projects, the EMT and the transformation leader should develop their own rankings for criteria to consider. However, it is important to focus on the customer in critiquing these business plans—any decision that is made should address the customer's needs and desires.

CREATE THE ROAD MAP TO CHANGE

The road map to change, commonly referred to as the implementation plan, is the single most important deliverable of this phase (see figure 6-4). Without a solid, detailed, and thorough road map to change, the implementation phase will surely encounter many otherwise avoidable problems. The key to the implementation plan is the answers to all the questions involving the hows of implementation. Required for every solution addressing each big idea, the implementation plan answers the following key questions: *Who* is going to do *what*, and by *when*? *How*? The implementation plan carefully lays out the path that must be taken, step by step, to turn the solution into reality. Furthermore, the implementation plan should include milestones, performance targets, and goals that will allow the teams and the organization as a whole to celebrate often and keep morale up. Details are extremely important in the implementation plan because this is the document people are going to adhere to in execution. According to Nissan's transformation leader, Carlos Ghosn, "You need to devise a plan with quality and depth—one that's detailed enough to execute…when it's time for action."[6] In spite of the importance of having a detailed plan, however, people must recognize that the road map to change is a living document that should be constantly scrutinized, adjusted, and changed as a result of the progress of the project.

FIGURE 6-4

Create road map to change

Collaboration to Create a Road Map to Change

The implementation plan is the next logical step after the approval of a business plan. Now that the EMT and the transformation leader have approved entering the particular market or developing the specific product, given the forecasts and cost estimates argued in the business plan, the question of how must be answered in depth according to the strategy outlined in the business plan.

On the other hand, the road map to change should not be limited to solutions that require business plans, such as entering a new market or developing a new product. Instead, implementation plans must be developed for every solution addressing each big idea. For example, even cost-cutting initiatives require an implementation plan that details exactly how much should be cut as well as where, when, and how.

Regardless of whether the implementation plan follows the approval of a business plan or not, creation of each road map to change often necessitates collaboration across rapid response teams. This is similar to collaboration for creation of business plans and should be directed by the PMO. The PMO should not only coordinate meetings between groups and arrange for collaboration but work with the EMT to ensure that the teams are all aligning their goals with one another's and toward the big idea. As with the collaborative effort involved in writing the business plan, one central team is still in charge of making the key decisions and combining all the input from the various rapid response teams. Timing and appropriate allocation of resources to these requests and projects is critical, given the increased complexity and interconnectedness of the team network.

Developing the Elements of the Road Map to Change

There are many elements of a road map to change—not only should it answer the questions about the details of implementation, it should also include sections explaining the goals and nongoals of the solution, the resources required, and anticipated problems or complications with implementation. Figure 6-5 highlights the key elements of a road map to change. We will discuss each of these elements later in the chapter.

The coaches can add significant value in the development of the implementation plans by asking the right questions. Sometimes, the teams overlook critical elements in their development of the plan. When the coach notices this, he should step in and guide the team in thinking about the right

FIGURE 6-5

Key elements of road map to change

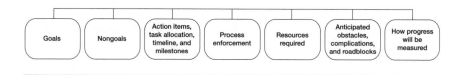

questions and coming up with answers that will lead to a more solid and useful road map. For example, for each task, the coach should make sure that the team knows who has ownership and how that person will ensure that the task gets completed. Although these are often questions the team members should think of on their own by now, the coach must be on his toes and catch gaps and flaws in the implementation plan. While he should not dictate the process or the answers, the coach's role in this is to oversee the process and make sure that the team is thinking critically about implementation.

Goals

By now, the teams should be familiar with the use of goals and cascading goals. In the implementation plan, each solution (regardless of the number of teams involved in developing the solution) should keep in mind not only corporate but also functional cascaded goals, in addition to the big ideas.

At this point, each particular implementation plan should include a new subset of goals whose aim is to achieve the functional goals. In essence, the goals used in the road map to change are one level deeper than the functional goals. As mentioned in the previous chapter, these goals are cascading goals that have cascaded down from the top level and broken down along the way to ensure manageability and alignment across the organization. People who read the implementation plan should have a more manageable set of goals than people who look at simply the team goals, yet by achieving the implementation plan goals, the employees are indirectly supporting the team goals (see "Waves of Change at Telefónica de España").

Nongoals

A list of nongoals is also an important element in the implementation plan. Although the term *nongoal* may sound paradoxical, nongoals clarify the direction and set the foundation for the final leg of the transformation. Nongoals are, essentially, things people should not be doing or options they should

WAVES OF CHANGE AT TELEFÓNICA DE ESPAÑA

At Telefónica de España, the transformation was broken down into year-long "waves," which were created by the executive team to meet the goals and priorities for that particular year. The waves could be decomposed into three or four large "blocks" of work, which were domains that together would build up to the transformational goals and performance for that year. These blocks of work represented the functional cascaded goals and were further decomposed into smaller projects, which together built up to that particular block.

According to Julio Linares, the transformation leader of Telefónica de España, "We discovered that this approach is a useful communication device: it helped people understand how the project they were working on would contribute to that year's targets and, therefore, to the overall transformation program."[7]

not be considering. Hence, a list of nongoals is a "not-do" list. These nongoals keep the rapid response teams focused and on track by preventing alternate distracting options from being discussed again after they have already been dismissed (see "The 'Not-Do' List at Procter & Gamble"). Especially when teams are coordinating and there are slight conflicts and disagreements regarding decisions, it is critical that members not look back on past options or dwell on decisions that have already been made. Rather, the better use of everyone's time is to focus on the chosen solution and to make sure that the particular choice is implemented as flawlessly as possible.

Action Items, Task Allocation, Timeline, and Milestones

This section is the heart of the road map to change. Here, not only are specific action items laid out and delegated to individuals and single owners, but so are deadlines and timelines as well as the expected duration of each task. Within the implementation plan, tasks must be specified in great detail to facilitate a smooth implementation. By reading the implementation plan, everyone should be extremely clear as to what their role is, in addition to when and how to approach the task. However, the team must also be prepared to accept that this section of the implementation plan is subject to the most change from unexpected obstacles. Because of the frequent changes, milestones are also important to note in the timeline of the implementation

THE "NOT-DO" LIST AT PROCTER & GAMBLE

At Procter & Gamble, CEO and transformation leader Alan G. Lafley recognized that in order to keep his teams focused and on track, he needed to develop a list of things team members were not to do. On this list were other options that the teams had previously considered as potential solutions but ultimately dismissed. However, Lafley's experience had shown him that these extraneous options often reappear in discussion even after another solution has already been chosen. Therefore, as he did when the corporate innovation programs were chosen, Lafley had his teams put on the not-do list these tempting options as well as other tasks that did not contribute to the chosen solution. When people were caught doing things from this not-do list, Lafley and his team would bring in both the people and the budget to refocus them on the "to-do" list.[8]

plan, for they provide an opportunity to recognize the progress made by individuals and teams. Importantly, milestones enable celebrations of this progress, which helps keep morale up.

Process Enforcement

It's one thing for people to know who owns what task, but it's another for those individuals to know how to enforce compliance and carry out the task. In developing the implementation plan, even without explicitly writing it down, the team must discuss how the owners are going to make sure that their task gets completed in time, and what will happen if it doesn't.

Furthermore, the team has to decide how it can enforce the new culture or processes throughout the company. How can they make sure the employees will follow the new rules and processes? While it's normal for people to naturally fall back into their familiar routine and process, the new processes need to be enforced for the effort to be successful (see "Process Enforcement at an Engineering Company").

Resources Required

An implementation plan must be clear and explicit about the requirements necessary for successful implementation and execution of the particular solution. The required resources considered should be not only monetary

PROCESS ENFORCEMENT AT AN ENGINEERING COMPANY

Through a series of discussions at an engineering company, the rapid response teams finally decided on using its program managers to enforce the processes throughout the organization.

To monitor process compliance, the program managers had to sign off at gates and on documents, as well as capture all the process gates and document sign-off requirements in the project plan. In instances of violation, after a certain grace period, the program managers had to report the violations first to the functional managers, who would then take corrective action. If corrective action was not taken or the violations were repeated, the program managers had to escalate the violations to the functional vice president. Through these clear stipulations, implementation and enforcement of the new processes were greatly facilitated.

resources but limitations on time and human capital. For example, if a company needs to hire new people, those employees should be considered in the required resources not only in financial terms (their salary) but also in the time and human capital required to adequately train them for their jobs. As such, training plans should be incorporated into the implementation plan as necessary. An appropriate estimate of the required resources is critical for prioritizing and integration.

Anticipating Complications, Obstacles, and Roadblocks

The detailed implementation plan should also anticipate complications and special requirements such as rollout and the detailed logistics behind the rollout plan. However, not only should these complications and roadblocks be anticipated, they should also be discussed and potential ways to address them should be brainstormed. Successful anticipation can also play an important role in preventing these complications from manifesting themselves. Implementation and execution are facilitated when these roadblocks are accurately predicted and addressed.

How Progress Will Be Measured

While many projects use milestones to measure progress, the implementation plan should detail how progress for this particular project will be measured. For example, does it depend on qualitative factors such as customer or employee satisfaction? Does it depend on revenue increase? How will the organization measure these factors? Will it conduct a survey? The team must identify how progress will be measured in order to set the expectations for the organization and set the ground rules for how implementation will work.

Integration of the Road Maps to Change

Not only does the PMO guide the collaborative development effort for each road map to change, it is also in charge of integrating the different road maps to change to create an overall big-picture transformation implementation plan. Again, this integration is critical for the success of the transformation effort. The PMO manages all logistical aspects of the implementation plans, from ensuring consistency among implementation plans submitted from different teams or networks of teams, to the use of templates, to planning the timing for implementation plans so that different plans that might constrain the same resources or send mixed messages to employees are not rolled out at the same time (see "Lack of Rollout Coordination at Best Buy"). Also, for solutions that are similar or complementary, integration of plans is critical to prevent duplicated effort and to maximize impact. Ultimately, the EMT and the transformation leader must sign off on each team's implementation plan as well as the integrated transformation implementation plan submitted by the PMO. Ideally, both team and integrated plans will be approved before the day 90 integration meeting, but in reality, problems often arise and delay the approval process.

LACK OF ROLLOUT COORDINATION AT BEST BUY

In its first transformation attempt, Best Buy launched a Standard Operating Platform (SOP) to be implemented across all stores. However, the numerous initiatives of the platform were not well integrated. As noted by a general manager from Houston, three major initiatives had rolled out at the same time without any consideration of timing or how the initiatives interacted with or affected each other. This simultaneous implementation of the three initiatives was extremely taxing on the store management and staff. As a result of the lack of coordination and prioritization among the initiatives, implementation of all three initiatives failed.[9]

Furthermore, in signing off on the integrated implementation plan, the EMT and the transformation leader are also responsible for prioritizing projects and allocating resources. Prioritization of projects should be carried out similarly to prioritization of the business plan. Resource allocation should mirror project prioritization—that is, projects high on the list should be the first to get their necessary resources. The EMT and the transformation leader, however, may want to consult the CFO for budgeting, as well as the CEO if he is not part of the EMT.

In order to coordinate and integrate the road maps to change, the PMO should host a meeting with all the project managers to ensure that project deadlines and implicit messages do not conflict with each other. In a meeting between relevant team leaders, project managers, and the PMO, the numerous project plans are combined into a coherent and logical integrated implementation plan.

Road Maps to Change in Practice

Now that you know how implementation plans work, how do you put everything together in practice? We will give you an example from the Nissan Revival Plan, developed through recommendations from the rapid response teams.[10]

The Nissan Revival Plan finalized by Ghosn was extremely precise and detailed. In relation to other performance goals and deadlines, the plan was very factual and quantified, to the point that there was no room for interpretation or even choice. In communicating the plan, Ghosn made the goals that would raise the quality level clear. The implementation plan was extremely detailed, with clear timetables and deadlines, and groups assigned to certain work. Furthermore, when the plan was articulated, it was also divided into clear sequences with milestones people could follow. Importantly, while the goals and the timetable for reaching these goals were nonnegotiable, the execution plan was. This gave employees the flexibility to adjust the implementation plan according to changes in the situation or when unexpected obstacles arose.

Nongoals were also evident in the Nissan Revival Plan, since Ghosn communicated to the company that discussion was to end once a decision had been made, and only slight adjustments (not substantial changes) could be made afterward. This indirect communication of nongoals focused the organization on moving forward in the effort and not turning back to rehash past decisions.

To make sure the implementation went smoothly and that employees implementing the road map to change were dedicated to the effort, Ghosn gave employees who disagreed with the implementation plan, whether about goals or tasks, the option of leaving the company.

PREIMPLEMENTATION

As this is the phase preceding the implementation phase, the rapid response teams should plant the seeds for a successful implementation beyond the creation of a detailed road map to change. Although these are items that should have been carried out throughout the transformation effort, it is especially important that deliberate steps be taken now to actively prepare the organization for implementation (see figure 6-6).

Rapid response team members, for example, should be promoting the transformation and setting the stage for implementation in their daily job function, with their regular teams. At this point, their job is to get buy-in from those around them, which can be accomplished through informal discussion and dialogue. Team members need to give people a heads-up about what's coming so people aren't completely in shock when the transformation leader makes his announcement. At the same time, however, team members must do this without sharing any confidential information. The implementation plans themselves, for both individual teams and the overall effort, should be kept private until the transformation leader makes his day 90 presentation. For the same reasons you wouldn't want parts of the recommendation leaking out to the public, you don't want that information to leak out internally. Rather, team members should focus on emphasizing continuous improvement, even amid the transformation effort. In this setting, continuous improvement is not synonymous with incremental improvement.

TIGER TEAMS

Throughout this phase, the tiger teams that have recently been created are working frantically to play catch-up, for they have to diagnose the situation

FIGURE 6-6

Preimplementation

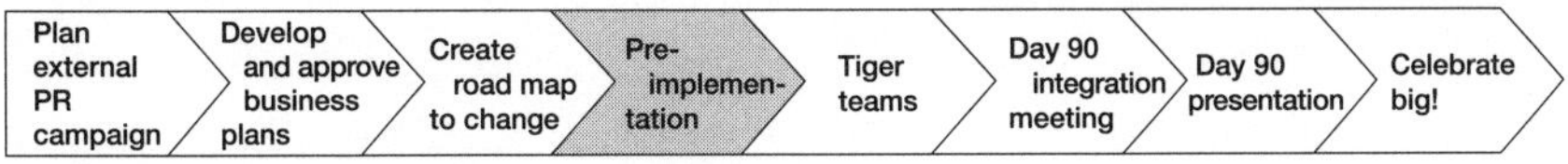

Tiger teams

| Plan external PR campaign | Develop and approve business plans | Create road map to change | Pre-implemen-tation | Tiger teams | Day 90 integration meeting | Day 90 presentation | Celebrate big! |

in their relevant area *and* develop recommendations by the day 90 integration meeting. Luckily, the scope of the teams is less than the typical rapid response team because the key areas should have already been covered and attacked by the original teams. The tiger teams are also typically more specific than the original rapid response teams because they're covering a particular area that was overlooked by the other teams. Furthermore, the work of tiger teams is facilitated because these teams can leverage off the work that has been done for the transformation effort thus far (see figure 6-7).

In this phase, tiger teams should have diagnosed their particular domain or task and developed a solution. While their recommendations will most likely not necessitate a business plan, the tiger team does need to create an implementation plan, with individual owners and a timeline. To ensure that the tiger teams can complete their tasks in a timely manner, the EMT should work very closely with them and make sure that all obstacles are removed immediately. By the end of this phase, the tiger teams should have a set of recommendations that are ready to be implemented. They will present with the other teams at the day 90 integration meeting, though only the content that is relevant to their analysis.

DAY 90 INTEGRATION MEETING

The day 90 integration meeting is the culmination of all of the work dedicated to the transformation effort and is where the final business plans are presented (see figure 6-8). However, the day 90 integration meeting should be run no differently from the other integration meetings. Each rapid response team is expected to present, and other teams and the EMT can then ask questions and challenge the recommendations. Just as the EMT had to give the big ideas the green light after the day 60 meeting before teams could move forward with that idea, the EMT must here give the road maps to change the green light before they can progress.

FIGURE 6-8

Day 90 integration meeting

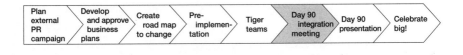

Each team should present the following:

- A recap of the issues found.

- Proposed solutions and recommendations (the business plans and/or road maps to change). In this section, teams can detail a specific project failure this solution will resolve.

- Progress to date.

- Any remaining actions (left over from the 90 days transformation) and their owner

- Prioritized list of processes to be implemented in the coming months.

- How the team ensures successful implementation.

- How progress will be measured.

- Planned timeline (similar to those in road maps to change, but this one should integrate across projects).

Ideally, all the loose ends should be tied up by the end of the day 90 integration meeting. Most business plans should have been approved by the time the meeting occurs, though the day 90 meeting is when teams officially get the green light on their projects from the EMT. The EMT also gives either yellow or red lights, as in the day 60 integration meeting. Business plans given the yellow light should go through another iteration, while projects given the red light can't be justified and should be stopped. Projects undergoing another iteration will hence get their final approval after the day 90 integration meeting.

For the projects that have gotten the green light, prioritization happens immediately after the day 90 integration meeting, and resources are allocated appropriately according to their implementation plan. With resource allocation, a buffer should be agreed on between the project owner and the EMT.

This means that a certain amount of leeway is given in terms of resources before the EMT has to make further approvals.

This day 90 meeting is also when the reorganization is first officially announced internally to those directly involved in the transformation. The reorganization is formally announced internally to the entire company in the day 90 presentation and publicly announced externally on the 91st day in the external PR campaign. Officially, handoff does not occur until the 91st day.

Announce the Reorganization

Throughout the first 60 days, the EMT and the organizational excellence team have been deliberating the reorganization of the company. Sometimes the reorganization can be as simple as moving key people around to increase their impact on the organization. Other times, reorganization requires restructuring the entire company and putting key employees in places they wouldn't have previously imagined. Regardless of the level of reorganization within the company, however, the EMT and the organizational excellence team should have been thinking of the people they want to place in key leadership roles—the top two tiers. While discussion about role assignments should take place within the EMT, the transformation leader has the final say as to who goes where.

In this phase of the transformation, the reorganization, along with new positions and people assigned to key positions, is announced, though the actual handoff process has not yet begun. With the announcement of the new organization comes one on the new compensation plans and performance review process and criteria. Sometimes, more dramatic reorganization of the company is incorporated into the transformation effort. At VeriSign, for example, the entire structure of the organization had shifted from a functional focus to a segment focus, resulting in a 70 percent change in the top leadership. All the top leadership positions had been filled by either internal or external hires by this point in the effort, and the new positions were announced in the day 90 integration meeting.

The official reorganization announcement should be executed carefully, for the situation and the decisions are delicate, especially for those who are leaving the organization. The reorganization should hence be carefully planned, and all those involved in it should know about the plans before they are officially announced within the organization. People need to be eased out of their old jobs and into their new jobs as necessary. One of the most difficult aspects of reorganization is ensuring that learning is transferred across the organization. Furthermore, the new hires and the people in new positions in the new organization should buy in to the transformation and understand the implementation plan.

DAY 90 PRESENTATION

The day 90 presentation is an internal companywide presentation hosted by the transformation leader. Though there are many ways to hold and communicate this presentation, the goal is to inform employees throughout the organization about the transformation effort, key findings, and next steps (see "Ghosn's Announcement of the Nissan Revival Plan"). After the day 90 integration meeting, the day 90 presentation is an official summary and explanation of the transformation effort to all employees (see figure 6-9). It is an opportunity to get the entire organization caught up on the work and recommendations from the transformation. Because all employees within the organization should speak the same language, the message may seem cryptic to outsiders. Therefore, as in all communication, the transformation leader should remember the importance of simplicity in developing an effective message. Honest communication about the company's problems is just as important in the internal PR campaign as it is in the external campaign. As a precursor to the

GHOSN'S ANNOUNCEMENT OF THE NISSAN REVIVAL PLAN

When Ghosn announced the Nissan Revival Plan in 1999, he made sure to communicate directly to the people—his presentation was given to the entire company by way of a video hookup. Through this effort, employees were introduced to the new vision for and direction of Nissan, for this was the first time in Nissan's history that the president spoke directly to everyone in the organization. Ghosn continued to communicate his plan in subsequent visits to company sites, constantly talking to employees at all levels in small groups.[11]

In this presentation, the transformation leader formally announces the reorganization again, though this time to the entire organization. Additionally, a major goal of the day 90 presentation is to share the new direction for the company with employees and reinvigorate them in support of this new direction.

FIGURE 6-9

Day 90 presentation

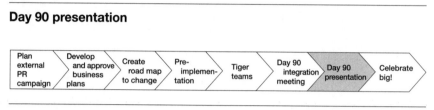

external PR campaign, however, the day 90 presentation should express goals higher than those announced externally, as mentioned earlier.

CELEBRATE BIG!

Having put forth all the hard work in this phase and developed implementation and reorganization plans as well as a public relations campaign, the transformation team members should feel appreciated for their time and effort and recognized for their accomplishments. After the day 90 integration meeting marking the end of the official transformation planning (the 90 days effort), the organization should therefore host a major celebration marking the beginning of a better future (see figure 6-10). Such a celebration not only symbolizes a new beginning but also serves to boost morale and renew the energy of employees.

This celebration can take the form of a retreat, allowing employees to relax and mentally and emotionally prepare themselves for the next step of the transformation, the implementation phase. It can also simply be an on-site celebration where employees get to talk to one another about anything.

All participants involved in the effort should be recognized for their hard work and accomplishments in front of the entire organization. For example, Bay Networks' transformation leader, Dave House, had individual teams stand up in front of everyone in recognition of their efforts and dedication. At the

FIGURE 6-10

Celebrate big!

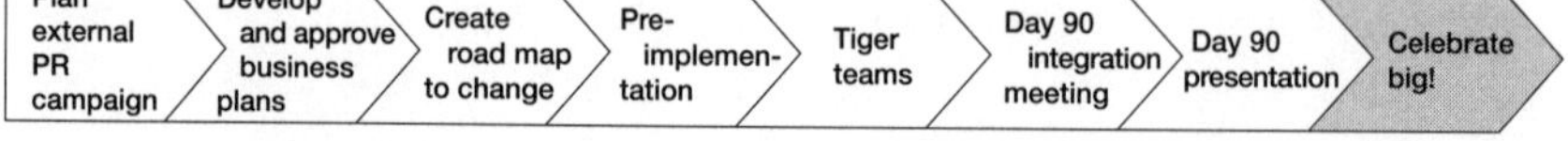

VERISIGN'S CELEBRATION

After the day 90 integration meeting, VeriSign made sure to recognize and highlight the role and importance of key leaders of the transformation effort at the major celebration. Each key participant was called up to the front of the group and personally thanked for his unique contribution to the effort. This personal expression of gratitude not only validates the employees' work, but it also motivates them to continue with their efforts because they know that they are being recognized for it.

Additionally, the celebration was an opportunity to informally discuss the key lessons participants learned during the transformation effort, as well as to get feedback about the progression of the transformation. In the discussion, participants expressed their astonishment at how much they had learned and accomplished, and the general consensus was that the transformation effort had been a wonderful and worthwhile experience. In particular, participants noted the sense of urgency that helped them think outside the box. Also notable was the participants' recognition of the important role teamwork and unity played in the transformation effort. As one employee noted, "If we are all united, there is no limit on where we can go." The cross-functional rapid response teams were a common topic of discussion. In their feedback, employees expressed the importance of the informal networks and cross-boundary communication. Furthermore, many members had originally thought that it would be impossible to go beyond functions and work with each other to solve problems on a level playing field, but gained a deep appreciation for the process by the end of their experience.

same time, however, key leaders playing particularly significant roles should especially be noted and thanked for their part in the effort.

In addition to providing special recognition, the celebration gives those involved in the transformation a chance to debrief and reflect on their efforts. In this discussion, the EMT and the transformation leader can not only get feedback from participants about the transformation but also assess the value added to employees as a result of the effort (see "VeriSign's Celebration"). It is important that people can talk about and analyze lessons they've learned from the transformation effort, even in an informal setting. Through the celebration in general and discussion in particular, participants involved in the effort can finally take the time to see how much they've grown and developed in just three months.

Despite the importance of a spirit of celebration at the end of this phase, however, some organizations make the mistake of declaring victory too soon. The celebration is not a time to become complacent or declare an ultimate victory—rather, it is a chance to recognize the progress the organization has made to date while acknowledging the hard work necessary for successful implementation. Thus, the celebration on "day 90" does not necessarily mean that it must occur on the 90th day of the transformation; in some cases, it behooves the company to hold off on celebrating the effort until the transformation is in a state ready to move on to implementation.

As important as this celebration is to officially mark the end of the 90 days transformation effort and unofficially kick off the implementation phase, this should only be the first (albeit the largest) celebration of many to come. In fact, the organization should frequently celebrate meeting its performance targets to maintain momentum and keep morale high.

CONCLUSION

In phase 3, the rapid response teams expanded on the big ideas selected from phase 2. Through their efforts, they created a business plan and an implementation plan to pave the road for implementation. Without these documents, implementation would be a trailblazing effort, where the teams might get lost every once in a while and be forced to backtrack at other times.

In phase 3, the teams should tie up loose ends while planning and preparing for the implementation phase. The external PR campaign should be planned in this phase, and the new organizational structure should be officially announced internally. The final recommendations made and given the green light for implementation are critical in addressing the problems identified in phase 1 and in carrying the organization through its problems into a brighter future.

Day 90 officially symbolizes the end of the 90 days transformation, providing employees with a sense of closure. The celebrations serve as a brief hiatus from the transformation effort, which will be continued with implementation and execution on day 91. The 91st day opens a new door in the transformation effort—the transformation implementation phase. Starting from the 91st day, changes materialize throughout the organization as stipulated by the implementation plans.

7

Transformation Implementation

Execution

*Every man has power to carry out
that of which he is convinced.*

—Johann Wolfgang von Goethe

On completion of the 90 days transformation effort, the company stands ready to embark on the most critical phase of the transformation effort. This "transformation implementation" phase, also called the execution phase, typically lasts from six to twelve months. However, it should not be construed as a phase that begins on the 91st day. Rather, implementation starts earlier and has been taking place throughout the transformation effort in the form of early wins and low-hanging fruit. This phase is different from those previous phases in that the entire transformation team and the organization as a whole are dedicated fully to implementation and execution, whereas implementation earlier was part of the larger picture. Now, implementation becomes *the* picture. Of course, in certain plans and ideas, implementation begins in this phase, but on the whole, the transformation implementation phase is where momentum on implementation picks up. In this way, it capitalizes on the early wins of the company, and momentum does not need to be regenerated from scratch.

During this phase, the company executes the implementation plans developed during the previous phase. Over the past 90 days, employees from across the company have come together to diagnose the organization and to develop a plan to restore the company's health. A compelling high-level strategy and vision inspired the creation of a set of implementation plans. Although this vision was critical in mobilizing a strong and motivated team, the actual success of the transformation effort hinges on the ability of the company to translate these plans into real changes and results. Failing in the implementation phase is like training extensively for a track meet but then tripping on your shoelaces in the race. Implementation is ultimately what matters, because unless you can implement your plans to fix the organization, the solutions are simply pieces of paper. In its hands, the company now has the checks that can propel it into the future. If it doesn't cash or deposit them, the checks are useless.

Both Dave House of Bay Networks and Carlos Ghosn of Nissan expressed the importance of execution in driving results. "At Bay Networks," House said, "I was all about execution."[1] Although strategy was important to House, his ability to choose a course of action and to mobilize people toward achieving it was one of his greatest leadership qualities. Ghosn exhibited some of the same qualities and reiterated this point, saying, "Execution is 95 percent of the job. Strategy is only 5 percent."[2] In a transformation effort, implementation can be seen as a seamless transition between the following phases: unfreezing, making the changes, refreezing, and maintaining the changes. While we don't focus on these particular phases, keeping them in mind will give you an overall idea of where you currently are and give you some insight into what steps you may need to take for the future.

In this chapter, we will start by describing the 91st day: the day after the official conclusion of the 90 days transformation effort and marking the beginning of transformation implementation (see figure 7-1). On the 91st day, the public relations (PR) campaign is launched (assuming that the organization decided to design one), and organizational rollout begins. Rollout not only means that the top two layers of the organization begin their new jobs, it also means the official disassembly of the rapid response teams. On the 91st day, the process integration czar is also formally introduced to the transformation team.

FIGURE 7-1

Chapter overview

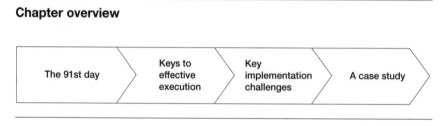

After our description of the 91st day, we will highlight several best-in-class execution practices, some that are more specific to a transformation effort than others. Effective execution is critical to successful implementation. Some keys to effective execution include maintaining momentum, creating a culture of accountability, and building a tool to measure and assess progress. After sharing these keys with you, we will move on and describe some of the more common barriers to implementation. These barriers, if anticipated and dealt with appropriately, will not have a significant impact on the implementation of your plans and ideas. With successful implementation, you plant the seeds of effective execution within your company so that it continues even beyond the transformation implementation phase.

THE 91ST DAY

Figuratively, the 91st day represents the beginning of the new organization and is when the ball really begins to pick up speed. It does not have to be exactly the 91st day of the transformation effort, but it is when the organization first takes its major, official steps into implementation (see figure 7-2). On this day, the external PR campaign is launched, organization rollout begins, and a process integration czar is introduced. Because it is important to get started on the right foot, the 91st day should not begin until the organization is ready.

Launching External Public Relations Campaign

In phase 3, the organization had to decide whether or not it wanted to launch an external PR campaign to tell the public about the changes the company is undergoing. Assuming that the organization decides to follow through with launching the external campaign, it has been going through different iterations of the campaign message throughout the last phase. Now, the transformation leader should finalize the message and the campaign should be launched.

FIGURE 7-2

The 91st day

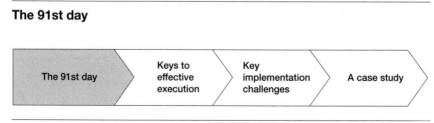

One of the most important results of the external PR campaign is its effect on the public's image of the company, for the transformation effort and the public's image of the company mutually affect each other. The transformation team shapes its public image through the PR campaign and by delivering on its promises. On the other hand, the public's image typically affects the transformation effort by influencing its momentum. According to Corrado Passera, the transformation leader of Banca Intesa, "[Your employees] will not believe you unless you can change the organization's image in the media."[3] Therefore, managing the relationship between a company and its customers, investors, and analysts is important in maintaining the momentum of the transformation.

Launching the external PR campaign may involve more than the transformation leader simply making a presentation. As mentioned in the previous chapter, there are many different means of communicating the campaign message, and often more than one have to be applied simultaneously (see "VeriSign's Public Relations Campaign"). While ideally the transformation leader himself should make the major presentations about the transformation, he may delegate certain presentations to a team for the sake of efficiency.

After the organization launches the campaign, however, the transformation team should not hold its breath and wish for a miracle. As mentioned earlier, the natural reaction from the public to such announcements and promises about the effort and the future of the company is usually skepticism. For example, Nissan's stock fell by 20 percent the day the Nissan Re-

VERISIGN'S PUBLIC RELATIONS CAMPAIGN

Immediately after the first 90 days, VeriSign launched an advertising PR campaign to communicate the new vision to its customers. By emphasizing its intent to deliver top products, the organization hoped to gain further client validation in its campaign.

The PR campaign was multipronged. First, VeriSign wrote and distributed two white papers that helped spread awareness of it new market-based strategy. VeriSign also advertised in business publications. Most importantly, Vernon Irvin went on road shows to the press, to clients, and to all industry and financial analysts, at which he educated the audience about VeriSign's offerings and value to the customer, all the while presenting VeriSign's future goals.

vival Plan was first announced.[4] Similarly, when investors became aware of the rapid changes being made at The Home Depot, they sent the stock price plummeting by 50 percent.[5]

As difficult as it sounds, don't let these negative initial reactions demoralize the transformation team and the organization. Instead, anticipate them and continue to strongly present why the new vision and corporate goals are both compelling and promising. Just as the transformation leader had to convince the company of the transformation effort and convert resisters into supporters, the business will have to slowly win and gain the confidence of the public. The opportunity is there if you seize it, because once the public starts being convinced of the success and impact of the transformation effort, its confidence can be leveraged to create even greater confidence among the general public.

While the public's conversion from resister to supporter is typically a natural, gradual process, there are some things you can do to accelerate the process. Because the public wants to see results, the organization should demonstrate that it can deliver on its promises. Namely, in its external campaign, the company should share the results of its early wins, especially the high-impact ones. In future press releases or presentations, the organization can continue to share the progress of the effort.

Another way to increase the public's confidence in the company is to maintain transparency. Over time, the organization should communicate its progress and provide updates in a predictable and timely fashion, and this can be done by various means, such as by regularly posting articles and press releases on its Web site. These updates should include the results, what's going well, what isn't going so well, and what actions the business is taking to mitigate those things that aren't going well. Investors and the public appreciate honesty, especially when it comes to information that people would naturally want to hide. Such honesty leads to improved credibility, which helps improve the company's image. By maintaining this transparency, the company can create an open and trusting relationship with its investors, analysts, and customers.

A layer of transparency, however, should be maintained not only with the public. Instead, it should also be maintained in internal communications within the company. While not all information needs to be available to everyone at all times, the right people should get the right information at the right time. This communication program should do exactly that. For example, the organization needs to communicate all major decisions internally and companywide (see "The Home Depot's 'HDTV'"), as well as communicate to employees where any information of interest can be found.

THE HOME DEPOT'S "HDTV"

At The Home Depot, Robert Nardelli created the company's own television program, called "HDTV" (Home Depot TV). Through this program, important information was "broadcast live to every store on a continuous basis." Furthermore, the company's live TV shows communicated weekly plans made by senior management to individual store managers.[6]

Organizational Rollout Begins

The second part of the 91st day is organizational rollout. Throughout phases 2 and 3, the organizational excellence team should have been working with the transformation leader to plan the new organization. At the end of phase 3, the new organization should have officially been announced to the transformation team and the organization at large. Even before this official announcement, however, relevant employees should have already been notified about the imminent changes, and appropriate action to facilitate a smooth handoff process should have been taken. On the 91st day, the employees, especially executives at the top two layers, are finally ready to step into their new positions, already understanding the roles and responsibilities associated with them.

Also happening on the 91st day, typically, is the disassembly of the rapid response teams. The teams are disbanded, and members return to the organization as missionaries of the transformation. The team members, especially pilots, typically return to positions of power so they can fully use their new skills and affect change effectively. As a result of organizational rollout, the right people should be in the right places to instigate and implement change. Let's first turn to the handoff process.

Handoff Process

On the 91st day, the top two layers of management start their new jobs. For those with positions that change, the old management engages in a handoff process, which aids the new managers in quickly becoming acclimated to their new positions. To ensure an adequate transfer of knowledge and expertise, the handoff process should be gradual and cooperative rather than abrupt and competitive. The two top layers of the organization should be replaced first to drive the proper changes from the top. These top two layers are partly responsible for the successful handoff and replacement of key managers and employees farther down in the organization. Throughout the rest of the implementation phase, the handoff process continues until the new organization is complete. Hence, the handoff trickles down throughout the organization, starting from the top.

The organizational handoff process should in no way interfere with the implementation phase of the transformation effort. Instead, putting the right people in the right positions should facilitate the implementation phase because these are the people with the right expertise and skill set to instill change in the organization. Hence, even though the positions and titles of some key players may change, they are still responsible for the tasks agreed on in the transformation implementation plan. In short, they are the same owners, just with a new job description.

In practice, the handoff process can have its challenges. In most cases, each position will have its unique job description and requirements and will require an individualized handoff strategy. Furthermore, different people have different methods of transferring expertise, and some people may be more resistant than others to changing positions in the organization. Each situation should be addressed individually, although open communication and an emphasis on the better future opportunities can facilitate the process.

Sometimes, the new organization will be drastically different from the previous organization, requiring much more coordination in the handoff process (see "Reorganization at ACI"). In these situations, the new organizational structure should be explained clearly to the entire organization, and new roles and the expectations of each role need to be especially clarified.

REORGANIZATION AT ACI

After a long series of discussions, the organization excellence team at ACI, along with the executive management team, decided to turn the organizational structure of ACI upside down and transform the company from one organized around business units to one organized around business functions. This new structure facilitated communication between business units, in addition to increasing efficiency and ensuring consistency in business processes. The organizational excellence team communicated its plan for this new organizational structure to the other cross-functional teams as they progressed in the transformation effort before solidifying it and communicating it to the rest of the organization.

For example, employees need to know exactly who to report to. In some instances, employees may resist the new organizational structure. To address these concerns, the transformation team and company leaders should explain the costs and inefficiencies of keeping the old structure and the benefits of adopting the new one. They should make it clear that the new structure is the result of extensive and intensive discussion and that they won't yield on the new structure.

There are instances, however, where a decision to restructure the organization has been made but the changes are not effective because of unanticipated factors. In these cases, the organization needs to recognize that the idea and plan did not materialize as expected, and the next step is to remedy the situation and find a more viable organizational structure. Changing the structure too often may not be beneficial to the organization, but sometimes these changes are necessary (see "Multiple Reorganizations at Hewlett-Packard").

Disassembling the Rapid Response Teams

At the end of the 90 days, the members of the rapid response teams should return to the new organization to serve as change agents. The organizational excellence team plays an important role in placing these members in positions where they can exert a higher level of responsibility and control.

The rapid response team members should be placed in positions of power and influence for a variety of reasons. First of all, the team members were initially chosen because of their leadership potential. Having been assessed, evaluated, and piloted throughout the transformation effort, these

MULTIPLE REORGANIZATIONS AT HEWLETT-PACKARD

At Hewlett-Packard (HP), transformation leader Carly Fiorina reorganized the organization into a "3-D" matrix cube, where each person had three bosses, one from each of three domains: region, business, and function. Although this ensured that each domain got important information, the new structure proved to be ineffective, inefficient, and difficult for decision making.

After her departure, the new transformation leader, Mark Hurd, acknowledged the ineffectiveness of the new organizational structure and changed it back to a "2-D" matrix. While these frequent organizational changes created turmoil in the company, reverting to a 2-D matrix was both beneficial and critical for the organization.

team members have proved themselves capable of leading the execution of their implementation plans. Even if the transformation leader had reservations at the beginning of the effort, these team members have acquired many skills applicable for execution throughout the process. Most importantly, these members should have demonstrated the discipline and dedication necessary for execution.

Furthermore, having been involved in developing the implementation plans, these members are in the most appropriate position to execute them. Not only does this decrease the risk of misinterpreting or misunderstanding the plan, it also ensures that the implementation has sufficient buy-in to be followed through in its entirety. They know the rationale behind the plans, as well as the owners and the timeline. At Nissan, for example, Ghosn involved over five hundred employees through the rapid response teams and subteams. Because these team members had played an important role in developing the implementation plans, buy-in was already achieved.

Disassembling the rapid response teams and reintegrating them into the new organization should be a smooth and seamless process. Members of rapid response teams carry with them the expertise gained from their engagement in the transformation effort and should share it with the new organization. Hence, reintegration should be a collaborative effort where knowledge is disseminated through all levels of the organization.

In some cases, former team members will replace incumbent managers and executives. Just as in the handoff process for the top two layers of the organization, a gradual handoff process is the most effective for middle and upper management. This was demonstrated at Nissan, where an entire generation of top managers was gradually eased out of power.[7] Even a drastic organizational overhaul can be smooth and seamless.

Introducing the Czar

One particularly important member of the transformation team is the new process integration czar, introduced on the 91st day. This person has been carefully selected from the transformation team and performs his czar duties on top of his daily job function and his other tasks for the transformation effort. Ideally, the process integration czar should be a senior vice president or above and should have a background in either quality or operations. Additionally, the process integration czar must be extremely detail oriented.

The role of the process integration czar is to ensure that implementation and key handoff nodes are of the highest quality (see "Disassembly and the Czar at VeriSign"). He is responsible for the quality of the entire transformation

DISASSEMBLY AND THE CZAR AT VERISIGN

At VeriSign, the rapid response teams were disassembled shortly after the day 90 integration meeting. However, the former team members had a vested interest in the implementation of their plan and action items. To ensure that the plans were implemented, a senior program manager who reported to a senior executive kept track of all the plans and their execution through completion. Although the program management office (PMO) from the 90 days effort did not undertake this major task, VeriSign assigned the job to someone with similar expertise in program management who could follow through on the plan to the end. Additionally, the new roles of the former team members gave them the authority to solidify the results of the implementation plan within their respective functions.

process, end to end. His role is to make sure that the interfaces between processes work well together and, at a high level, that implementation progresses as planned. He should also be able to resolve issues, make sure everything is documented appropriately, and ensure that people are adequately trained. Because only one person is performing these duties above and beyond most members of the transformation team, he should keep track of quality from a high level and step in mainly when issues arise.

KEYS TO EFFECTIVE EXECUTION

As Ram Charan claimed, "Execution is not just tactics—it is a discipline and a system. It has to be built into a company's strategy, its goals, and its culture."[8] Similarly, A. G. Lafley, former CEO of Procter & Gamble, said that the challenge in achieving excellent execution is learning to "unpack" the idea. "You're not going to get it unless you have disciplined strategic choices, a structure that supports the strategy, systems that enable large organizations to work and execute together, a winning culture, and leadership that's inspirational. If you have all that, you'll get excellent execution."[9] Therefore, effective execution is not just an aspect of the organization. Rather, it's a culture, a mind-set, and something that drives every decision and action in the organization (see figure 7-3).

Execution is central to an effective implementation phase. For implementation to be successful, the transformation team and the organization as a whole need to be able to execute. Otherwise, all the work and effort that has

FIGURE 7-3

Keys to effective execution

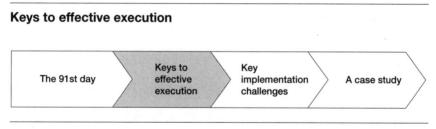

been put into the transformation phase thus far has gone to waste. On the other hand, though effective execution is critical in the transformation implementation phase, elements of it should have been developed throughout the transformation effort. The following tools for execution aren't things the transformation leader pulls out and introduces just for implementation—they take time to build and develop throughout the organization.

Many different factors go into effective execution. In our research, we have been able to parse excellent execution into the most critical elements: alignment with the strategic vision, choosing passionate leaders, maintaining momentum, building a tool to measure and assess progress, developing a culture of accountability, creating a learning culture, being flexible and taking risks, and communicating (see figure 7-4).

While some of these factors aren't specific to the transformation, they have tremendous effect on the success of the effort and are hence worth mentioning.

Alignment with the Strategic Vision

Throughout the transformation effort, all the decisions have been made with the strategic vision in mind, whether directly via the transformational goals or indirectly through cascading goals (see figure 7-5). In effective execution,

FIGURE 7-4

Key elements of effective execution

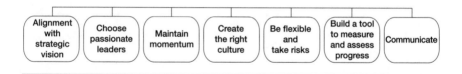

FIGURE 7-5

Execution via alignment with strategic vision

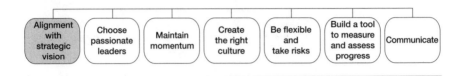

all decisions and actions should still align with the strategy of the organization and the transformation. An article published by the Harvard Business School noted that maintaining a focus is one of the keys of effective execution and that the characteristics that help an organization maintain its focus are "a realistic attitude, simplicity, and clarity."[10] These are all things that should characterize an effective strategic vision.

To maintain focus on the strategic vision, the organization must clearly and repeatedly communicate the company's overarching strategy. Every employee in the organization must understand, embrace, and internalize the strategy. In the same way that a culture of effective execution must be ingrained in the DNA of the organization, so must the driving strategy of the organization. Employees should at all times know the goals of their specific project and have an idea of how it contributes to the overarching strategy of the company.

Choose Passionate Leaders

As we have seen thus far, a strong coalition of employees led by passionate and involved leaders has been critical to driving the transformation effort. Going forward, the company will need leaders to remain committed to the plans laid in the 90 days effort. The leaders need to be involved, reliable, and passionate despite any potential changes (see figure 7-6).

FIGURE 7-6

Execution via choosing pasionate leaders

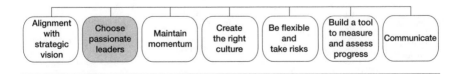

More important than passion, of course, is ability. Leaders should first and foremost be selected and assigned for their ability to lead and motivate others. Moreover, they should be focused on execution in order to drive it down through the layers of the organization.

Many of the companies we studied were known for their passionate and results-oriented leaders. Execution is a particularly important focus for leaders. As Larry Bossidy said, "The leader of the organization must be deeply engaged in [execution]. He cannot delegate its substance."[11]

The focus on execution should not lie only in the transformation's or organization's leader, however. It must exist in all leaders of the organization, whether they be of functional groups, of business units, or of projects. The focus on execution must trickle down throughout the company.

Maintain Momentum

In the road ahead, the organization will inevitably encounter many obstacles to implementation. The company will need to remain agile and open to change while continuing to drive the transformation effort forward. Therefore, momentum from the first three phases must be carried over to overcome these obstacles and keep the company on its toes.

Maintenance of momentum is also critical because it usually decreases and stalls in the implementation phase. Often, companies find themselves more relaxed after the planning stages end, because they feel they have overcome a major milestone with the end of the 90 days effort. The transition to the implementation phase also marks a significant change in the nature of participants' role in the effort, from planning to execution. This break in the planning routine, coupled with uncertainty of the future, leads to hesitation and creates a speed bump that temporarily stalls momentum. Therefore, the company should take steps to maintain the momentum developed during the transformation effort.

The three most important tools for maintaining momentum are (1) addressing resistance, (2) celebrating often, and (3) using a rewards system (see figure 7-7).

Address Resistance

Just as resistance in the form of friction works against a rolling ball and decreases both its speed and its momentum, resistance works against the momentum of the transformation effort. In an organizational change effort, this resistance to change may stem from both internal and external sources.

FIGURE 7-7

Execution via maintaining momentum

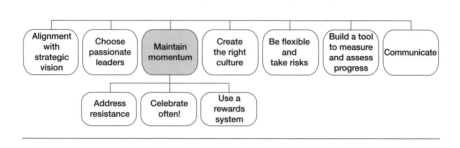

Internal resistance typically results from employees who do not internalize the transformation effort, and can typically be addressed in one of two ways. First, the organization should try to help employees internalize the effort by enforcing and reinforcing the new culture, by communicating the need for change, and by communicating the company vision. Though these efforts should have been practiced throughout the transformation effort, trying them one last time at this point will hopefully catch those remaining resisters who somehow slipped through the cracks in the initial screenings for employees resisting the change. If these efforts are ineffective, then these employees should be given the chance to leave on their own accord, although every effort should be taken to facilitate a smooth transfer of expertise. Those who don't want to leave but are willing to compromise need to ensure others that despite their different opinions, they will not deliberately stall the transformation.

Former cross-functional rapid response team members can play a very important role in addressing internal resistance in a company. The organization already has buy-in from the rapid response team members, who can champion the transformation effort throughout the organization. As they move into their new positions, these team members can address resistance and get buy-in from others. Furthermore, as they enter their new positions, a successful and seamless handoff process here is extremely important in maintaining momentum, for an unsuccessful handoff process can lead to a choppy transition to the implementation phase.

The organization will most likely also face external resistance, which is typically manifested in lack of public support and confidence in the company. One of the most effective remedies for external resistance is time, coupled with open communication and delivered results. Sometimes, it takes time before the market justly reflects the performance of the organization. By being prepared for this negative public reaction, companies can maintain morale and momentum despite external resistance. As discussed earlier, the external PR campaign can be effective in addressing and decreasing external resistance and skepticism.

Celebrate Often!

Morale is critical to maintaining momentum, and thus should be carried over from the day 90 celebration. As mentioned in the chapter on phase 3, celebrations are an important and effective means of maintaining and even increasing morale. According to an extensive study conducted by Cross, Baker, and Parker, people are energized in engagements marked by progress, and celebrations are an effective way to announce and recognize the progress made.[12] Frequent celebrations acknowledging successes, especially of short-term wins, are critical for keeping employees motivated and encouraged, as well as for neutralizing skepticism about the effort. Examples of good short-term wins to celebrate include receiving good customer feedback and meeting minimilestones. Such celebrations make employees realize that their sacrifice is paying off, for no one wants to keep working without knowing whether their work is having its desired effect. Celebrations are particularly effective because morale and momentum are maintained best when people feel recognized for their effort and hard work. According to GE's former CEO Jack Welch, "As a great leader share great wins you have as a result of great work they [your employees] have done."[13]

At the same time, however, holding too many celebrations may backfire, because people may become numb to the effects of the celebrations and find them superficial. We will also recap the additional caveats that were described at the end of the previous chapter. Praise is most effective when it is sincere and when it's not given out too freely, and premature celebrations must be avoided. Victory should not be declared too soon, for that may lead to complacency and hinder future progress.

Use a Rewards System

Celebrations, however, are not the only tools available for acknowledging successes. Rewards, if used correctly, are also an effective means of maintaining momentum and morale. To be useful, a rewards system must reinforce the desired behavior. Hence, the leader must clearly define the desired behavior before creating a rewards system around it. For example, the leaders of Best Buy strongly believed that "to make new behaviors stick, [you need to] align them with new priorities for reward and recognition. New behaviors are the paychecks of change. Cash them."[14]

A rewards system can be used in parallel with celebrations, as in the case of SAS (see "Thoughtful Rewards at SAS"). One important thing to remember is that rewards should be given publicly, and criticisms privately. Public rewards and acknowledgments that recognize an individual's accomplishments are extremely useful tools for increasing morale in an organization and encouraging similar behavior in the future. Because criticisms detract from morale if used improperly, they should be given in private, where the reasoning and expectations behind the criticisms, along with their implications, should be openly discussed. In this way, criticisms can actually also be an effective means to maintain momentum for the transformation effort.

THOUGHTFUL REWARDS AT SAS

To thank and reward employees for all the hard work they had put into the transformation effort, SAS, an airline company, decided to send each of its twenty thousand employees a package during the holiday season in December. In each package was a gold wristwatch with a second hand in the shape of an airplane, a memo explaining the more liberal regulations governing free trips for employees, a "little red book" called *The Flight of the Century* (different from the first book, titled *Let's Get in There and Fight*, which detailed the vision of the company), an invitation to a party, and a thank-you note for all the work the employees had done to transform SAS from its worst loss ever to its biggest profit in history.

SAS had divided its reward plan into two phases, visible in the package. The first phase was awarding "an individual symbol of recognition," represented by the watch. The second phase was the party. Both of these rewards had an implicit underlying message. The watch tied directly to the company's goal to become the world's most punctual airline, and the party symbolized the fact that SAS is a collective group, and that everyone played a role in the transformation. This package hence not only motivated employees to work harder because they were being appreciated and recognized for their work, but also reemphasized the key values and goals the transformation and the organization were trying to promote.[15]

Create the Right Culture

The type of culture embraced by an organization is a key determinant of its transformational success, because it serves as the self-regulating cycle that enforces the key aspects of the effort.

A Culture of Accountability

An organization should be able to rely on its employees to deliver on promises and not fall behind schedule, even without constantly using a tool to measure progress. For this to happen, the organization must have a culture that automatically guides people toward effective execution and holds them accountable for their promises (see figure 7-8). Accountability ensures that deadlines are met, tasks are completed, and quality is upheld. In effect, a culture of accountability ensures that the people who make the baby not only deliver it but also take care of it. By creating a culture of accountability, you are weaving one of the key principles of excellent execution into the DNA of your organization. People who feel accountable for their tasks and actions inevitably strive for better quality and push for timely completion. By creating an execution-oriented culture, a culture of accountability is also very effective in maintaining momentum and increasing morale and confidence, both internally and externally.

As mentioned earlier, momentum is also maintained by an appropriate rewards system. At the same time, however, if used correctly, rewards are effective in enforcing and reinforcing a desired behavior (see "Behavioral Maps at Best Buy") and holding individuals accountable for their actions. Performance-based rewards help encourage the desired behaviors, and lack of rewards can increase accountability by reducing undesirable attitudes and behavior in the organization.

FIGURE 7-8

Execution via creating the right culture

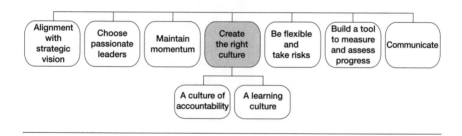

BEHAVIORAL MAPS AT BEST BUY

To change the entire culture of the organization and encourage employees to behave in the desired way, leaders at Best Buy first developed behavioral maps, which were detailed descriptions that showed patterns of new behaviors. These behavioral maps were important in clarifying the desired behaviors in the new organization. In order to ensure that employees were willing to behave as desired and continue to learn, Best Buy created opportunities that allowed employees to act in this new way and also provided constructive feedback. This feedback empowered employees and held them accountable for their actions. Additionally, feedback can help redirect employees toward the right course.

Even without the rewards, performance reviews can also increase accountability and improve execution. These performance reviews may fall under the category of project reviews, which may also have the additional benefit of addressing skepticism about an individual or a group's ability to execute (see "Measuring Progress in Human Resources at The Home Depot"). Furthermore, these performance or project reviews further increase accountability if

MEASURING PROGRESS IN HUMAN RESOURCES AT THE HOME DEPOT

Division presidents expressed to Dennis Donovan, executive vice president of human resources (HR) at The Home Depot, their skepticism about the HR department's ability to actually deliver what it had promised. In response to their skepticism, Donovan held his HR staff accountable and required that they submit detailed plans for each project they were responsible for. Additionally, he required that they meticulously document their progress every month. According to Donovan, "Everyone on the HR team project-reviews every single process area, and they do it religiously. That's how we focus on the 'execution' part."[16] These actions helped alleviate the skepticism of the division presidents, as well as improve morale and confidence throughout the HR department and the organization as a whole.

they are conducted publicly. Public commitments have a strong effect on people's sense of responsibility because their personal image and reputation are suddenly also at stake.

Additionally, accountability can be increased through simplicity. Simplicity, in the form of a clear message, role, or responsibility, has the benefit of reducing interfering noises and the opportunity for excuses. A central aspect of a culture of accountability is refusal to tolerate excuses, misses, and slips in the schedule. Employees need to be confident about setting their goals and meeting them (see "Lack of Accountability at Hewlett-Packard" for an instance where this was not the case). In a culture of accountability, people take responsibilities for their actions, whether they are proud of them or not. Through the good and the bad, people need to be held responsible. Employees cannot be fair-weather fans of accountability.

Even though it is important for leaders to investigate why certain projects are behind schedule and why execution failed, it is just as important for them to distinguish between the real reasons and the excuses. Knowing the truth behind the obstacles and problems people face enables leaders to prevent the same situation from happening again in the future. Learning about the excuses, however, teaches the organization nothing. In differentiating between a reason and an excuse, leaders should emphasize that the point of digging behind the missed target or deadline is not to find someone to punish

LACK OF ACCOUNTABILITY AT HEWLETT-PACKARD

During the Carly Fiorina era, Hewlett-Packard lacked a culture of accountability, partly because of its centralized structure. No one took responsibility for any project or sponsored any goal. In fact, in 2003, the company didn't even set a sales quota! Without this goal, no one could be held accountable for not meeting target sales. Even more astonishing, it took three years before the company finally fired the head of sales for not doing his job and setting a quota. Furthermore, the leaders of the business units that worked with the sales staff were only given control of 30 percent of the costs under Fiorina.[17] When pressured about their performance, they responded, "You can't hold us accountable when only 30 percent is in our control and 70 percent is out of our control!"

or blame but to improve the organization and help the particular employee by finding and removing relevant obstacles. In order for this to occur, the leadership team must first know the staff and its capabilities, because in some instances, the implementation plan and task may not have been realistic to begin with, given the skill set and workload of the employee. In a culture of accountability, the organization must dig deep to identify the problems, fix them, and learn how not to make them again.

A Learning Culture

In a culture of accountability, employees are willing to learn from cases where execution failed. This learning culture is extremely important to effective execution. Every organization makes mistakes, some more costly than others. One of the main differences between a company that succeeds in its implementation phase and a company that fails is what happens after those failures. Looked at from the right perspective, failures can be wonderful learning experiences. Successful companies conduct a "failure analysis," which forces them to learn from their past mistakes. In this analysis, the organization not only analyzes the failure but also develops potential solutions and learns how to avoid making those same mistakes again or similar mistakes.

One important aspect of failure analyses is asking, Why? For example, when a company does not execute correctly, leaders should ask, Why? Why did execution fail? Was it lack of support? Why did we miss the deadline? What can we do to ensure that this doesn't happen again? Asking the right questions is critical to failure analysis. In a way, the failure analysis resembles the detective work done in phase 1. In both cases, a deep analysis must be conducted to look at the symptoms and analyze the root of a problem. As mentioned in the previous section on accountability, in asking the right questions, you have to know that you're getting the right answers. These answers must be honest and hit on the key points.

However, failure analysis is only one aspect of a learning culture. For effective execution, employees must be willing to learn at all times, not just after a failure. Hence, it is important to create an entire culture where every interaction or experience is an opportunity to learn, not just from your own experiences but from others' as well. Two-way communication must be established in order for learning on all fronts to occur. Additionally, two-way communication is particularly useful in providing feedback, which further promotes the learning culture in the new organization by helping shape new behaviors and actions.

Be Flexible and Take Risks

While excellence in execution is about discipline, it is not enough to encourage routine behaviors. Execution also requires taking risks and being adaptable and flexible (see figure 7-9). Situations and environments often change, and unexpected things often occur. By being ready to adapt to these changes in the environment, the organization will be more likely to turn obstacles into opportunities and not let these problems thwart execution. According to Jan Carlzon, CEO of SAS, an organization should "run through walls."[18] In particular, don't let minor obstacles stand in your way, and don't give up too early. Often, companies let minor barriers break down effective execution, but in many cases, these barriers can be overcome through persistence and adaptability.

Execution requires taking risks. Many times, there are various ways to execute an idea or principle. Choosing one idea over another requires evaluating the trade-offs between the choices and taking a risk by choosing one. However, the safest choice may not always be the best option. Carlzon notes, "Taking small steps . . . won't be enough when you're peering over the edge of the chasm . . . Not only must those in top management learn to leap the chasm, but risk-taking must ripple throughout the *entire* organization.[19] Furthermore, sometimes one method of execution may prove ineffective. At that point, the team or organization must be flexible and consider the other alternatives (see "Effective Execution at Bay Networks").

Build a Tool to Measure and Assess Progress

Effective execution hinges on your ability to measure whether or not progress is being made at the appropriate pace (see figure 7-10). The most popular tool for assessing progress is the balanced scorecard, also called the change scorecard.

FIGURE 7-9

Executing via being flexible and taking risks

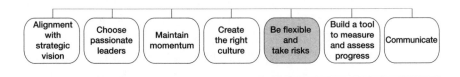

EFFECTIVE EXECUTION AT BAY NETWORKS

Dave House stressed the importance of execution in transforming Bay Networks. He said, "I was all execution." He explained further, "In any task, there can be ten ways of doing it. Eight of them may work, and you can spend a lot of time debating which one will be more effective. But the power of execution is picking one of them and getting everyone behind it. If one method ends up being ineffective, you can figure that out early on and change the method."[20]

FIGURE 7-10

Building a tool to measure and assess progress

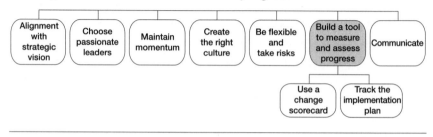

Use a Change Scorecard

A change scorecard is a management tool that breaks down the overall strategic vision of the company into several perspectives by which performance is measured. It uses cascaded goals and metrics to ensure that targets are being met on various fronts. In short, it consists of a document or an interface that tracks the progress made toward different cascaded goals that, when combined, build up to the greater strategic goal of the organization. According to John Kelly, president and CEO of Crown Castle International, a telecommunications company, "The [balanced scorecard] provided [a] tangible link; it showed our people what they need to do to help implement the strategy."[21] The four main strategic perspectives most commonly addressed in the balanced scorecard are the financial or shareholder perspective, the customer perspective, the internal perspective (such as internal processes), and the perspective on the company's ability to innovate, learn, and grow.

In a transformation effort, when you are trying to change the natural, routine behaviors of employees, you need to find ways to make people actively adopt the new mind-sets and behaviors. A scorecard not only makes sure people understand the new behaviors you expect, but provides a way to enforce them and measure the organization's progress toward a new DNA.

To enforce progress toward the goals determined in the scorecard, the leadership team should regularly assess progress on a dashboard. Performance toward targets can be rated by red, yellow, or green lights, each symbolizing how near people are to the mark. A red light signals to the organization that more energy needs to be dedicated to that area, whereas a green light means everything is going as planned. A balanced scorecard should be transparent, and everyone in the organization, not just top executives, should be able to see the progress made toward the goals. At the same time, however, change scorecards should only be shared with the relevant parties because of proprietary information. Larry Brady, executive vice president of FMC Corporation, noted in an interview that one of his managers said, "Unlike monthly financial statements or even [my] strategic plan, if a rival were to see [my] scorecard, [I] would lose [my] competitive edge."[22]

The transformation team should develop a high-level, corporate-level scorecard that has the key targets of the transformation effort with the relevant cascaded goals as well as the key performance indicators. People who know how the transformation effort is progressing are more likely to focus their efforts and continue the progress. In addition to the high-level transformation scorecard, however, individual business units or functions also often need a scorecard to measure the smaller-scale progress toward the goals. In these instances, the teams need to ensure that the different scorecards still send a clear and consistent message and do not overwhelm the employees (see "Ineffective Use of Scorecards at Best Buy").

A scorecard is not a static entity. Rather, it has to be dynamic, changing with the constantly evolving goals of the business. A scorecard that is frozen in time soon becomes outdated. Although a scorecard is important in focusing the organization, it is only effective if it focuses the organization on the right goals and factors. Furthermore, a scorecard is only as good as its metrics. For each of the main perspectives, the organization has to select certain metrics against which to measure performance and progress. These metrics should capture the essence of the strategy or goals without being either too broad or too narrow.

Track the Implementation Plan

A scorecard is an effective tool for measuring the continual progress and performance of employees toward the targets and goals set by the

INEFFECTIVE USE OF SCORECARDS
AT BEST BUY

Before its transformation in 1999, Best Buy was using a scorecard to measure the performance of each of its store managers. Although Best Buy recognized the value of measuring performance using these scorecards, the company failed to do so in a systematic way. It gave managers too many requirements, often issuing up to thirty different scorecards, each with its separate, and often contradicting, requirements. Furthermore, the company tracked business results rather than the behaviors that actually produced these results. Add to that the fact that bonuses were tied to these measures of performance, and "beating the scorecard" quickly became each store manager's mission. Hence, because the scorecards were inappropriately applied, they were largely ineffective and even detrimental to the company.[23]

transformation team, and it is important in affecting behavioral change throughout the organization by focusing and aligning everyone. However, the actual progress of the action items on the implementation plans developed by the rapid response teams must also be continually assessed.

To specifically assess the progress of the transformation effort and ensure that implementation is progressing as scheduled, the PMO should integrate the action items and their respective deadlines from the transformation implementation plan into a document or spreadsheet. With respect to the deadlines, this spreadsheet should have two columns: one for the originally planned deadline and the other for the adjusted deadline. Inevitably, circumstances will arise that push projects behind schedule, but the key is not to let things get out of control and not to let these misses become the norm.

The PMO should host a biweekly meeting (similar to the weekly meetings during the 90 days effort) where teams can update the EMT and the rest of the transformation team on the progress of their action items. This meeting increases accountability and commitment because the pilots and owners are responsible for the progress made on the implementation plan. Each team should go through each of its action items and report on the progress made since the last meeting, including whether the item is on time or delayed and why. Owners who keep falling behind schedule on their action items need to explain why their schedules are slipping and what they will do about it. In this way, the PMO and the transformation team can ensure timely implementation of the implementation plan.

Communicate

As something that has been emphasized throughout the transformation effort, communication should not break down at this point. Effective execution is facilitated by strong, open communication, in which people can talk openly about the problems and obstacles they're encountering without worrying about being blamed for the problems they're facing (see figure 7-11). Open and honest communication keeps everyone up to date with the latest news on the transformation and the company, and it helps give the right people the right information at the right time. People should be comfortable stepping up and communicating when an issue arises, and they should feel comfortable asking for help when necessary. Additionally, many cases of misunderstanding are overcome only through open communication, and many problems are mitigated through communication. Lines of communication should remain open throughout implementation and beyond, especially across functions and boundaries.

KEY IMPLEMENTATION CHALLENGES

All organizations will encounter complications with implementation, although some will overcome these obstacles more easily and gracefully than others. Knowing what are the most common problems faced by companies in the implementation phase enables you to anticipate and address these problems before they become unmanageable (see figure 7-12). For an organization to survive and grow, it must learn from its mistakes and be persistent and willing to keep trying, despite a few setbacks—that is, it needs to have a learning culture and be willing to take risks, as stated previously. Many of the organizations we studied had previously undergone transformations and turnarounds, some of which were successful and some of which weren't. Regardless, each learned from past mistakes and was able to address the obstacles in the subsequent iteration. There is no single "ultimate" transformation. Organizations keep changing, and the key is to make it to the next transformation.

FIGURE 7-11

Execution via communication

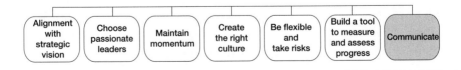

FIGURE 7-12

Key implementation challenges

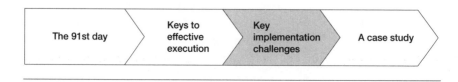

Knowing and addressing these key implementation challenges increases the probability that your company will make it to the next effort.

Underestimating Complexity of Implementation and Execution

Implementation requires extreme attention to detail and a solid understanding of the nuances of the organization. At the heart of implementation in a transformation effort is changing the behavior of employees, which is no simple task. Without the proper use of tools and without processes in place, the company will find that inertia and habit counter attempts to change. As Best Buy noted after its first failed attempt at transforming the company, "We didn't fully understand the complexity of behavioral change and how much time it takes to implement."[24] Given the opportunity, most people will gladly fall back into their comfortable routine. Behavioral change takes a lot of energy and deliberate action. Performance-based rewards as well as frequent open and honest communication usually simplify and streamline the change process.

Further complexities of implementation include coordinating between the short term and the long term and having employees juggle the transformation effort and their immediate jobs. Often, people say that one of the most difficult aspects of implementation is making all the planned changes on top of meeting quarterly numbers. Successful companies can do both, because suffering a failure in either domain is not a viable option.

Underestimating the Power of Internal Resistance

As mentioned in the last section, people are sometimes very difficult to change. Throughout this book, we have mentioned the power of internal resistance in undermining a transformation effort. Employees who resist the effort will create otherwise avoidable roadblocks and obstacles for the transformation, and this will be especially devastating in the implementation phase. Internal resistance can spread throughout an organization, and people who might have bought in to the effort may suddenly question it. An organization that is not unified is also inconsistent, and inconsistency in the organization, especially at the top, will send a damaging message: either that management isn't serious about implementing the change or that management is unwilling to contribute to the effort. Neither message has a positive effect on the transformation effort.

Resistance in implementation often stems from not getting either adequate or appropriate buy-in from the organization. For implementation to be successful, people have to understand the change and internalize it early on, even before they are approached with the particular details of the implementation plan. They need to know how the transformation will affect them in order to prepare themselves adequately for it.

Sometimes, resistance stems from a lack of understanding. If employees were not involved in the development of the plan, they can easily misinterpret it. Additionally, they need to know the details about how to implement the plan. A high-quality implementation plan can easily be translated into action, as well as ways of enforcing the new, desired behavior. To facilitate the process, however, the person responsible for implementing the plan should have had a say in developing it—hence the value of rapid response teams. This will help increase not only understanding of the plan but also the buy-in for implementation. In Best Buy's initial attempts at transforming the company, where external consultants developed a plan to be implemented, the organization found only 44 percent true compliance.[25] This internal resistance, though not blatantly obvious, manifested itself in the poor implementation of the plan.

In some instances, resistance starts surfacing partway through implementation, especially if people don't feel that they're getting the results they expected. This can start as a remnant of the original internal resistance, but it can also represent dissatisfaction with the progress of the implementation. To take advantage of the momentum carried over from the 90 days transformation effort and to overcome a sense of slow progress, the transformation team should front-load the implementation. By putting a significant amount of work up front, the team will give people a stronger sense of progress and help fight the burnout that typically appears in the later stages of implementation. This will take advantage of the enthusiasm and new ideas associated with implementation in the beginning and fight internal resistance from the get-go.

Another effective way to address the problem of internal resistance is to deal with people who will not change. Banca Intesa, for example, replaced 70 percent of its branch managers in three years, embracing the philosophy of investing in new people instead of expending time and energy in changing the outlook of traditional employees.[26] Similarly, GE's former CEO Jack Welch similarly got rid of employees who did not align with GE's culture, even if they could perform. By the end of his era, GE had only 90,000 employees, compared to 420,000 when Welch first joined the company.[27]

Ineffective Coordination of Implementation Activities

Implementation of the plans developed in the 90 days transformation effort is extremely difficult and complicated. Thus, coordination between different programs is especially critical and important. (See "Lack of Coordination of Rollout at Xerox" for an example where ineffective coordination caused the programs to fail.) As mentioned in the chapter on phase 3, Best Buy had not coordinated between efforts in its first transformation effort, resulting in three major initiatives rolling out at the same time and fighting for resources and priority.[28] Because of this lack of integration and coordination, implementation of all three initiatives failed. Without communication and coordination, various initiatives that would otherwise be successful will fight against each other and most likely fail.

LACK OF COORDINATION OF ROLLOUT AT XEROX

In 1997, Xerox hired Richard Thoman as CEO and engaged in an urgent transformation effort. As a result of the effort, the company launched two massive, critical initiatives in parallel: (1) reorganize the thirty thousand–person sales force and (2) consolidate the administration and billing of customer orders from thirty-six centers to three. Because Xerox was incapable of carrying out these two parallel efforts, chaos ensued as customer orders were missed and the sales force was overworked, trying to both straighten out customer orders and be retrained to sell solutions rather than products. Furthermore, Thoman didn't have the authority to appoint his own leadership team, and he lacked the support of the existing team, which was skeptical of his vision from the beginning.[29]

When thinking about how to roll out the different implementation plans via the transformation implementation plan, the transformation team, the PMO, and the EMT should assess the plans that are complementary and will benefit from concurrent rollout. At the same time, the team should analyze the plans that vie for the same resources and should not be rolled out at the same time, either because of limited resources or because it may confuse the employees. The priorities of the different projects and plans are important, but success is highly dependent on coordination among them.

Overpromising and Underdelivering

The transformation team and the organization are constantly under external pressure to deliver and perform. With such a spotlight on them, the organization has a strong temptation to make promises it may not be able to deliver on. Credibility in implementation is extremely powerful and difficult to regain once it is lost.

Overpromising is usually related to an overemphasis on the public image of the company. Though it works in the short term if the public believes you, it actually hurts you in the long term. If you constantly don't deliver on your promises, the public will lose faith in you and your company and will stop hearing your promises altogether. To fight the urge to overpromise, you must realize that a strong performance speaks for itself, with or without flashy announcements and promises. As explained by Dennis Cain, a thirty-two-year veteran of Hewlett-Packard, "Don't talk about what you're going to do. Just do it, and then let other people talk about it."[30]

Another way to combat overpromising is by assigning the role of devil's advocate to an executive, since overpromising is often also related to a disconnect from reality (see "Overpromising at Lucent"). By having someone constantly challenge you, you are more likely to be brought down to Earth and less likely to make unrealistic promises that the organization knows it cannot achieve. At the same time, however, you must strike a balance between making promises that are too easily achievable and those that are impossible. This middle ground consists of stretch goals, which are extremely effective in motivating an organization.

Running Ineffective Meetings

While this may seem like a minor point in discussing implementation challenges, running ineffective meetings is a problem that ties directly to one of

OVERPROMISING AT LUCENT

Richard McGinn was appointed CEO of Lucent Technologies in 1996, and he immediately promised investors high growth. He began to set unrealistic goals and wanted to target markets in which Lucent didn't even have products yet! Additionally, he ignored the harsh reality that Lucent lacked the capability to get products to market fast enough. Even worse, McGinn's team warned him against setting such unrealistic goals and encouraged him to set more realistic and attainable ones. Because McGinn ignored their input and feedback, he alienated his team and no longer had the support necessary to drive change.[31]

the more well-known problems of execution: lack of time. People have only twenty-four hours in a day to juggle around, and by adding the task of implementation, they often get overwhelmed. However, many employees fail to realize that much of their time spent in meetings can actually be reallocated to implementation without much impact on their other work, if the right measures are taken to make the meetings more efficient.

One way to combat ineffective meetings is to teach people how much easier their lives would be if they held more-effective meetings. Sometimes, this can be done in a training course or through on-the-spot, real-time learning through coaching. One aspect of particularly ineffective meetings is decision making. We all know of those meetings where considerable debate is undertaken but not everyone there is even relevant to the discussion. Those debates should be taken offline, and only relevant employees should be present at the meetings. Running more-effective meetings and having a better decision-making process can also improve implementation by encouraging people to be more efficient and productive overall, throughout the organization.

FINAL THOUGHTS: A COMPARISON

Having summarized the basics of successful implementation, we will now compare two corporate transformation efforts within the same company in the same decade: one that was largely unsuccessful and one that can be deemed preliminarily successful (see figure 7-13). The leaders of these two efforts differed drastically, and the variation in outcome can be attributed to effective execution or the lack thereof.

FIGURE 7-13

A case study

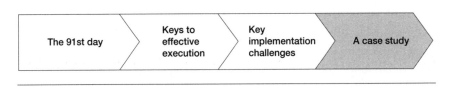

Hewlett-Packard, a technology company providing products, services, and solutions, has faced numerous problems in the past decade. Its hopes were raised when Carly Fiorina joined the company as CEO in 1999, but within six years, HP was disillusioned, and Fiorina was forced to resign from the company. When Mark Hurd joined the organization in 2005, skepticism ensued, and many doubted his ability to turn HP around. As this book goes to press, Hurd's transformation by all accounts has been a success since early 2005, when Hurd joined.

In this section, we compare the approaches of these two recent leaders of HP. Most experts will say that Fiorina's downfall was not due to lack of vision but lack of execution and implementation. According to Pat Dunn, who serves on HP's board of directors, "It was not a difference over strategy but over execution; the board feels execution is of the primary importance moving forward."[32] Although Fiorina's efforts were largely unsuccessful, it can be said that she paved the road for Hurd, creating a strong vision for the company and kick-starting several projects.

The Beginnings

When Carly Fiorina joined HP, she hit the ground running. According to an executive at HP, "Carly was looking so far ahead, you sometimes couldn't run fast enough to keep up with her. You had to build bridges to follow along quickly." Initially, she spent a disproportionate amount of time spreading her vision for the new organization. During her first six months on the job, Fiorina was constantly on the road, hosting numerous coffee talks and speaking about her plans and vision for the future. These coffee talks, however, were extremely impersonal, and Fiorina never took the opportunity to get to know the employees and hear their gripes on an individual level. She was very focused on creating a good image of herself and selling her vision for the company, both internally and externally.

Mark Hurd, however, entered HP on a mission to learn. For the first few months, he didn't take any major action. Rather, he investigated the situation and diagnosed the company by meeting with employees at all levels and spending time with customers to see what it felt like to be a customer of HP. Within the first three months alone, Hurd had met with over one thousand customers. Although he also hosted coffee talks at many company locations, his primary goal was not to create an image and vision for himself and the company but to identify the major pain points of the company. In his coffee talks, he used a flip chart to get everyone learning about the numbers of the company, such as revenue goal and net profit goal. He wanted the data to speak for itself and drive change from the bottom up.

Organizational Focus

Fiorina focused her efforts on rallying the organization behind her new vision. She entered HP with grand new plans to change and improve the company, and always maintained a big-picture perspective. Because of her flashy public image, by the dazzle of marketing, people never questioned the what she was aiming for, but the how. In fact, she even refused to name a chief operating officer to help her implement the details of her strategy.[33]

Hurd, however, was focused more on operations and execution than on creating a vision, for he believed that the vision would come after he fully diagnosed the situation. For example, he didn't make any drastic changes in strategic direction in his first five months at HP. As Todd Bradley, executive vice president of the Personal Systems Group summarized, "Mark seemed . . . far more focused on creating value through operational performance than just pitching grand visions."[34] At the same time, however, Hurd may not have been able to focus on the operational aspects of the company had Fiorina not developed and championed a vision for the new organization in her tenure, since both aspects are critical in driving change in an organization. According to Hurd, "When I came aboard, there was a lot of work already done. This was not a one person show."[35]

Leadership and Management Style

Fiorina's leadership and management style generated tremendous controversy at HP. "She was everything HP wasn't—charismatic, bold, even glamorous."[36] As a visionary, Fiorina had a tendency to aim high and set goals that seem unattainable. While this sometimes worked for her, it also sometimes worked against her. For example, she set a target growth of 15 percent for fiscal year 2000 for the organization. Even though many of the employees didn't believe that such a growth rate was attainable amid a reorganization and strong competition, HP sales actually did end up increasing by over 15 percent.[37]

On the other hand, sometimes she would stretch the goals so far, they actually were unattainable and unrealistic. When Fiorina asked the heads of business units and functions to bring her a plan, she often sent the plan back for another revision and more aggressive targets. After several iterations, Fiorina would finally be satisfied by the plan, but the new plan was so far beyond the original plan that the developer no longer bought in to it. As a result, he would miss the target, but there would be no consequences for this failure to plan and execute.

Hurd's leadership style differs drastically from Fiorina's style. When he asks for a business plan or target, he clearly demands that his people bring him a plan they can meet, and tells them they have to meet their plan or be prepared to face the consequences. Thus, he holds people accountable, not only for setting targets but for meeting their numbers. At the same time, Hurd, known for being driven by numbers and hard data, does not simply accept any number and target presented to him. If they're unreasonable or illogical, Hurd will challenge people on their numbers and assumptions. Hence, Hurd leads and manages indirectly through numbers, letting them drive his analysis and decisions.

Relationship with the People

Fiorina's glamorous and flashy style, though attractive, isolated her from many of her key executives because of its sharp contrast and opposition to the "HP Way." Realizing that she only needed approximately 15 percent of the organization to be committed in order to carry out her vision, she focused her efforts on getting the 15 percent. Because she did not get enough buy-in and was isolated from her employees, they never executed her vision, contributing significantly to her downfall. Even though she was isolated from people, however, she was dedicated to her employees and tried to develop the existing talent rather than hire from outside. She wanted instead to use the strengths of the existing people.

Hurd, more similar in many ways to the founders of HP, more successfully connected with people at a rudimentary level and hence motivated the organization. By being simple, clear, and consistent, Hurd was able to rally the organization and create a data-driven organization supported by analytics and accountability. Unlike Fiorina, Hurd was willing to bring people in from the outside, for he believed that the right people would lead to the right strategy. For example, in two years, Hurd has gradually replaced over 60 percent of its executive council.

Organizational Structure

As mentioned earlier in the chapter, both Fiorina and Hurd changed the organizational structure of the company during their tenure. Fiorina organized the company into a 3-D matrix cube, where employees had to respond to three bosses: one each from business, function, and region. The reorganization also involved combining the entire organization into two front-end sales and marketing organizations and two back-end research and development and manufacturing organizations.[38] Even though the new structure was designed to integrate many different businesses and divisions and encourage communication, Fiorina did not get adequate support from the organization. In fact, executives and divisional managers strongly opposed the reorganization, questioning its practicality and the resulting unclear accountability. According to one executive, "I don't know anyone who was in favor of it other than Carly. She just did it."[39]

Hurd, however, reversed the reorganization and reverted to a 2-D matrix. As a result, business heads had more control of their units and were held more accountable. Business unit leaders also got control of 70 percent of the costs associated with their operations, up from 30 percent during Fiorina's tenure.[40] By decentralizing the organizational structure of HP, Hurd has clarified the responsibilities of employees and decreased the opportunity to blame others for poor performance. This organizational structure has helped build a culture of accountability.

Rewards and Compensation

Fiorina used various tools to measure and assess the progress and performance of employees and plans alike. With the Compaq–HP merger, for example, she created a balanced scorecard to measure the success of the integration. Fiorina also tried to establish a standard rewards and compensation plan, which many ironically found incomprehensible. The compensation plan included numerous statistics, some that were beyond employees' control, such as the company's performance relative to the Standard & Poor's 500 stock index.[41]

Hurd has revamped the rewards and compensation process and simplified it so that employees are rewarded according to the performance of both their business units and HP. This new compensation plan has been highly effective in motivating employees and aligning them to the overall goals and strategy of the organization.

Impact

Even though Fiorina had many successes during her tenure at HP, the general consensus is that she did not perform up to par. With the serious challenges of the Compaq–HP merger, Fiorina was forced out in 2005. In fact, HP's stock rose 7.5 percent the day she announced her resignation.

Hurd's transformation is currently looking very optimistic. (See the appendix for a table that compares the data when Hurd first joined with more recent data.) As of May 2007, stock prices, revenue, and profit all exceeded investors' expectations. In response, Hurd said, "We gained share, but that's not our sole objective. We want to run a better business."[42] In 2006, HP posted $91.7 billion in annual revenues, surpassing IBM as the world's largest technology corporation in sales.[43]

CONCLUSION

Throughout this chapter, we have discussed the 91st day and focused on successful implementation and effective execution. Implementation is a critical part of the transformation effort and should not be overlooked. In fact, the transformation effort hinges on effective execution, for until the plans are executed, they have minimal impact on the organization. Ideally, through this transformation effort, effective execution will be instilled in the DNA of the organization. An organization that can execute effectively will be more successful in the long run than one that cannot.

Some of the keys to effective execution are choosing passionate leaders, maintaining momentum, creating a culture of accountability, creating a learning culture, building a tool to measure and assess progress, being flexible, and communicating. Companies that can execute effectively will have not only a more successful transformation effort but also a more successful organization as a whole. Implementation cannot be overlooked or discounted. The keys to a winning organization are a strong strategy combined with effective execution.

THE END OR THE BEGINNING?

With the conclusion of transformation implementation comes the ultimate conclusion of the 90 days effort. Throughout the transformation effort, employees have been challenged to extend beyond their comfort zone and adopt new perspectives or ways of thinking. Through this experience, employees, leaders, and executives alike have grown and developed into better business-people. They have seen that through their hard work, they can make a change and drive quantum leaps in performance in the organization.

As mentioned early in the book, the keys to the success of the 90 days transformation are that it's all-encompassing, integrative, and fast and gets passionate buy-in from the organization. The rapid response teams are the drivers of the transformation effort, conducting the analysis, developing the appropriate recommendations, and then going into the company and implementing the plans. Only through rapid response teams can the organization analyze all aspects of its operations and improve them in parallel with such speed. Only through rapid response teams can the transformation leader get such buy-in from all levels of the organization so quickly. Additionally, these rapid response teams break down the boundaries of the organization and open up lines of communication.

With the conclusion of the transformation, the leader should reflect on the effort and look at what he would have changed. The effects of a transformation will last as long as the company continues to adapt, execute, and anticipate trends in the market. Sometimes, however, conditions change, and the organization may once again find itself slipping. If this is the case, the company should reflect on the transformation effort and the keys that helped drive excellent performance. The company can look back on the key lessons learned from this effort and implement them.

However, it's only a matter of time before change is required again. The question then is, How do I continue to change before I have to? The beauty of the 90 days model is that it spins out an army of change agents with informal networks and experience working across numerous boundaries, and who have internalized change and the change process. By creating an organization of change leaders that think outside the box, the company will be better prepared to change in the future, for employees will be less resistant and more experienced.

Organizations inevitably grow and change. But if the tools and skills learned from the transformation can be internalized, the organization will no longer be afraid of change. Instead of fighting it, the company will be able to harness and use the energy coming from the change to its benefit. It will be able to work with the change and morph it to fit its needs. Instead of being something to be feared, change becomes something that is empowering. Change promotes growth. And that is the ultimate power of transformations.

Appendix

Transformation Performance Index Model

In this section we describe an innovative quantitative model that assisted us in distinguishing successful corporate transformations from unsuccessful ones. This then allowed our research team to perform indepth and rigorous study of the companies' various practices and paths that affected their respective outcomes.

The task of defining success, however, is not as simple and straightforward as it may seem. For example, many different factors are indicative of success. How do you balance, prioritize, and select the variables that appropriately and effectively illustrate a successful transformation effort? And once you've selected some key indicators of success, how do you reconcile the data when some variables illustrate clear success but others don't? When is it appropriate for one variable to outweigh another, and when is it not? And most importantly, how do you standardize the evaluation process so it becomes objective and unbiased? These are some of the challenges our research team faced in the development of the transformation performance index model; we address them in the following sections.

RESEARCH TEAM AND ANALYSIS
PROCESS OVERVIEW

The transformation performance index model was developed by a panel of experts led by the author. This panel of experts included:

- The CFO of a billion-dollar company, with senior management background in one of the Big Five accounting firms as an auditor

- A former partner of a well-known consulting firm, with over twenty years of experience in organizational change

- An expert in company valuation who works for a large hedge fund on the East Coast

- A finance expert at Stanford University

The panel was selected according to managerial and financial expertise in the most important and relevant performance measures to determine success or failure in transformation. This panel of experts went through numerous iterations of the model before reaching the final version. The numbers engaged in considerable discussion and debate throughout all stages of the development process, from challenging assumptions underlying the original draft of the model to selecting and prioritizing the indicators of success. They endorsed the final transformation performance index model presented in this appendix.

Once the panel members completed the development of the model, they selected a random sample of companies that underwent a transformation and whose criteria fit the constraints of the model (see the following section for details). With the model developed and the sample selected, the research team, composed of five graduate students at Stanford University with significant background in finance and accounting, gathered the necessary data and conducted the analysis of the companies.

With the companies quantitatively analyzed and categorized into successes and failures, the research team then proceeded to assess the practices and methods used in the organizations' transformations, identifying connections between these practices and methods and the outcome of the transformation effort. In particular, the research team was interested in identifying best-in-class practices associated with transformation efforts.

This entire research process, including development of the transformation performance index model, spanned more than ten years.

SAMPLE

The panel of experts initially started with a list of over five hundred companies that had undergone changes in the past twenty years. The panel used the companies' annual reports, quarterly presentations, and 10Ks, as well as archival sources such as business journals (*BusinessWeek*, *The Wall Street Journal*) and news articles, to identify the companies that underwent change efforts that fit the constraints of the model. The most common reasons for a company's exclusion from our analysis were the following:

- The company underwent incremental, not transformational, change.

- The company was not a public company.

- The starting date did not fit the constraints of the model.

- Some data was available but incomplete.

We will explain each of these criteria at the end of this section, along with why exclusion based on these criteria is warranted.

The constraints of the model led to the natural emergence of the final sample of fifty-six companies. These companies were picked blindly, without any preconceived notions about the impact of the transformation. We didn't conduct the analysis having already chosen the companies. Rather, the analysis and the data spoke for themselves.

Another note about our final sample, representing a wide variety of industries, is that although we believe that it is a random, representative sample, we recognize that it is not exhaustive. Indeed, many companies or organizations underwent transformations that fit our constraints but were not included in our analysis. In later sections, we will explain how we know that the sample is fair and representative.

Let us now return to the main reasons companies were excluded from our analysis and the rationale behind the development of these constraints.

Incremental, Not Transformational, Change

Because the research team wanted to analyze the impact of organizational transformations on the company's performance, we needed to first define what constituted a transformation. After looking at various definitions, the team concluded that the basic premise of a transformation is a fundamental, often radical, shift in the company's functioning. This stands in sharp contrast to incremental change, when an organization makes smaller, more gradual changes. Unlike incremental change efforts, transformations tend to have more drastic effects on a company.

To identify whether a company had actually undergone a transformation and not simply incremental change, the research team and panel of experts looked for words such as *transformation*, *radical change*, and *reengineering* in each company's archival sources and descriptions about its change effort. Once the sources of these words were identified, the panel of experts sifted through them to make sure that the usage of the words accurately and appropriately defined a transformation effort. On further research, we learned that many companies in our original list of over five hundred had actually undergone incremental change rather than a transformation.

Nonpublic Companies

To compare companies objectively in a standardized way, the panel of experts decided to use several common financial metrics to assess the impact of the various transformation efforts. Therefore, private companies and government enterprises were not included in the analysis because of their absence in capital markets and the lack of available and accessible public information about their financial performance.

Starting Date

A key question in developing the constraints of the model was, Which of the transformations are relevant in today's world? The panel of experts noted that since the early 1990s, a major shift in the entire corporate environment has transformed both the way companies are run and the way business is conducted. Such a shift needed to be taken into consideration when selecting an appropriate boundary for a starting date for companies to be analyzed.

In the 1990s, the entire landscape shifted from an industrial, international economy to an informational, truly global economy, a shift that was facilitated and accelerated by the advent of the World Wide Web and rapid globalization. An organization in the 1990s, amid these changes, needed to address numerous new management challenges and reexamine its culture because of the ready access to information. Companies had to rethink what they were doing and how to address the different challenges they were encountering.

This major shift resulted in what we call a postmodern or post-Web world, dominated by postmodern companies. In this new, hypercompetitive environment, market transitions are a lot faster, and the cycle of innovation has gotten shorter and shorter. Because people can innovate from anywhere in the world now, new products and services are appearing more and more frequently, resulting in further competition. This landscape change also saw the rapid adoption of e-mail and work group tools and the rising power of real-time information.

To make the findings of our research relevant to today's postmodern corporation, the panel of experts decided that the companies analyzed needed to be part of this post-Web world. Therefore, their transformation efforts needed to occur in the mid-1990s and beyond, when the landscape had already shifted in major ways. In order to standardize the model and take this into account, the expert panel decided that transformations that occurred before 1995 should be discarded, because that is approximately the time of the shift.[1]

Interestingly, in the discussion about this major landscape shift, the panel of experts noticed a more recent major event that had an impact on the corporate environment. This event occurred around the turn of the century and is commonly known as the *dot-com bubble*, which saw unprecedented heights in company valuation by financial markets in the years before 2000, followed by an equally remarkable decline in the years after 2000. The prebubble phase was characterized by abundance, the postbubble by scarcity. The question then fell to the research team: do the tools adopted in the postbubble environment reflect a major shift where former techniques and processes are no longer relevant in today's postbubble correction period? In other words, does the dot-com bubble reflect another major shift in the landscape? After considerable debate and discussion, the experts finally decided that they didn't need to make the decision—they would let the data speak for itself.

To identify the starting year for the transformation efforts, the panel of experts sifted through the archival sources to identify cornerstone events that signaled the beginning of the effort. Often, this occurred simultaneously with the entry of a new CEO to transform the company. Other times, a company might have made a public announcement about the effort and reflected on when it began. Not only did identified companies have to begin their effort in 1995 or afterward, they also needed to have public information available one year before the transformation began, because of the way the model was developed. This year before the transformation would provide a baseline measurement for analysis.

Duration of Available Data

The effects of the transformation effort typically start appearing in the financial performance of the company within two to three years. However, the focus of a transformation is not just to maximize short-term gains but also to create sustainable new processes. A period of five years can illustrate sustainability of the operations and allow the transformation to further translate to financial returns in a way that is still tied to the effects of the transformation. However, a period shorter than three years cannot fairly and accurately show the impact of the transformation on the performance of the organization. Hence, most of the companies were analyzed over a period of three to five years, depending on the start date and the availability of the data and the situation of the company. Data was sometimes unavailable because of acquisitions or mergers within the assessed time frame. If there was not enough available data for the entire three-year minimum period for analysis, the company was discarded.

We provide a list of companies analyzed after we describe the model, the fundamentals, and the evaluation process.

ANALYSIS 1:
AN INTRODUCTION TO THE MODEL

Because a transformation effort is typically undertaken to drastically improve an organization's performance, we can assume that the effort should have an impact on the financial performance of the company.

The transformation performance index model uses eleven financial criteria (hereafter referred to as *fundamentals*) in five areas to assess the relative success of the numerous transformation efforts. These fundamentals are categorized as primary and secondary, with the primary criteria being the most important indicators of an effort's success. A primary analysis using only the primary fundamentals is first conducted to separate the clear successes and failures. For the mediocre companies, a secondary analysis including the secondary fundamentals is subsequently conducted to distinguish between the efforts that were average, above average, and below average. The transformation efforts of each company are compared with each other by representing all analyzed companies on a normal distribution curve and looking at the percentile each company falls under.

Table A-1 shows the main steps taken to analyze the companies in our model. We will explain some of the key terms both below and in the following sections.

Fundamentals

Each company's transformation effort is evaluated using fundamentals in five categories: operational performance, common equity performance, productivity, financial condition (liquidity and solvency), and return on investment. The fundamentals are categorized into two sets, or "buckets": (1) primary fundamentals and (2) secondary fundamentals. Primary fundamentals are those considered most crucial from a financial perspective and potentially most responsive to the transformation. Operational performance and the performance of the company's common equity in capital markets (stock market performance) are considered primary fundamentals. Secondary fundamentals include the less crucial, yet still financially important fundamentals of productivity, financial condition, and return on investment.

TABLE A-1

Conducting the analysis

For each company:

1. For each fundamental:
   a. Gather the relevant financial data.
   b. Calculate a percentage value for the fundamental. Depending on the particular fundamental, this percentage may reflect either absolute change (either positive or negative) or an industry-benchmarked average change over the period of the transformation.[a]
   c. Translate the percentage value into a preliminary semantic value. This can be done using the formula described later.
   d. Adjust the preliminary semantic value as necessary to obtain the final semantic value. Adjustments should only be made to semantic values that reflect negative impact of the transformation.

2. Conduct a primary analysis by calculating the weighted sum of the adjusted semantic value for only the primary fundamentals. This weighted average will give you a primary index score for the company.

3. Conduct a secondary analysis by calculating the weighted sum of the adjusted semantic value for both the primary and secondary fundamentals combined (primary fundamentals weighted more heavily than secondary fundamentals). This will give you a secondary index score for the company

To categorize companies:

1. From both the primary and the secondary analyses, create a normal distribution curve based on the mean and standard deviation of the respective index scores of all the companies combined.

2. Calculate the percentile of each company from the primary analysis, using the primary index score and the generated distribution.
   a. Companies ranked in the 70th percentile or above are clear successes.
   b. Companies ranked in the 30th percentile or below are clear failures.

3. Calculate the percentile of each company from the secondary analysis using the secondary index score and the generated distribution of all companies, but categorize only the companies that were not categorized in the primary analysis using this secondary analysis percentile.
   a. Those ranked in the 66th percentile or above are above average.
   b. Those ranked between the 33rd percentile and the 66th percentile are average.
   c. Those ranked in the 33rd percentile or below are below average.

[a]To calculate the percentage value for the starting year, data from a so-called base year must first be obtained.

For each fundamental, we calculate a percentage value reflecting either absolute change (positive or negative) or the industry-benchmarked average change over the period of transformation. We consider industry benchmarks for those fundamentals that make sense only in the context of the firm's primary industry. Benchmarking relevant fundamentals also takes into account surges in the general market, such as those experienced during the dot-com bubble. To earn points, companies still have to perform better than their counterparts, measured by the industry average. In sum, the percentage value, whether it reflects an absolute change or was benchmarked against the industry average, captures the magnitude and the direction, either improvement or worsening, of change in the underlying fundamental during the period of the transformation.

Semantic Value for Each Fundamental

For a given fundamental, the calculated percentage is then scaled and normalized into a *semantic value*. A semantic value is a numerical representation of the perceived performance of a given fundamental during the transformation period that lets us directly compare the companies. This numerical representation is a number between −10 and 10, inclusive, where 0 implies neutrality, positive values imply desirable results, and negative numbers reflect less desirable results.

Evaluation and Categorization Process: An Overview

Categorization is a two-step process. In the first step, clear successes and failures are identified. Those companies whose transformation results in the first step do not qualify them as either outright successes or outright failures are considered for further review in the second step. After the secondary analysis, the remaining companies not ranked in the primary analysis are categorized as either average, above average, or below average. Both the primary and secondary analyses require the same steps—the only difference is the amount of data that is analyzed in each. The secondary analysis uses both primary and secondary fundamentals, whereas the primary analysis is restricted to the primary fundamentals.

Analysis is based on index values, which are the weighted sum of all the semantic values of the underlying fundamentals for one particular company. Because of their importance in indicating a company's performance, primary fundamentals are given more weight than secondary fundamentals. These resulting index values represent the overall financial impact of the transformation, where higher, more positive index values reflect stronger transformation performances, negative values reflect weaker performances, and 0 reflects essentially neutral results.

We emphasize that the index scores are a *weighted sum* of the fundamentals. In some cases, a company may score highly on one fundamental but poorly on another. For example, stock price, while generally a good indicator of a company's performance, is not always accurate. Most businesspeople know that sometimes the stock price gets ahead of the company, and sometimes the company gets ahead of the stock price. Therefore, stock price is not the only primary fundamental in our model. Rather, we look at numerous indicators, such as the price-earnings (P/E) ratio and revenue. Creating an index value using the weighted sum of these indicators gives a more balanced and accurate reflection of the company's performance.

The index scores allow the transformations in different companies to be compared directly by standardizing performance of the transformation on a common financial basis. Since the relevant financials are benchmarked relative to the company's own industry, the comparison is fair and takes into account the differences in industry structures that companies have to deal with. For example, a company in a high-growth industry would need to have higher absolute growth or performance figures than a company in a mature or stable industry to receive a higher score on the index.

The biggest advantage of using an index value is the ability to conduct cross-company comparisons. For this purpose, we calculate the mean and standard deviation of the index values of all the companies and use the results to generate a normal distribution curve, ultimately producing percentile values for each company. (See figure A-1 for an illustration of a normal distribution curve, relevant standard deviations, and the corresponding percentiles.) This normal distribution curve is important because it indirectly and statistically expands our sample size according to the mean and standard deviation. Assuming that the mean and standard deviation are representative of all the companies in the world that fit our constraints, the calculated percentiles will reflect how a particular company's transformation ranks against all the other transformations in the world, even those that weren't analyzed in our data set.

The logical question would then be, How do you know whether your mean and standard deviation are representative of companies in the world at large? In the beginning, when there are few data points, any addition will significantly affect the mean of the data set. However, as more and more data points are added, each additional data point has a smaller and smaller effect on the mean and standard deviation. A sample can be considered representative for the purposes of the model when additional, random data points that are added do not significantly affect the normal distribution curve.

The mean (M) lies at the peak of the graph at the 50th percentile, where the standard deviation is 0. Using a normal curve allows the placement of each company's index value with respect to the curve to generate a corresponding percentile value. For example, if the index value of a given company is

FIGURE A-1

Normal distribution percentiles

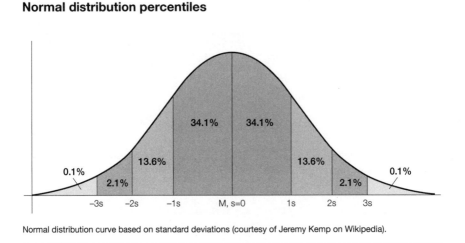

Normal distribution curve based on standard deviations (courtesy of Jeremy Kemp on Wikipedia).

1 standard deviation (1s) above the mean, then the company's percentile will be 50 percent + 34.1 percent = 84.1 percent, meaning the company's transformation effort did better than 84.1 percent of the transformations out there. If the company's index value is 2 standard deviations (2s) above the mean, then its percentile will be 50 percent + 34.1 percent + 13.6 percent = 97.7 percent, meaning only 2.3 percent of the transformations out there, whether they were included in our sample or not, performed better than that company's. Hence, we use this normal distribution percentile to rank the perceived financial impact of the transformation process in the transformed companies. In this way, the transformation efforts of different companies can be objectively ranked using a standardized process.

The following three main sections explain in further detail the three areas mentioned above: fundamentals, the semantic value, and the evaluation and categorization process.

THE FUNDAMENTALS

Table A-2 summarizes the key information for the fundamentals used in our analysis. We next describe each fundamental.

Those with the evaluation metric "benchmarked average" refer to the fact that analysis using those fundamentals was benchmarked against industry levels, as described previously. These benchmarked fundamentals are more dependent on the particular industry the organization is in, whereas other

TABLE A-2

Fundamentals breakdown

	Fundamental	Evaluation metric	Success indicator	Primary or secondary
Operational performance	Revenue growth	Percentage change	Higher	Primary
	EBIT margin (net)	Percentage change	Higher	
Stock market performance	Stock price	Stock price CAGR over transformation period[a]	Higher	Primary
	Price-earnings ratio	Benchmarked average	Higher	
	Price-to-sales ratio	Benchmarked average	Higher	
Productivity	Revenue/employee	Benchmarked average	Higher	Secondary
	Income/employee	Benchmarked average	Higher	
Financial condition (solvency and liquidity	Debt/equity ratio	Benchmarked average	Lower	Secondary
	Current ratio	Benchmarked average	Lower	
Return on investment	Return on equity (ROE)	Percentage change	Higher	Secondary
	Return on assets (ROA)	Percentage change	Higher	

[a]CAGR stands for compound annual growth rate, the year-over-year growth rate applied to a part of a company's activities over a multiple-year period. The formula for calculating CAGR is (current value/base value) $\times$ (1/# of years) − 1.

fundamentals, those analyzed using "percentage change," can be appropriately assessed independent of the industry. For a transformation effort to be considered successful with respect to a metric that is benchmarked against the industry average, it has to perform above the industry average. As mentioned before, such benchmarking also takes into account changing market conditions.

The success indicator refers to whether a higher or a lower number reflects success. In the factors that are benchmarked against the industry average, companies with higher values than the industry average are penalized for some fundamentals, but lower values are penalized for others. "Higher" in the success indicator column hence means that a higher number reflects the success of the company's transformation effort for that fundamental.

Primary fundamentals are given a weight of 2, whereas secondary fundamentals are given a weight of 1. These weights reflect only the relative importance of a parameter, compared with other parameters, in the score, rather than the absolute significance of the fundamentals in evaluating a company's performance.

Category: Operational Performance

The most basic, yet most important analysis of a company is that of its revenue and profitability trends. The two metrics thus used here are considered as primary fundamentals.

Fundamental: Revenue Growth

Revenue is obviously a fundamental indicator of a company's operational performance. A high growth rate can be attributed to a number of factors, including the company's ability to deliver the right products and services to the market, to price them correctly, or to carry out its sales and marketing plans. For each year in the transformation period, year-to-year revenue growth is first calculated, followed by the average value of the annual growth rates.

Fundamental: Earnings Before Interest and Taxes (Operating) Margin

A company with high revenue growth rates can still lose money for various reasons, such as inefficient operations or uncontrolled increases in expenses to support revenue expansion. To better gauge a company's operational efficiencies, we consider earnings before interest and taxes (EBIT) as a margin of revenue.[2] High EBIT margins indicate efficient operations, because a high percentage of revenue is left even after subtracting the cost of goods sold (COGS), selling, general, and administrative (SG&A) activities, research and development (R&D), and other operational expenses. For each year of the transformation period, year-to-year changes in the EBIT margin were calculated, and the average value of the annual EBIT margin changes was then used.

Category: Stock Market Performance

The most common way to assess a company from an investment perspective is to analyze its stock market performance. The stock price and price ratios reflect the market's estimation of a company's future. The stock performance also shows the changing business environment in which the company operates. In this analysis, we use the stock price compound annual growth rate (CAGR) and an average of price ratios, both P/E and price-to-sales (P/S), benchmarked against industry levels. Stock price and P/E are considered primary fundamentals since they are the most frequently used parameters for capital market analysis. P/S is used to complement the P/E ratio and is especially useful in cases where analysis is not possible because of negative earnings. While direct comparisons of prices and ratios between companies and industries are meaningless, benchmarked metrics allow us to transform such apples-to-oranges comparisons into apples-to-apples comparisons.

Fundamental: Stock Price

The stock price is a direct measure of how much a company and its future are valued by investors. An increase in the stock price indicates investors' belief in the growth potential of the company, since the price is the present value of expected future cash flows.

Fundamental: Price-Earnings Ratio

The P/E ratio is a much better indicator of the value of a stock than the market price alone. It estimates how fast and how much a company and its industry are expected to grow. A P/E greater than the industry average indicates that the company is expected to grow faster than its competitors. This results in a positive effect on the company's score in the analysis.

Fundamental: Price/Sales

The P/S ratio shows how much investors value every dollar of a company's sales. P/S, though not the most frequently used ratio, is very effective in analyzing companies when they have negative income, since the P/E ratio becomes meaningless in these cases. P/S benchmarking is also used for spotting recovery situations and for double-checking that a growth company is not overvalued.

Category: Productivity

Productivity is a measure of a company's management and task force performance, as compared with the primary industry in which the company operates. The two metrics mentioned below are benchmarked against industry averages and are used as part of the secondary analysis.

Fundamental: Revenue per Employee

This fundamental tells us how effectively the company's task force can generate revenue for the company, compared with the rest of the industry players.

Fundamental: Net Income per Employee

This fundamental shows us how cost-effective the company's task force is in its operations, compared with the rest of its industry players.

Category: Financial Condition (Solvency and Liquidity)

This analysis primarily helps us understand the company's long-term and short-term financial viability. The two parameters used here are the debt/equity ratio, which tells us about the extent of a company's financial leverage, and the current ratio, which tells us about the company's ability to meet short-term liabilities, such as debt and payables. The higher the D/E ratio, the more liquid the company is. Since the ratios tend to vary in different industries, they are benchmarked against the industry average. Solvency and liquidity fundamentals are considered secondary and therefore are given lower weights, since they are not absolute measures of an organizational transformation and are vulnerable and susceptible to such things as "cosmetic accounting changes."

Fundamental: Debt/Equity

The D/E ratio is a measure of solvency. While D/E tells little about the company's growth prospects, it does indicate the financial strength of the company and its ability to survive a tough period. A high D/E may be due to debt financing for growth, though it adds volatility to future earnings because of increased interest liabilities. While some amount of debt is good for a company, since it provides a tax shield and allows the company to pursue additional growth opportunities, debt also results in increased risk for shareholders. Hence, a balance between debt and equity financing needs to be made. Because of the relatively greater risk of having too much debt, companies with a higher D/E than the industry average are penalized. The metric is a secondary fundamental, since it is only indicative and not an absolute measure of a company's growth, efficiency, or financial performance.

Fundamental: Current Ratio

This secondary fundamental is a measure of the efficiency of the company's liquidity and operating (cash) cycle and refers to the company's ability to turn its products and services into cash. The higher the current ratio, the more capable a company is of meeting its current liabilities, which are due within a year. While a lower ratio doesn't mean that the company will go bankrupt in the near future, it doesn't indicate a healthy financial condition, as the company may run into liquidity problems. Companies with a current ratio lower than the industry average are hence penalized.

Category: Return on Investment

The final part of the score is return on investment, which refers to the company's ability to extract positive, high returns on money invested in the company in the forms of equity and capital assets deployed for the company's operations. The two parameters used are return on assets (ROA) and return on equity (ROE). While the two measures are somewhat similar, together they paint a clearer picture of the company's performance than they do individually, by indicating how balanced the financing structure is, such as the balance between debt and equity financing. For example, a high ROE could result from highly leveraged growth of the company, which would be indicated in a significantly lower ROA. For each year in the transformation period, year-to-year changes in ROA and ROE are first calculated, and then the average values of the annual growth rates are calculated. Profitability metrics are considered secondary fundamentals because they can be "artificially boosted" by changes to the capital structure and may not be a direct result of operational improvements during the process of transformation.

Fundamental: Return on Equity

This is a measure of how well investors' money is used for generating profits and growing the company, and hence investors' share in the company. ROE also indicates how efficiently a company is able to grow without raising additional equity capital. However, there is a limit to the ROE without the addition of capital in the form of either equity or debt, and ROE is significantly dependent on the industry. While ROE is a good performance indicator when benchmarked against the industry average, it does not take into account the entire capital structure of the company, primarily debt financing for operations and growth.

Fundamental: Return on Assets

ROA tells us how much profit was generated by management for every dollar of the company's assets, both debt and equity, regardless of the size of the company. A high ROA is a sign of good financial and operational performance. However, a highly leveraged company will show a much higher ROE than ROA, since the portion of equity in the total assets reduces with increasing debt. Thus, ROA would indicate whether a high ROE is a true indicator of the company's future, or whether it is misleading because of a leveraged position. ROA and ROE together, when benchmarked against the industry, are good indicators of both efficiency in using the available capital to grow the company and the long-term financial health of the company.

THE SEMANTIC SCALE

Absolute figures for the previously described fundamentals do not allow for any comparison between companies, either on individual parameters or taken together. Therefore, a semantic scale was used to create a standard scale on which percentage scores could be normalized and transformations could then be compared. It translated performance on different metrics relative to each other to a single dimensionless metric. This final semantic scale ranges from –10 to 10, with –10 being extremely poor, 0 being neutral, and 10 being extremely good.

To transform the former values into the semantic scale, we first translated all the absolute numbers to percentage values to document the percentage change from one year to the next. Hence, a base year needs to be used to measure the progress of the first year of the transformation. After this, we used the function shown in figure A-2 to convert the percentages into a preliminary semantic scale, where x is the percentage value calculated for a given fundamental. The higher the value of x, the higher the semantic score and the better the performance on that metric.[3]

At this point, the performance index ranges from 0 to 10, with 0 being poor performance, 5 being neutral, and 10 being outstanding. For example, when $x = 0$, meaning there was no change in the fundamental (for better or for worse), the preliminary semantic score returned by the function is 5. Figure A-3 shows how an absolute number, the x-axis, can be translated to the preliminary semantic scale, the y-axis. As in the formula, 0 percent on the graph corresponds to a 5 in the preliminary semantic scale. Negative scores on the semantic scale means the company performed worse after the transformation than before, while positive values mean performance improved.

FIGURE A-2

Semantic scale

$$10 \cdot \left(\frac{1}{1 + \frac{1}{2^x}} \right)$$

Semantic scale conversion

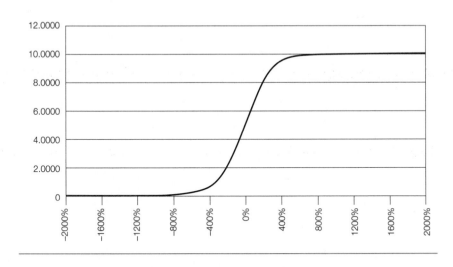

Scores with performance values equidistant from this neutral score of 5 should be weighted equally when calculating the overall semantic scale. Hence, for scores below 5, 10 (a perfect score) was subtracted to give them a negative score. For an example of how the integers changed from the preliminary semantic scale to the final semantic scale, see table A-3.

Hence, values equidistant from neutral multiplied by the weight result in the same number, only with different signs. This means that a score of –8 and 8 are of the same magnitude in impact, only the former was negatively impacted and the latter positively impacted. This will make future calculations and values more intuitive.

Figure A-4 is a graph that converts an absolute value to the final adjusted semantic value. This semantic value was used in calculating the total index score. The x-axis represents the absolute value, whereas the y-axis represents the final, adjusted semantic value.

TABLE A-3

Final semantic scale conversion

Preliminary	0	1	2	3	4	5	6	7	8	9	10
Final	–10	–9	–8	–7	–6	0	6	7	8	9	10

Adjusted semantic value conversion

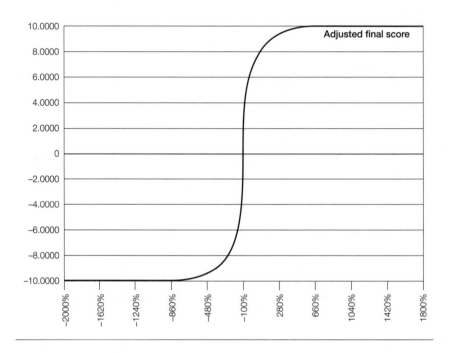

As visible in both the table and the graph, a final semantic score of −5 and 5 cannot actually be achieved. However, this does not affect our analysis and the overall index. Through the adjustments made to the preliminary semantic scale, however, a negative score symbolizing a poor transformation effort is represented by a negative number, rather than a number between 0 and 5. This not only makes the later analysis more intuitive but also facilitates the evaluation process.

THE EVALUATION PROCESS

As discussed in the overview of the evaluation process, evaluation is done in two steps: a primary analysis followed by a secondary analysis. Although a secondary analysis is conducted on all the companies to attain the mean and standard deviation necessary to generate a normal distribution curve, only the companies left uncategorized after the primary analysis, the average companies, are categorized in the secondary analysis.

Primary Analysis

Once all the fundamentals have been converted to the semantic values and adjusted for negative performance, an index value based on the weighted sum of the primary fundamentals is generated. The model contains five primary fundamentals whose semantic values are scaled by a factor of 2, resulting in an index ranging from –100 to 100.[4]

To enable cross-company comparisons, the average and standard deviation of index values are used to generate a normal distribution curve, as described earlier. According to the generated normal curve, a percentile value is associated with each company. The percentile value ranks the company's financial performance with respect to other firms, assuming that the financial performance of the transformation follows a normal distribution curve. Using the resulting percentiles, we categorize the transformation impact on the primary fundamentals, as shown in table A-4.

When we graphed the data, there was a break or inflection point at the 70 percentile. Similarly, at the lower end there was another inflection point at the 30 percentile. Thus, in the primary analysis, a passing grade of 70 percent reflects success, although scoring below 70 percent does not automatically imply failure. Instead, we differentiate between failures (those with scores below 30 percent) and those in the average range, which are categorized pending further analysis. All the companies are then put into another analysis incorporating the secondary fundamentals, although only the average companies are then rated. The new analysis will illustrate whether the impact of the transformation effort is visible in the other fundamentals.

Remember that these percentiles are based on a normal distribution curve and do not represent percentiles with respect to our research sample. Hence, more than 30 percent of our sample can fall in the 70th percentile, which isn't intuitive to the amateur statistician. Similarly, over 30 percent of our sample may attain scores, or percentiles, below 30 percent.

TABLE A-4

Primary analysis categorization

Percentile	Transformation results
Less than or equal to 30%	Failure
Between 30% and 70%	Mediocre—final rating pending further analysis
Higher than or equal to 70%	Success

Secondary Analysis

In the secondary analysis, the rating involves generating a new set of index values based on the weighted sum of both primary and secondary fundamentals. The index will range from −160 to 160, with a weight of 2 given to the primary fundamentals and a weight of 1 given to the six secondary fundamentals.[5] Similar to the primary analysis, the average and standard deviation of the newly generated index values for all the companies is used to create a normal distribution curve, and comparison is done using the resulting percentile values.

There are two basic differences in the evaluation: (1) although all the companies undergo a secondary analysis, only mediocre performers, those that ranked between 30 percent and 70 percent in the primary analysis, are rated again; and (2) we follow different metrics to categorize the companies' transformation efforts. The remaining companies are now categorized as average, above average, and below average, creating the third, fourth, and fifth buckets. In this way, we can differentiate the companies according to terms alone. Average companies, as well as those above and below average, were ranked in the secondary analysis, whereas successes and failures were finalized in the primary analysis. The companies deemed mediocre in the primary analysis were categorized using the criteria in table A-5.

Our procedure did not allow for inconsistent categorizations based on the primary and secondary analyses, because only the mediocre companies were ranked in the secondary analysis. However, in instances where companies ranked differently in the primary and secondary analyses, the primary analysis was given more weight. For example, assume company A performs in the 65th percentile in the primary analysis and company B scores in the 75th percentile. In the secondary analysis, company A scores 68 percent, and company B scores 60 percent, for whatever reason. Company B is ranked as a success, and company A is above average. This is important because the primary fundamentals are more telling than the secondary fundamentals,

TABLE A-5

Secondary analysis categorization

Percentile in secondary analysis	Transformation results: category
Less than or equal to 33.33%	Below average
Between 33.34% and 66.66%	Average
Higher than or equal to 66.66%	Above average

which are subject to "window dressing." They are also clearer indicators of a company's performance, which lies at the heart of what a transformation effort should address.

DETAILED RESULTS AND IMPLICATIONS

In this section, we will share the findings through a series of graphs and tables, accompanied by explanations. To begin, table A-6 is a list of the companies we analyzed quantitatively using the model explained above, narrowed down from an original list of over five hundred companies. These companies reflect a representative sample of companies in the world at large, for the mean and standard deviation used to generate the normal distribution curve remained steady and changed only slightly when the final five to ten companies

TABLE A-6

Companies analyzed

	Company	Stock symbol	Years[a]
1	3Com	COMS	2001–2005
2	3M	MMM	2000–2004
3	Abbott Laboratories	ABT	1999–2003
4	Agere Systems	AGR	2002–2006
5	Amdocs	DOX	2002–2006
6	Apple	AAPL	2001–2005
7	Archer Daniels Midland	ADM	1999–2003
8	Avaya	AV	2001–2005
9	Barclays	BCS	1999–2003
10	Bay Networks	BAY	1995–1997
11	Best Buy	BBY	2002–2006
12	Boeing	BA	1996–2000
13	Brocade Communications Systems	BRCD	1999–2003
14	Brunswick	BC	2000–2004
15	Caterpillar	CAT	2003–2006
16	Corning	GLW	2001–2005
17	DaimlerChrysler	DCX	2000–2004
18	Dell	DELL	1997–2001
19	Delta Air Lines	DALRQ	1999–2003
20	Dun & Bradstreet	DNB	2000–2004
21	Eastman Kodak	EK	2000–2004
22	Electronic Data Systems	EDS	2003–2006

(continued)

TABLE A-6 (continued)

Companies analyzed

	Company	Stock symbol	Years[a]
23	EMC Corp.	EMC	2001–2005
24	Ford	F	1999–2003
25	General Electric	GE	1995–1999
26	General Electric	GE	2001–2005
27	General Motors	GM	2000–2004
28	Hewlett-Packard	HPQ	1999–2003
29	Hilton Hotels	HLT	1997–2002
30	IBM	IBM	1996–2000[b]
31	Ingram Micro	IM	2000–2004
32	Intel	INTC	1997–2001
33	Lucent	LU	2000–2004
34	McDonald's	MCD	2003–2006
35	Motorola	MOT	2004–2006
36	New York Times	NYT	2002–2006
37	Nissan	NSANY	2000–2004
38	Nokia	NOK	1999–2003
39	Nordstrom	JWN	2000–2004
40	Nortel Networks	NT	1998–2002
41	Office Depot	ODP	2000–2004
42	Procter & Gamble	PG	2000–2004
43	Quest Communications	Q	2002–2006
44	RadioShack	RSH	1999–2003
45	Redback Networks	RBAK	2001–2005
46	Sanyo	SANYY	2001–2005
47	Schering-Plough	SGP	2003–2006
48	Sony	SNE	1999–2003
49	Symbol Technologies	SBL	2003–2006
50	Telefónica de España	TEF	2000–2004
51	The Home Depot	HD	2000–2004
52	Time Warner	TWX	2000–2004
53	Tyco International	TYC	2002–2006
54	VeriSign	VRSN	2002–2006
55	Whirlpool	WHR	1999–2003
56	Xerox	XRX	2001–2005

[a]Note that the dates in this table and in subsequent tables are inclusive. Therefore, the years 2000–2002 are considered a three-year transformation period in our analysis.

[b]Lou Gerstner joined IBM in 1993. IBM was included in the analysis despite the fact that its starting date was before 1995 because of the notoriety of the effort. Had we used an earlier date in our analysis, IBM actually would have had a better ranking than it did (see the following tables). This is because when Gerstner joined IBM, it was at a low point in its history, and the company's performance had improved slightly by 1996, the time we started our analysis.

were added. (The explanation for generating the normal distribution curve and how to identify when a sample is representative was given earlier.)

Of the fifty-five companies listed, we analyzed fifty-six transformation efforts (the two efforts from GE were analyzed separately). An additional company, ACI (a pseudonym), was also used in the research but not analyzed because it was a private company. By most accounts, though, ACI's transformation was a success (discussed later).

Through a primary analysis of the companies, we identified the mean and standard deviation for our sample, shown in table A-7.

Using this data, we developed the normal distribution curve and corresponding percentile values for the range of scores (see figure A-5). The curve with triangles, a cumulative curve, reflects which percentile each score represents. For example, a score of 0 translates to a percentile of approximately 30 percent.

TABLE A-7

Primary analysis mean and standard deviation

Mean	7.38
Standard deviation	26.08

FIGURE A-5

Normal distribution curve for primary fundamentals

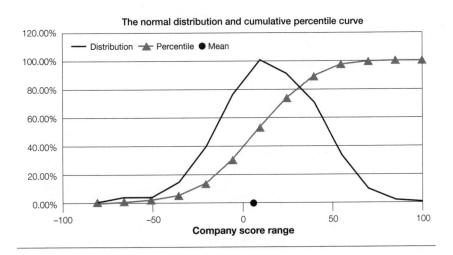

The normal distribution and cumulative percentile curve

As a result of the primary analysis, eighteen companies were labeled as successes, and twenty were labeled as failures. Tables A-8 and A-9 chart these companies, their scores, and their relative percentiles. As a reminder, the percentiles reflect their ranking with respect not to the analyzed sample but a normal distribution curve based on the mean and standard deviation. We assumed that according to our sample, other transformation efforts, had we analyzed them, would have fallen onto our distribution curve, given our mean and standard deviation. Hence, a company scoring 70 percent does not mean that the company did better than 70 percent of the companies in our data set. Rather, the company performed better than 70 percent of the companies in the overall, projected data set.

Companies with successful transformation efforts made up 32 percent of our data set, while failed transformation efforts made up 36 percent of our sample. Note that even though we used the 70th percentile to categorize successful companies, successes in our sample were in fact representative of the 80th percentile, for all the successful companies scored above 80 percent.

TABLE A-8

Successful transformation (primary analysis)

Score	Company	Years	Percentile
57.20	Bay Networks	1995–1997	97.06%
55.28	Telefónica de España	2000–2004	96.53%
54.48	3M	2000–2004	96.29%
40.53	General Electric	1995–1999	89.48%
33.75	Apple	2001–2005	83.99%
33.64	VeriSign	2002–2006	83.89%
33.35	Nissan	2000–2004	83.62%
33.12	The Home Depot	2000–2004	83.42%
32.92	Abbott Laboratories	1999–2003	83.21%
32.05	IBM	1995-1999	82.36%
31.60	Best Buy	2002–2006	81.91%
31.43	General Electric	2001–2005	81.74%
31.36	McDonald's	2003–2006	81.67%
30.98	Procter & Gamble	2000–2004	81.28%
30.83	Brunswick	2000–2004	81.13%
30.76	Nokia	1999–2003	81.06%
30.22	Brocade Communications Systems	1999–2003	80.49%
29.57	Symbol Technologies	2003–2006	79.80%

TABLE A-9

Failed transformations (primary analysis)

Score	Company	Years	Percentile
(7.82)	Ford	1999–2003	27.67%
(8.48)	Hilton Hotels	1997–2002	26.84%
(9.55)	Hewlett-Packard	1999–2003	25.52%
(10.72)	RadioShack	2000–2004	24.09%
(10.81)	Barclays	1999–2003	24.00%
(11.26)	DaimlerChrysler	2000–2004	23.47%
(11.85)	Lucent	2000–2004	22.78%
(11.91)	Redback Networks	2001–2005	22.71%
(11.98)	Agere Systems	2002–2006	22.63%
(12.67)	Whirlpool	1999–2003	21.85%
(14.33)	Qwest Communications	2002–2006	20.02%
(15.50)	Electronic Data Systems	2003–2006	18.79%
(16.95)	Schering-Plough	2003–2006	17.34%
(25.19)	Eastman Kodak	2000–2004	10.47%
(30.77)	General Motors	2000–2004	7.10%
(30.94)	New York Times	2002–2006	7.01%
(32.08)	Nortel Networks	1998–2002	6.44%
(33.59)	Delta Air Lines	1999–2003	5.75%
(57.99)	3Com	2001–2005	0.61%
(60.51)	Avaya	2001–2005	0.46%

Our primary analysis left us with 32 percent of the sample, the mediocre companies, to be categorized after the secondary analysis was completed. We then conducted a secondary analysis on all the companies, using both primary and secondary fundamentals, and found the mean and standard deviation for the data set, shown in table A-10.

TABLE A-10

Secondary analysis mean and standard deviation

Mean	3.86
Standard deviation	36.3

FIGURE A-6

Normal distribution curve for secondary fundamentals

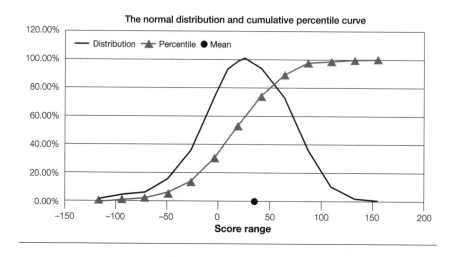

As with the primary analysis, we developed a normal distribution curve and identified corresponding percentile values for the scores using this data (see figure A-6).

With this data, we then distinguished among companies that had above average, average, and below average transformation efforts. Companies that scored 66.66 percent or above were rated above average, those that scored between 33.33 percent and 66.66 percent were rated average, and those that scored 33.33 percent or below were rated below average. In tables A-11, A-12, and A-13, we detail which companies scored above average, average, and

TABLE A-11

Above average transformation (secondary analysis)

Score	Company	Years	Percentile
32.56	Caterpillar	2003-2006	78.54%
32.42	Archer Daniels Midland	1999–2003	78.42%
32.10	Boeing	1996–2000	78.17%
30.22	Amdocs	2002–2006	76.61%
29.99	Motorola	2004–2006	76.42%
29.37	Intel	1997–2001	75.88%
29.28	Xerox	2001–2005	75.81%

TABLE A-12

Average transformations (secondary analysis)

Score	Company	Years	Percentile
18.94	Dun & Bradstreet	2000–2004	66.10%
13.26	EMC Corp.	2001–2005	60.22%
7.81	Sony	1999-2003	54.33%
4.28	Time Warner	2000–2004	50.46%
(2.02)	Tyco International	2002–2006	43.56%
(8.91)	Ingram Micro	2000–2004	36.25%
(10.25)	Corning	2001–2005	34.87%
(10.88)	Office Depot	2000–2004	34.23%

below average in our secondary analysis. Of our entire sample, 9 percent were above average, 16 percent were average, and 4 percent were below average. These below average companies still fared better than our failure companies, which were labeled in the primary analysis.

Analyzing the Bubble

As we mentioned earlier, the research team questioned the effect on the data of the technology bubble that occurred around the turn of the millennium. We now pose the question again: did the dot-com bubble reflect a major shift in the landscape, where prebubble tools and techniques are no longer relevant in today's postbubble economy?

In table A-14, we illustrate how the prebubble and postbubble companies were categorized. We defined prebubble as transformation efforts that began before the year 2000 and postbubble as those that began in the year 2000 or after.

TABLE A-13

Below average transformations (secondary analysis)

Score	Company	Years	Percentile
(14.59)	Dell	1997–2001	30.56%
(24.64)	Nordstrom	2000–2004	21.62%
(28.59)	Sanyo	2001–2005	18.57%

TABLE A-14

Bubble breakdown by absolute numbers

	Success	Failure
Prebubble (total: 18)	6 companies	7 companies
Postbubble (total: 38)	12 companies	13 companies

One of the first things you may notice is that there are more postbubble successes than prebubble successes. Does that mean that postbubble companies fared better than prebubble companies did? Not necessarily, because there are also more postbubble failures than prebubble failures. Because our sample contained more postbubble than prebubble companies, both successes and failures were more likely to be postbubble. In this case, looking at percentages simplifies the comparison (see table A-15).

These percentages refer to successes and failures either prebubble or postbubble. Looking only at successes, we can see that the percentage of companies that were successes was comparable in the prebubble and postbubble phases (33 percent versus 32 percent). This logic can be extended to the failure cases.

But what are the implications of this, and how does this answer the original question posed by the panel of experts?

We can tell intuitively from the data that these prebubble and postbubble distinctions don't make much sense. Why? Such continuity in the data, in spite of the prebubble-postbubble recategorization, indicates that there was no significant change in the corporate environment prebubble and postbubble, at least not one that affected the success of transformation efforts. Regardless of whether the efforts began prebubble or postbubble, a similar percentage of companies were successful, and a similar percentage were not. Hence, the dot-com bubble didn't change the rules of the game or completely shift the landscape. This important conclusion tells us that the tools and practices identified in the book do not depend on the prebubble-postbubble

TABLE A-15

Bubble breakdown by percentages

	Success	Failure
Prebubble (total: 18)	33% (= 6/18)	39% (= 7/18)
Postbubble (total: 38)	32% (= 12/37)	35% (= 13/37)

classification. Rather, these tools and practices remain relevant to all companies in today's postmodern world.

EXCEPTIONS TO OUR QUANTITATIVE MODEL

Throughout this appendix, we have described in depth the quantitative analysis as conducted by the transformation performance index model. We have also mentioned how researching best-in-class practices fits with the quantitative analysis and how, combined, these have formed the premise of our book.

There are, however, some exceptions regarding the inherent connection between the model and the qualitative research—we researched some of the companies without having first analyzed and categorized them using the transformation performance index model. ACI, for example, couldn't be analyzed using the model because appropriate data was unavailable. However, the effects of its transformation could be seen in other ways—through some key financial performance indicators. In another example, Hewlett-Packard, though a public company, undertook a recent transformation led by Mark Hurd. As this book goes to press, however, Hurd's transformation effort hasn't hit the three-year mark and so could not be analyzed through our model. Although neither ACI or HP could be ranked with the other companies by score and percentile, key indicators of success are still clearly visible.

ACI

A midsize systems integration and consulting company based in India, which we will name ACI (Asian Company Inc., a pseudonym), did not have any of the performance indicators necessary for analysis, because it was a private company.

Revenue and net income for ACI, however, are extremely telling. As a result of the transformation, revenue increased threefold and net income increase fivefold in only three years. This percentage increase in revenue was 50 percent greater than that of the company's fastest-growing rival. Furthermore, within two years, turnover was reduced by 50 percent. Such performance factors identify ACI as having a successful transformation effort.

Hewlett-Packard

As this book goes to press, Hewlett-Packard (HP) is currently undergoing a transformation, led by CEO Mark Hurd. However, because the transformation began in 2005, the research team could not justify assessing it with the

TABLE A-16

HP performance

	Metric	Q1 '05	Q1 '07	Percent change
Primary fundamentals	Revenue	$21.5 billion	$25.1 billion	16.7%
	EBIT margin	4.89%	7.82%	59.9%
	Stock price	$20.47	$43.28	111.4%

transformation performance index model using less than three years of data. Preliminary results and financial indicators, however, indicate that the transformation is successful. In table A-16, we give several key metrics and compare the situation of the company when Hurd entered in 2005 with the situation as of February 2007. In the second quarter of 2007, net revenue was up 13 percent year-over-year to $25.5 billion, with a record cash flow from operations of $4.2 billion. HP's strong financial performance is clear from its significant increases in revenue, EBIT margin, and stock price in just a few years.

ANALYSIS 2: CRITICAL SUCCESS FACTORS THROUGH QUALITATIVE INDUCTIVE ANALYSIS

There were 18 successful and 20 failed company transformations in our sample. Thus our research team developed 38 detailed case studies of the successful and failed companies. Our goal was to identify factors that distinguished successful transformations from failed ones. The cases represent different industries, geographies, and company sizes.

Data Collection

For each company case, an average of 10 people were interviewed. The number of interviewees ranged from 7 to 14 people. The average number of interviews was 23, since some people were interviewed more than once. For each company case, we also examined an average of 3,580 company archival pages, including proxy statements. Further, the research team studied an average of 26 articles in the popular press that were written about each company's transformation efforts.

Interviews

The people who were interviewed were executives, senior managers, managers, and employees who were involved in the transformation. Care was taken to have representation from all functions, including strategy, marketing, sales, technology, human resources, manufacturing, and finance for developing each company case. Each interview was semistructured—balanced with open-ended and focused questions—and took 1 to 1.5 hours. The information was analyzed at the end of each interview.

Data Analysis

The research team triangulated the data using multiple sources of data from interviews, archival data, and articles regarding each company. The categories were derived from iterative and simultaneous activities of collecting, coding, and analyzing the data. Thus the categories were grounded and rooted in observation. Coding included detailed coding of line-by-line data to develop some early categories. Later, the research team focused on more selective coding related to categories that were converging.

We observed that more than $2/3$ of interview respondents mentioned at least $1/3$ of categories during the interviews. The three grounded categories were all-encompassing and integrative, speed, and full buy-in, especially from the top layers of the organization during transformation. In the chapters, we decided to separate all-encompassing and integrative categories to provide a richer explanation for the readers.

These factors and categories appeared more commonly in the successful transformation efforts than they did in the failed transformation efforts and differentiated between the successful and unsuccessful companies. Applying the ANOVA statistical tool, we found statistical significance between the successful and failed companies in applying the three categories. Thus, successful transformations typically were all-encompassing, integrative, and fast and had full, passionate commitment and buy-in, especially at the top layers of the organization.

In table A-17, we detail the top companies from our quantitative analysis and highlight the success factors found in the various companies. By fast, we mean that the planning of the transformation was six months or less, and execution took place within a year. Full buy-in refers to real commitment and understanding from the organization. People who have complete buy-in are fully involved and engaged in execution.

You may have noted that some of these companies did not have all the critical success factors. We then looked at the situation behind these companies and their transformation efforts to gain a deeper understanding. We were interested in the following question: why were some of these companies successful despite the absence of some of these critical success factors?

Critical success factors in the successful companies

	All-encompassing and integrative	Fast	Full buy-in, especially at the top layers
Bay Networks	X	X	X
Telefónica de España	X	(3 waves)	X
3M	X	X	X
General Electric (1995–1999)	(4 main areas)	X	X
Apple	X	X	X
VeriSign	X	X	X
Nissan	X	X	X
The Home Depot	X	X	X
Abbott Laboratories	X	X	X
IBM	X	X	X
Best Buy	X	X	X
General Electric (2001–2005)		X	X
McDonald's	X	X	X
Procter & Gamble	X	X	X
Brunswick	X	X	X
Nokia		X	X
Brocade Communications Systems	X		X
Symbol Technologies	X	X	X

- *Telefónica de España.* Telefónica de España is a rare case in which the transformation effort occurred in three distinct waves that were all integrated serially. Each wave, including implementation, lasted a year, and this clear sequence of waves addressed many different aspects of the organization. Every wave focused on growth, competitiveness, and commitment. While the waves didn't change radically from year to year, the efforts and focus within each wave changed to address the new environment and meet the new goals and targets. Each wave can be considered fast, and goals were cascaded within each wave. Although this isn't how we traditionally define *integrative*, the transformation effort as a whole integrated the various aspects of the organization.

- *General Electric.* Although the Jack Welch era is known as an era of perennial transformation, General Electric undertook a holistic transformation effort from 1995 through 1999. In this effort, employees saw major changes throughout the company in four major areas: accelerated globalization, fanatic focus on product services, Six Sigma, and digitalization. Transformations in these four areas led to an integrative, cross-functional effort throughout the company.

- *Nokia.* In response to changing market conditions that reflected a convergence between the telecommunications, wireless, gaming, Internet, and software industries, Nokia changed its strategy, created new business units, and changed its incentive structures. Hence, although the effort didn't attack every single aspect of the organization, it looked at the key parts that needed to be changed in response to the changing market. In embracing the convergence the organization saw in the market, Nokia proactively undertook a change effort.

Now that we have looked at the successful efforts, let us turn to the situation in the failed transformation efforts. Table A-18 lists the companies that performed the worst in our quantitative analysis and the critical success factors present in these companies.

As you can see, companies with failed transformation efforts lacked many of the critical success factors identified and present in the successful companies—in fact, some companies had none of the critical success factors at all! In some of these cases, the presence of one or two of these factors still didn't indicate success. Thus, individually taken, these critical success factors are important but may not be sufficient to drive an effort to success. Ultimately, many different factors need to come together and be aligned before a company can be successful.

Some companies that did not perform well in our analysis may have had better performance after the time period we analyzed. In these cases (and all others), we disregarded the performance outside the time period of analysis because it may have reflected numerous factors other than the transformation effort. Our interest was in how the transformation effort affected the performance of the organization, and the dates analyzed were the ones found to be relevant to our research.

CONCLUSION

Through the development of the transformation performance index model detailed in this appendix, our research team has been able to standardize and objectively categorize companies' transformation efforts into different levels

TABLE A-18

Critical success factors in the failed companies

	All-encompassing and integrative	Fast	Full buy-in, especially at the top layers
Ford	X		
Hilton Hotels			
HP (1999–2003)	X		
RadioShack			X
Barclays	X		
DaimlerChrysler			
Lucent			
Redback Networks			X
Agere Systems	X		
Whirlpool	X		X
Qwest Communications			
Electronic Data Systems			X
Schering-Plough		X	
Eastman Kodak			X
General Motors			X
New York Times			
Nortel Networks	X		
Delta Air Lines			
3Com			X
Avaya			

of success. This has then allowed us to identify the best-in-class practices—those commonly associated with the successful transformation efforts. These analyses have provided the framework for the tools and practices discussed in the book. They have also given us numerous real-life stories to share with you. We hope you have enjoyed learning about these practices as much as we had studying them, and we encourage you to try them out in your organization!

Notes

Introduction

1. Rajat Gupta and Jim Wendler, "Leading Change: An Interview with the CEO of P&G," *McKinsey Quarterly*, July 2005, www.mckinseyquarterly.com.

2. Ibid.

3. Michael Hammer and Steven Stanton, *The Reengineering Revolution* (New York: HarperCollins, 1995).

4. Dennis Donovan, interview by author, April 2006.

5. See the appendix for a detailed explanation of the research methodology and the transformation performance index model used to assess the relative success of transformation efforts from various companies. The appendix also details the findings from both the quantitative and the qualitative studies.

6. See the appendix for detailed findings and results.

7. Interview with Dave House, conducted November 2005.

Chapter 1

1. 90 Days Transformation is a registered trademark of Tabrizi LLC.

2. See the appendix for detailed findings and results from the quantitative and qualitative analysis.

3. MacWorld, Boston, 1997, http://YouTube.com/watch?v=PEHNrqPkefl.

4. "The Best and Worst Managers of the Year," *BusinessWeek,* January 12, 2004, www.businessweek.com/magazine/toc/04_02/B38650402best.htm.

5. Carly Fiorina, Business Biographies, answers.com. www.answers.com/topic/carly-fiorina.

6. Bill Leonard, "GM Drives HR to the Next Level: GM Undergoes a Transformation, and HR Helps to Steer the Changes—Strategic HR—General Motors Corp.; Human Resources—Company Profile," *HR Magazine*, March 2002, www.findarticles.com/p/articles/mi_m3495/is_3_47/ai_84238037/pg_2.

7. Paul A. Eisenstein, "Transformation at General Motors: Putting Passion Back into Product," The Car Connection, August 19, 2002, www.thecarconnection.com/Auto_News/Auto_News/Transformation_at_General_Motors.S175.A5203.html; and Tim Keenan, "Location Is the Focus of GM 2000 Plan," *Ward's Dealer Business*, December 1997, www.findarticles.com/p/articles/mi_m0FJN/is_n4_v32/ai_20230610/pg_2.

8. "Troubled GM to Cut 25,000 Jobs," *CBS News*, June 7, 2005, www.cbsnews.com/stories/2005/06/07/ap/business/main700105.shtml.

9. Leonard, "GM Drives HR to the Next Level."

10. Robin Gareiss, "Chief of the Year: Ralph Szygenda. General Motors' Hard-Driving CIO Has Revved the Engines of the Carmaker's Once-Stagnant IT Systems," *Information Week*, December 2, 2002, www.informationweek.com/story/IWK2002 1127S0011/1.

11. David Magee, *Turnaround: How Carlos Ghosn Rescued Nissan* (New York: HarperBusiness, 2003), 11.

12. Lou Gerstner, Interview with Dan Farber and Robert Joss, November 19, 2002, http://zdnet.com.com/1601–2-966420.html.

13. Andrew Haeg, "A Leaner 3M," *Minnesota Public Radio*, April 22, 2002.

14. What we will hereafter often refer to simply as VeriSign's transformation was actually a transformation effort engaged in by VeriSign's largest division, formerly known as VeriSign Telecommunications Services (VTS). After the transformation, VTS was renamed VeriSign Communications Services, or VCS.

15. VeriSign, "VeriSign Intelligent Infrastructure Drives Telecommunication Innovations for European Operators," news release, February 14, 2005, www.verisign.co.uk/verisign-inc/press_20050214_2.html.

16. Reggie Helton, "Movers & Shakers Interview with Vernon Irvin, Executive Vice President and General Manager of VeriSign Communications Services," Frost & Sullivan, www.frost.com/prod/servlet/exec-brief-movers-feature.pag?mode=open&sid=32398897.

17. Magee, *Turnaround*, 44–49.

18. Ibid, 79.

19. Leigh Kimmel, "Apple Computer, Inc.: A History," 1998, www.geocities.com/Athens/3682/applehistory.html.

20. P. Indu and Vivek Gupta, "The Transformation of Apple's Business Model," ICFAI Center for Management Research, 2006.

21. Jai Singh, "Dell: Apple Should Close Shop," www.cnetnews.com, October 6, 1997.

22. "The 100 Top Brand 2006," *BusinessWeek*, 2006, http://bwnt.businessweek.com/brand/2006.

23. AAPL, Google Finance, March 14, 2007, http://finance.google.com/finance?q=AAPL.

Chapter 2

1. For the remainder of the book, male pronouns are used to refer to males and females.

2. Carlos Ghosn and Philippe Riès, *Shift: Inside Nissan's Historic Revival* (New York: Doubleday, 2005), 175.

3. Rajat Gupta and Jim Wendler, "Leading Change: An Interview with the CEO of P&G," *McKinsey Quarterly*, July 2005, www.mckinseyquarterly.com.

4. Ghosn and Riès, *Shift*, 93.

5. Richard D. Austin and Richard L. Noland, "IBM Corporation Turnaround," Case 9–600-908 (Boston: Harvard Business School, 2000), 1.

6. Louis V. Gerstner Jr., *Who Says Elephants Can't Dance? Leading a Great Enterprise Through Dramatic Change* (New York: HarperBusiness, 2002), 11.

7. David Magee, *Turnaround: How Carlos Ghosn Rescued Nissan* (New York: HarperBusiness, 2003), 83.

8. Gerstner, *Who Says Elephants Can't Dance?* 77.

9. Ghosn and Riès, *Shift*, 133–134.

10. Gerstner, *Who Says Elephants Can't Dance?* 12.

11. Ghosn and Riès, *Shift*, 86–90.

12. Steve Jobs, presentation, MacWorld Conference, 1997.

13. Dave House, presentation at Stanford University, January 31, 2007.

14. A. Leshinsky, "Can HP Win Doing It the Hurd Way?" *Fortune*, April 2006.

15. Leshinsky, 2006.

16. Interview with HP, conducted by B. Tabrizi, J. Castilo, and A. Mak, December 2005.

17. Interview with HP, 2005.

18. Ghosn and Riès, *Shift*, 129.

19. Ibid., 132.

20. Gerstner, *Who Says Elephants Can't Dance?* 41.

21. Ibid., 25, 43, 46; and Austin and Noland, "IBM Corporation Turnaround," 7–8.

22. Doug Garr, *IBM Redux: Lou Gerstner and the Business Turnaround of the Decade* (New York: HarperBusiness, 2000), 59.

23. Magee, *Turnaround*, 62.

24. Gerstner, *Who Says Elephants Can't Dance?* 77.

25. John Kotter, "Leading Change: Why Transformation Efforts Fail," *Harvard Business Review*, March–April 1995.

26. Ghosn and Riès, *Shift*, 99.

27. Gerstner, *Who Says Elephants Can't Dance?* 77.

28. Janet Lowe, *Jack Welch Speaks: Wisdom from the World's Greatest Business Leader* (New York: Wiley, 2001), 98.

29. Gerstner, *Who Says Elephants Can't Dance?* 77.

30. James Collins and Jerry Porras, "Organizational Vision and Visionary Organizations," *California Management Review* 34, no. 1 (Fall 1991): 30–52.

31. Ibid.

32. Austin and Noland, "IBM Corporation Turnaround."

33. Ghosn and Riès, *Shift*, 134.

34. Interview with Dave House, November, 2005.

35. Jennifer Reingold, "Bob Nardelli Is Watching," *Fast Company*, December 2005, 76.

36. Giancarlo Ghislanzoni and Julie Shearn, "Leading Change: An Interview with the CEO of Banca Intesa," *McKinsey Quarterly*, Number 3, 2005.

37. Jan Carlzon, *Moments of Truth* (New York: HarperCollins, 1987), 26–27.

38. Gerstner, *Who Says Elephants Can't Dance?* 35.

39. Ibid., 36.

40. VeriSign Case, Stanford University, unpublished, 2005.

41. Ibid.

42. Michael Y. Yoshino and Masako Egawa, "Implementing the Nissan Renewal Plan," Case 1–303-111 (Boston: Harvard Business School, 2003), 8.

43. VeriSign Case, Stanford University, unpublished, 2005.

44. Steve Jobs, MacWorld Confrence, n1997, http://youtube.com/watch?vv=PEHNrqPkefl.

45. Interview with Sam Shiffman, Manager, 3M, April 26, 2007.

Chapter 3

1. Interview with Ava Butler, 2003.

2. Elizabeth Gibson and Andy Billings, *Big Change at Best Buy: Working Through Hypergrowth to Sustained Excellence* (Palo Alto, CA: Davies-Black Publishing, 2003), 22.

3. "25 Lessons from Jack Welch," 1000ventures.com, http://www.1000ventures .com/business_guide/mgmt_new-model_25lessons-welch.html.

4. Carlos Ghosn and Philippe Riès, *Shift: Inside Nissan's Historic Revival* (New York: Doubleday, 2005), 102–103.

5. Ibid.

6. Gibson and Billings, *Big Change at Best Buy*, 22.

7. VeriSign Case Stanford University, unpublished, 2005.

8. Ibid.

9. Magee, *Turnaround*, 70–71.

10. Magee, *Turnaround*, 102–105; Ghosn and Riès, *Shift*, 66–76; and Carlos Ghosn, "Saving the Business Without Losing the Company," *Harvard Business Review*, January 2002.

11. Gibson and Billings, *Big Change at Best Buy*, 16.

12. VeriSign Case, Stanford University, unpublished, 2005.

13. Ibid.

14. Ibid.

15. Magee, *Turnaround*, 77.

16. VeriSign Case, Stanford University, unpublished, 2005.

17. Ibid.

18. Magee, *Turnaround*, 70–71.

19. Gibson and Billings, *Big Change at Best Buy*, 7–9.

20. VeriSign Case, Stanford University, unpublished, 2005.

21. Gibson and Billings, *Big Change at Best Buy*, 21.

22. Magee, *Turnaround*, 70.

Chapter 4

1. Louis V. Gerstner Jr., *Who Says Elephants Can't Dance? Leading a Great Enterprise Through Dramatic Change* (New York: HarperBusiness, 2002), 203–205.

2. Ibid., 210–211.

3. Carlos Ghosn and Philippe Riès, *Shift: Inside Nissan's Historic Revival* (New York: Doubleday, 2005) 134.

4. Elizabeth Gibson and Andy Billings, *Big Change at Best Buy: Working Through Hypergrowth to Sustained Excellence* (Palo Alto, CA: Davies-Black Publishing, 2003), 19.

5. Ibid., 17.

6. John Kotter, "Leading Change: Why Transformation Efforts Fail," *Harvard Business Review on Point*, March–April 1995, 1–10.

7. Rajat Gupta and Jim Wendler, "Leading Change: An Interview with the CEO of P&G," *McKinsey Quarterly*, Web exclusive, July 2005.

8. David Magee, *Turnaround: How Carlos Ghosn Rescued Nissan* (New York: HarperBusiness, 2003), 9.

9. Gerstner, *Who Says Elephants Can't Dance?* 50.

10. Jan Carlzon, *Moments of Truth* (New York: HarperCollins, 1987), 22–23.

11. Carter McNamara, "Organizational Culture," Free Management Library, www.managementhelp.org/org_thry/culture/culture.htm.

12. Michael Warshaw, "Have You Been House-Trained?" *Fast Company*, October 1998.

13. Patricia Sellers, "Home Depot: Something to Prove," *Fortune Magazine* www.mutualofamerica.com/articles/Fortune/2002_06_27/homedepot1.asp; Home Depot's "Big Disappointment": Sales, January 17, 2003, www.businessweek.com/bwdaily/dnflash/jan2003/nf20030117_1318.htm; Carol Hymowitz, "Home Depot's CEO Led a Revolution, but Left Some Behind," *The Wall Street Journal,* March 16, 2004, B.1, http://proquest.umi.com/pqdweb?did=579550851&sid=1&Fmt=3&clientId=12498&RQT=309&VName=PQD.

14. Gerstner, *Who Says Elephants Can't Dance?* 196.

15. Ibid., 199.

16. Carlos Ghosn, "Saving the Business Without Losing the Company," *Harvard Business Review*, January 2002, 6.

17. Mark Tatge, "Prescription for Growth," *Forbes*, February 17, 2003, 4.

18. Gerstner, *Who Says Elephants Can't Dance?* 53.

19. Michale Amdt, "3M's Rising Star," *BusinessWeek Online*, April 12, 2004.

20. "Closer Look: The Minnesota Intiative Foundations," 2005. The McKnight Foundation, www.mcknight.org/feature/mifs.aspx.

21. Interview with Dave House, November 2005.

22. Gerstner, *Who Says Elephants Can't Dance?* 190.

23. Under the leadership of VeriSign's CEO Stratton Sclavos, the problems men-

tioned in this customer care section were addressed and solved in the later phases of the transformation.

24. Magee, *Turnaround*, 98.

25. Benham Tabrizi, *Becoming a Real-Time Enterprise* (McGraw-Hill, 2006).

26. Richard Blake, "The Fixer-Upper," *Institutional Investor* (International Edition), January 2004, 14.

27. Interview with Nardelli, www.chiefexecutive.net/nardelli.htm.

28. "Flowchart," iSixSigma Dictionary, www.isixsigma.com/dictionary/Flowchart-431.htm.

29. "Basic Tools for Process Improvement—Module 6: Flowchart," iSixSigma, www.isixsigma.com/offsite.asp?A=Fr&Url=http://quality.disa.mil/pdf/flowchrt.pdf.

30. See www.isixsigma.com/offsite.asp?A=Fr&Url=http://www.sytsma.com/tqmtools/flow.html.

31. In reference to the final four items, see Michael Lee Smith, "BOLO (Be On LookOut) List for Analyzing Process Mapping," iSixSigma, www.isixsigma.com/library/content/c040301a.asp.

32. F. John Reh, "Benchmarking," About: Management, http://management.about.com/cs/benchmarking/a/Benchmarking.htm.

33. Paul Kaihla, "Best-Kept Secrets of the World's Best Companies," *Business 2.0*, March 16, 2006, http://money.cnn.com/magazines/business2/business2_archive/2006/04/01/8372806/index.htm.

34. See www.aluenet.com/pdf/benchmarking_Sitnikov.pdf (pg. 4).

35. "Fast-Cycle Benchmarking," *Harvard Management Update*, April 1, 1999.

36. Magee, *Turnaround*, 111–112.

37. Larry Bossidy and Ram Charan, *Execution: The Discipline of Getting Things Done* (New York: Crown Business, 2002).

38. See http://encyclopedia.lockergnome.com/s/b/Benchmarking.

39. Ibid.

Chapter 5

1. Leander Kahney, "Straight Dope on the iPod's Birth," *Wired*, October 17, 2006.

2. Mark Hurd, "Address to Channel Partners" (HP America Partner Conference, Las Vegas, Nevada, June 19, 2006), www.hp.com/hpinfo/execteam/speeches/hurd/06apc.html.

3. David Magee, *Turnaround: How Carlos Ghosn Rescued Nissan* (New York: HarperBusiness, 2003), 77–79.

4. VeriSign, "VeriSign Acquires Unimobile Assets, Expands Communication Services Offerings," news release, March 22, 2004, www.verisign.com/verisign-inc/news-and-events/news-archive/us-news-2004/page_004017.html.

5. VeriSign, "VeriSign Successfully Completes Acquisition of Jamba! AG," news release, June 3, 2004, www.verisign.com/verisign-inc/news-and-events/news-archive/us-news-2004/page_004007.html.

6. Verisign, "VeriSign Acquires Unimobile Assets."

7. Louis V. Gerstner Jr., *Who Says Elephants Can't Dance? Leading a Great Enterprise Through Dramatic Change* (New York: HarperBusiness, 2002), 219.

8. Ibid., 220.

9. Ibid., 202.

10. Carlos Ghosn and Philippe Riès, *Shift: Inside Nissan's Historic Revival* (New York: Doubleday, 2005), 108.

11. Pui-Wing Tam, "Task of Two H-P Executives: Make a Behemoth Bigger," *Wall Street Journal*, November 15, 2005.

12. Kevin Allison, "HP Chief Outlines His Expansion Strategy," *Financial Times*, December 14, 2005.

13. Josep Isern and Julie Shearn, "Leading Change: An Interview with the Executive Chairman of Telefónica de España," *McKinsey Quarterly*, August 2005, www.mckinseyquarterly.com.

14. Pui-Wing Tam, "Hurd's Biggest Challenge at HP: Overhauling Corporate Sales," *Wall Street Journal*, April 3, 2006.

15. Giancarlo Ghislanzoni and Julie Shearn, "Leading Change: An Interview with the CEO of Banca Intesa," *McKinsey Quarterly*, 2005, 3.

16. Vanessa L. Facenda, "Cowboy Culture/GE Mentality," *Retail Merchandiser* 42, no. 8, August 2002, 23.

17. Carlos Ghosn, "Saving the Business Without Losing the Company," *Harvard Business Review*, January 2002, 10.

Chapter 6

1. Carlos Ghosn and Philippe Riès, *Shift: Inside Nissan's Historic Revival* (New York: Doubleday, 2005), 134.

2. Louis V. Gerstner Jr., *Who Says Elephants Can't Dance? Leading a Great Enterprise Through Dramatic Change* (New York: HarperBusiness, 2002), 88–92.

3. David Magee, *Turnaround: How Carlos Ghosn Rescued Nissan* (New York: HarperBusiness, 2003), 127.

4. Michael Y. Yoshino and Masako Egawa, "Implementing the Nissan Renewal Plan," Case 1–303-111 (Boston: Harvard Business School, 2003), 5.

5. Giancarlo Ghislanzoni and Julie Shearn, "Leading Change: An Interview with the CEO of Banca Intesa," *McKinsey Quarterly*, Number 3, 2005.

6. Carlos Ghosn, "Nissan Motor Co.," *Fast Company*, June 2002, 80.

7. Josep Isern and Julie Shearn, "Leading Change: An Interview with the Executive Chairman of Telefónica de España," *McKinsey Quarterly*, August 2005, www.mckinseyquarterly.com.

8. Rajat Gupta and Jim Wendler, "Leading Change: An Interview with the CEO of P&G," *McKinsey Quarterly*, July 2005, www.mckinseyquarterly.com.

9. Elizabeth Gibson and Andy Billings, *Big Change at Best Buy: Working Through Hypergrowth to Sustained Excellence* (Palo Alto, CA: Davies-Black Publishing, 2003), 7–8.

10. Ghosn and Riès, *Shift*, 111–112, 123.

11. Yoshino and Egawa, "Implementing the Nissan Revival Plan," 8.

Chapter 7

1. Interview with Dave House, November 2005.

2. Lindsay Brooke, "From Here to Infiniti: Carlos Ghosn Surprised the Industry by Meeting Nissan's Revival Plan Targets a Year Ahead of Schedule. Now Comes the Fun Part—Selling New Product," *Automotive Industries*, March 2002, www.findarticles.com/p/articles/mi_m3012/is_3_182/ai_84377729/pg_2.

3. Giancarlo Ghislanzoni and Julie Shearn, "Leading Change: An Interview with the CEO of Banca Intesa," *McKinsey Quarterly*, Number 3, 2005.

4. David Magee, *Turnaround: How Carlos Ghosn Rescued Nissan* (New York: HarperBusiness, 2003), 82.

5. Jennifer Reingold, "Bob Nardelli Is Watching," *Fast Company*, December 2005, 76.

6. Ibid.

7. Carlos Ghosn and Philippe Riès, *Shift: Inside Nissan's Historic Revival* (New York: Doubleday, 2005), 152.

8. Larry Bossidy and Ram Charan, *Execution: The Discipline of Getting Things Done* (New York: Crown Business, 2002), 6.

9. Rajat Gupta and Jim Wendler, "Leading Change: An Interview with the CEO of P&G," *McKinsey Quarterly*, July 2005, www.mckinseyquarterly.com.

10. Melissa Raffoni, "Three Keys to Effective Execution," *Harvard Management Update*, February 2003.

11. Bossidy and Charan, *Execution*, 6.

12. Rob Cross, Wayne Baker, and Andrew Parker, "What Creates Energy in Organizations?" *MIT Sloan Management Review*, Summer 2003.

13. Janet Lowe, *Jack Welch Speaks: Wisdom from the World's Greatest Business Leader* (New York: Wiley, 2001), 98.

14. Elizabeth Gibson and Andy Billings, *Big Change at Best Buy: Working Through Hypergrowth to Sustained Excellence* (Palo Alto, CA: Davies-Black Publishing, 2003), xiii.

15. Jan Carlzon, *Moments of Truth* (New York: HarperCollins, 1987), 113–114.

16. Andrew R. McIlvaine, "Retooling HR," *Human Resource Executive Online*, www.hreonline.com/HRE/story.jsp?storyId=4222054.

17. Peter Burrows, "HP Says Goodbye to Drama," *BusinessWeek Online*, September 2, 2005, www.businessweek.com/technology/content/sep2005/tc2005091_4868_tc119.htm.

18. Carlzon, *Moments of Truth*, 78.

19. Ibid., 78, 82.

20. Interview with Dave House, Novemenber 2005.

21. John Kelly, "One CEO's Journey: Reflections on a Scorecard-Driven Transformation," in *Balanced Scorecard Report* (Boston: Harvard Business School, July–August 2002).

22. Ibid, 10.

23. Gibson and Billings, *Big Change at Best Buy*, 200.

24. Ibid., 10.

25. Ibid., 9.

26. Ghislanzoni and Shearn, "Leading Change."

27. Christopher Bartlett and Meg Wozny, "GE's Two-Decade Transformation: Jack Welch's Leadership," *Harvard Business Review*, February 25, 2004.

28. Gibson and Billings, *Big Change at Best Buy*, 7–8.

29. Bossidy and Charan, *Execution*, 40–41.

30. Burrows, "HP Says Goodbye to Drama."

31. Bossidy and Charan, *Execution*, 41–45.

32. John Oates and Drew Cullen, "Carly Fiorina Quits." *Register*, February 8, 2005.

33. Ellen O'Brien and Todd Weiss, "Fiorina Steps Down—HP Seeks Change," *CIO News*, February 9, 2005, http://searchcio.techtarget.com/originalContent/0,289142 ,sid19_gci1052673,00.html.

34. Burrows, "HP Says Goodbye to Drama."

35. Timothy Prickett Morgan, "Hurd on the Street: HP Cuts 14,500 Jobs in Reorganization," *Linux Beacon*, July 26, 2005.

36. Peter Burrows, *Backfire: Carly Fiorina's High-Stakes Battle for the Soul of Hewlett-Packard* (Hoboken, NJ: John Wiley & Sons, 2003), 135.

37. Michael Beer, Rakesh Kharana, and James Weber, "Hewlett-Packard: Culture in Changing Times," Case 9–404-087 (Boston: Harvard Business School, 2005), 10.

38. Ibid., 9.

39. Ibid.

40. Burrows, "HP Says Goodbye to Drama."

41. Ibid.

42. Rex Crum, "H-P Climbs After Profits Rise 51 Percent," *MarketWatch*, May 17, 2007.

43. C. Pettey, "Gartner Says Hewlett-Packard Takes Clear Lead in Fourth Quarter Worldwide PC Shipments and Creates a Virtual Tie with Dell for 2006 Year-End Results," 2007, www.gartner.com/it/page.jsp?id=500384.

Appendix

1. The one exception here is IBM, which was included because of the notoriety of its effort. Although Lou Gerstner initiated the transformation in 1993, starting the analysis from 1993 rather than 1995 would have only improved the company's performance according to the model.

2. EBIT = revenue – cost of goods sold – operating expenses.

3. The exceptions to this formula were the D/E and current ratios. Since lower D/E and current ratios are preferable, the function used is $10 \cdot (1/(1+2^x))$, and the lower the score, the better the performance on those fundamentals.

4. Since the maximum score per fundamental is 10, the highest possible index for the primary fundamentals is (score) · (number of fundamentals) · (scaling factor) $= (10) \cdot (5) \cdot (2) = 100$.

5. The maximum value that can be attained is (max weighted primary index) + (max weighted secondary index) $= \{(\#$ primary fundamentals$) \cdot [($max score per fundamental$) \cdot ($weight$)]\} + \{(\#$ secondary fundamentals$) \cdot [($max score per fundamental$) \cdot ($weight$)]\} = [5 \cdot (10)(2)] + [6 \cdot (10)(1)] = (100) + (60) = 160$ total maximum score.

Index

Note: page numbers followed by *f* indicate figures; page numbers followed by *t* indicate tables; page numbers followed by *n* indicate material in endnotes.

About the Author

Dr. Behnam Tabrizi is Consulting Professor at the Department of Management Science and Engineering at Stanford University. His work includes research and consulting on organizational transformation, cross-boundary/functional management, time-to-market acceptance, and acquisition and integration. Key projects include rapid transformation to greatness, designing effective organizations, sales transformation, cross-functional effectiveness, real-time enterprise, and excellence in product/service definition. His research on more than one hundred companies with McKinsey and Co. around the globe regarding "Accelerating Transformation: Process Innovations in Companies around the Globe" was called a "pioneering work" by Tom Peters in *Forbes*, *Chicago Tribune*, *The Washington Post*, and *San Jose Mercury News*.

As a frequent traveler to China in the past three years, Dr. Tabrizi worked with over three hundred CEOs of the largest private and public Chinese companies on their corporate transformation. He has also served as a member of the doctoral committee at Harvard Business School and has taught at the Stanford Graduate School of Business and the Stanford Graduate School of Business Executive program in "Leading and Managing Change." He has been interviewed by BBC and C-SPAN regarding his recent work on transformation. *Rapid Transformation: A 90-Day Plan for Fast and Effective Change* is Dr. Tabrizi's fourth book on transformation and change.

Dr. Tabrizi received the prestigious *Administrative Science Quarterly* 2001 Award (with Professor Kathleen Eisenhardt) for scholarly contribution for a paper published five years earlier, which had great influence on subsequent theory and research in the field of management and which deals with the fields of strategy, marketing, organization, and operation. He has also received the Stanford School of Engineering Tau Beta Pi award, from among over two hundred faculty members, for Excellence in Undergraduate Teaching, as well as the Industrial Engineering and Engineering Management Teacher of the year award.

In the winter of 1994, Dr. Tabrizi taught the first Web-based course in the world, at Stanford University. Among his notable past and current consulting clients are Applied Materials, Hewlett-Packard, Intel, IBM, IDC, Nokia, GAP, Motorola, Lucent, Agilent, Oracle, Cisco, Li & Fung, Nortel Networks, Clarify, Haier, Verisign, and many mid-size and small companies. He serves on the board of Catapult Ventures and has served on the board of iChatterbox.com (sold to Covia Inc.) and WebMBO (merged with Realm Corp.), as well as the advisory boards of several startups.

Professor Tabrizi received a BS in Computer Engineering from University of Kansas, an MS in Electrical and Computer Engineering from University of Illinois, Urbana, and an MS in Engineering Management and a PhD in Strategy, Organizations, and Technology Management from Stanford University, Management Science and Engineering.